The Rapture Was REAL?!

And You Were Left Behind... Now What?

Letters to You From Jesus

To Give You HOPE and INSTRUCTION

as given to Clare And Ezekiel Du Bois
and Carol Jennings

Published by Heartdwellers.org

ISBN 13: 978-1518838842

ISBN 10: 1518838847

This volume includes messages given from September 2014 to October 2015

Other Still Small Voice venues are:

Still Small Voice Youtube channel:

https://www.youtube.com/user/claredubois/featured

Still Small Voice Facebook: Heartdwellers

Blog: https://heartdwellingwithjesus.wordpress.com/

Blog: www.stillsmallvoicetriage.org

TABLE OF CONTENTS

Foreword

I'm so sorry. I just wish I could have told you. I just wish you could have known somehow. I wish you had listened. I wish you could have cared. I wish you could have known! I'm so, so, so sorry. But we had to go.

I wish we could have seen you more, have been with you more, given you more. And now you have to face the most horrible, terrible times that have ever come upon this Earth very soon. You didn't believe us…really.

But now it's happened, and everything else IS coming. Just like the Scriptures say. The Bible IS TRUE. Never doubt it again. There is one way still to escape the worst. Turn to Jesus NOW. While you can. It seems to make no sense, but the things of God really do, because His mind is so much higher than yours. You can't do this anymore on your own.

Only HE knows everything. Only He can save you. He made you. He made you because He loved you. He's the only one that ever can or ever will love you completely and perfectly. He knows everything that is really good for you, and everything that's going to hurt you. And He knows what will surely kill you.

All He wants is for you to be happy, to be protected, to be FREE. Truly free, to become so completely happy and fulfilled. It's all been prepared for you. He's been waiting, waiting to help you. To keep you from being trapped in the most terrifying place of horror and never-ending torture: Hell.

Yes, Hell is REAL.

God did not set it up for you. YOU were not made to go there EVER.

You were made for a place where you'll never be hurting or lonely, tired or hungry, with absolutely no such thing as pain. Only to be more happy and forever young and free, than even you could ever imagine.

FOREVER.

It's your choice. It's all in your hands now. To live – or to die. To suffer forever worse and worse – or to be guaranteed to be so awesomely happy, loved and protected forever.

This is all we can ask you now: please tell Jesus you're sorry and ask Him to come and take over your life now. Give it to Him. He will RUN to save you.

Clare and Ezekiel du Bois

October 3, 2015

INTRODUCTION

What WAS the Rapture, Anyway?
And Who Was it For?

Prophetic Message to My Bride

September 1, 2014

The Lord is calling His Bride, or His potential Bride to repentance. She's not ready for the Rapture. And He is wanting to prepare her. And, as I have shared in a previous teaching, part of the reason the economy in this country is slumping and the Lord is allowing it, is to get His Bride back from the world. To get her mind off of the things of the world and onto Him.

So, you know, we have a lot of prosperity Christians in this country, people who talk about prosperity - that you're not really a successful Christian if you don't have the faith to be prosperous. Nothing could be further from the truth, because prosperity and money was the last thing on the Lord's mind in the New Testament. In the Old Testament, it was sometimes a mark of favor from God, but in the New Testament, the Lord set a standard.

He didn't choose to be born as a king, or a prince, or to live like a king or a prince. He chose a simple life, an unpretentious life. A life that was not entrenched in the things of the world.

So, He's looking for a Bride who resembles Him. And as I examine my heart every day before the Lord, and I realize the areas where I fall short, I'm writing those things down for you as well. Because I think we can help each other, by recognizing some things about ourselves and sharing them.

Here's the message the Lord gave me:

"The beautiful people, as a group, are not My Bride. I'm looking for the lowly, contrite and devout. Those persecuted for the sake of righteousness. I am looking for those who resemble Me. That is what My Bride looks like. I want to give great hope to the lowly and marginalized. They are My beauties. They are the ones who most resemble Me on the Earth. I'm sorry to say it, but many of My Christians resemble the beauty queens of Babylon – or in your day, Hollywood.

"I know you get tired of Me saying it, but this is not Hollywood – this is Heaven. And the souls here bear no resemblance whatsoever to the ones you call great on this Earth.

"Summon My Bride and My people to repentance. I am by no means saying that a lovely person by the worlds' standards cannot be My Bride – but in her personal life, she will resemble Me. Crucified, rejected, passed over, scorned. Bearing the scars caused by the callous contempt of others in her heart. My heart is drawn to such as these. They carry their pain with quiet dignity, yet from the outside, you would never recognize them. These are My chosen ones. Along with the little, the frail, the rejected, and the marginalized.

"I know I'm repeating Myself – but this couldn't be more relevant, more important.

"I want all to know that what I am looking for in a potential Bride, is NOT the well-groomed Christianeze. Rather, the very, very little ones. Bring to Me all those who have deemed themselves unworthy of My Crown. Instill in them a quiet confidence that they indeed belong to Me and are worthy. They are My Bride. They are My Chosen Ones.

"And those who are still standing around waiting to be hired are VERY important to Me. They will indeed be paid the same wage as those who were chosen first, and ahead of all the lowly and undesirable ones."

So, that's the Lord's message right now to His Bride and to His Church. And I'm beginning a series on who is the Bride of Christ where I'm counting on the Holy Spirit to reveal more and more to me the attributes of those who are going to be Raptured, because they truly ARE His Bride. They truly resemble Him.

Until then, God bless you.

Left Behind in Nuclear War: Sequence of Events Before and After the Rapture

September 2, 2014

As it was in the Days of Noah, so it will be at the Coming of the Son of Man. For in the days before the Flood, people were eating and drinking, marrying and giving in marriage up to the very day Noah entered the Ark; they new nothing about what would happen until the Flood came and took them all away. Matthew 24:37

You will hear of wars and rumors of wars but see to it that you are not alarmed. Such things must happen but the end is still to come. Nation will rise against nation and kingdom and Kingdom. There will be famines and earthquakes in various places All these are the beginning of birth pangs. Matthew 24:6

Song:

When the mountains shake the seas, then you'll come to rescue me, for Your love will not be shaken in the storm.

When we're shattered to the core, in the dreaded crypt of war, the hearts of men will fail them in the storm.

With the piercing trumpet's cry, lightening rips through crimson skies, and all who have been waiting will arise.

Vindication fills the skies, clouds of saints ascend on high, as the King in all His grandeur takes His Bride.

It is written in I Corinthians 15, *"Behold, I tell you a mystery; we will not all sleep, but we will all be changed, in a moment, in the twinkling of an eye. At the last trumpet, for the trumpet will sound, and the dead will be raised imperishable, and we will be changed. For this perishable must put on the imperishable, and this mortal must put on immortality..."*

"This is how it will be at the coming of the Son of Man. Two men will be in the field; one will be taken, and the other left. Two women will be grinding with a hand mill; one will be taken and the other left. Therefore keep watch, because you do not know on what day your Lord will come. But understand this: if the owner of the house had known at what time of night the thief was coming, he would have kept watch and not let his house be broken into. So you, also, must be ready, because the Son of Man will come at an hour when you do not expect Him." The words of Jesus in Matthew 24

Song resumes:

In the tattered robes of war, those left standing at the Door will weep in Outer Darkness…in the Storm.

Now this absence of the Light, it will set the lost aright as they cry aloud for answers…in the Storm.

So despite the bolted Door, be repentant and implore, for His Mercy will restore you in the Storm.

(A mother's words the moment after her one-year-old baby is taken in the Rapture) "I'm so confused, so lost, so terrified! Oh somebody, help me, please! Please! What's going on? Everywhere I turn, parents are holding empty clothes in desperation, weeping bitterly.

"Oh, this can't be happening. I'm in a nightmare. I'm going to wake up…. I'm going to wake up!! "But no...it's real. I'm not dreaming. No one knows what's happened. I can't stop trembling. I'm in shock. Only moments ago she was safe here in my arms. The sun glistened off her golden hair and she laughed at the wind.

"We were so happy, she was so innocent. Now her dress lies limp on my arm, her little sandals on the ground. Is she no more? Oh, somebody help me…what happened? What happened??

"If there is a God and He is Real, tell me what happened to my angel, my little girl, tell me…where is she?

"…No, it can't be, she's been Raptured?? Oh, that's just a myth - a fairy tale, that can't be it. No intelligent person believes that stuff. But…she's gone and everywhere…our children are gone…

"Is it aliens? Could it be…all the children…
Raptured? But why? Why, God? Why??"

Song finishes:

So trim your lamp, tend to your light. It's not too late to get it right, He's standing here beside you, take His hand.

For He's coming at an hour…you know not when.

SECTION ONE
The Lord's Own Words for You

Post Rapture Letters from God #1

October 7, 2014

"I am calling out to you, speaking comfort to your heart. I've not left you, nor will I ever leave or forsake you. I know acutely the terrible loss you feel, at times even a sense of betrayal overtakes you. All of your questions of "Why, and where, and why am I still here, why was I left behind and what am I ever to do now?"

"You must resist the temptations to simply dive back into the world and get really busy, and take advantage now of many so-called new and exciting opportunities and careers due to the mass vacancies in every aspect of industry, business, and all-around money ventures.

"NO, even in your pain and bewilderment, draw back from these things. Pull back away from your unstable world and seek Me with all your heart ten times the more. Strongly call out to Me with true repentance and a sincere change of heart and I will help you. I will calm your fears, and welcome you back with open arms.

"You're not lost. In the coming days you will see more and more just how much I still truly love you. If a mother forsakes her child, I will not abandon you. I am forever here to save you.

"You are still My child, so very, very precious and cherished by Me.

"You are still My treasure, and I am with you even now."

Post Rapture Letter from God #2

October 7, 2014

"The question burning in your mind, 'But why? Oh, my Lord, why? Why, why was I left behind?'

"My child, you were never meant to be excluded from the Rapture. It was My merciful provision for all of My children, indeed My Church, My body, My Bride. You were to be part of the evacuation that took place to keep you from having to live in and witness the most horrible time of suffering upon the Earth that has ever been or ever will be.

"You began well, however, in time you began to become more and more entrenched in the world. Though still a Christian in name and affiliation, you began to draw more and more away, often to many distractions and pastimes.

"The times we used to share became less and less. You knew that you were beginning to compromise more and more with the world over your faith and so you stopped speaking to Me.

"That, combined with your new relationships and your new liberal ways of thinking caused you to begin looking at other souls around you, and judging them. You began to look down on them and the things that they held dear, even going as far as holding in scorn and contempt the joy that they expressed at the nearness of My coming.

"By the time I arrived, all you could do was stand in fear and shame for the very thing which you distained to believe had just happened right in front of you.

“Because you did not believe, you did not watch and pray, and I came as a thief in the night and you were not prepared.

“I could not take you.”

Post Rapture Letter from God #3

October 7, 2014

"You ask of Me, 'What now?'

"Stay close, stay ever so close to Me now. Pray for the grace to always have Me in your heart and mind, My name ever on your tongue.

"You must hold tightly to the hem of My garment and never for a second let Me go again. Develop the habit of thanking Me always and everywhere. Have me ever before your mind's eye. This you must pray for also and I will give it. I am with you already, as it is, but you need to be able to sense Me, feel Me, and interact with Me, speaking to Me always as your most trusted friend.

"I am keenly interested in your every thought and feeling so long as you strive to stay lowly and humble, being very little in your own eyes.

"I will forever be your most trusted Friend and confidant. Nothing draws Me more closely than very small and childlike souls. I stay closer to them than their own skin, and I will be with you.

"I know that you are still in a great state of bewilderment and the rest of the world around you is in a terrible state of disarray. But I also know that already you're beginning to feel an inexplicable, supernatural peace and calm within. I will continue to give you this gift and you will be able to think and reason with remarkable clarity.

"Do not worry about your needs. As you can see, I have provided for you in every way. People will continue to give to you everything that you will need, seemingly out of the blue, and you will quickly begin to experience just how truly beautiful a real life of faith is even during these most extraordinary circumstances.

"Nothing is out of My control and nothing is allowed without My consent. I have made every provision for you ahead of time. You have no need to be anxious at all, only keep your heart and eyes on Me. You are my precious, precious child and I will not allow anything or anyone to harm you. I have set my angels all about you to watch over you day and night. Not only will you be provided for, but you will know My loving care and the surety of My faithfulness as I bring an overabundance for you to help others with.

"You will begin to meet others who, like you, have repented as well, and through their own brokenness have been fully restored in profound humility and whose hearts are solely for Me and the Kingdom of God alone.

"I will gather again My people as a mother her little children and I will bring them through this time of trial and testing victorious. They will shine like the stars in the firmament of heaven, twice refined. They will rule and reign with Me as they have persevered and come through gloriously, the Time of Tribulation."

What Do I DO NOW?? Surrender to Love

October 25, 2015

At this point, you are probably asking yourself, "So what do I do now??"

Our Best Advice: Just talk to Jesus the same way you would talk to any other friend; but more than a friend - a Very Intimate Friend. He is the kind of Friend that You can talk to about anything, and everything, and He will never back away. So He's here for you. Right now, in this moment. Simply open your heart to Him, sharing all of your hopes and dreams, your fears and disappointments.

Last, but not least, give yourself fully and unreservedly to Him. He is the one who created you, and He knows far and beyond that which is for your ultimate good, for your total fulfillment and true lasting happiness.

"How," you may ask, "do I actually DO it?"

The main thing is that it genuinely and sincerely come from your heart. He is not looking for fancy words or formal prayers.

He LOVES You - just the way you are, right now.

So be yourself, and approach Him comfortably and naturally. Tell Him that you are sorry for your sins, and ask Him to take your whole life now, and everything in it.

Tell Him that you truly want to receive Him into your heart as your lord and Savior, and that you give yourself, fully and unreservedly, into His loving care, now and forever.

You have now become a New Creation in Christ! The Old Life has passed away, and now in this moment, you have been wonderfully REBORN !! You are as clean, pure, and innocent as a Newborn Baby, with absolutely no spot, stain, or wrinkle! You have just been given a brand new soul, a brand new life, - AND the PROMISE of the most beautiful life that will never end, in Heaven, where you will be Young and Free and Happy Forever!!!

Ezekiel

SECTION 2

Prophetic Dreams of What Will Happen At the Rapture or Soon Afterward

Rapture Dreams from Ezekiel #1

September 30, 2015

Clare: I'm going to interview Ezekiel du Bois, (some of his music is on the internet) and he's had three rapture dreams. He's coming from a background, a spiritual/religious background, that the rapture wasn't really taught or discussed. So, these dreams were quite an eye-opener for him. And he's going to tell us about them.

So, tell me about the first dream. You had a dream that shook you.

Ezekiel: Yeah, it kinda woke me up, so to speak.

Clare: Yeah, it shook me, too. But I'm going to wait for you to share your experience before I tell about mine.

Ezekiel: In the dream there was a small group of us and somehow we just knew that the Lord was coming back NOW, like SOON, like IMMEDIATELY. And we couldn't wait - we just couldn't wait.

Clare: You didn't hear anything on the radio that He was in Israel or coming around the globe and...?

Ezekiel: No. No.

Clare: Nothing. You just had an inner unction that the Lord was coming.

Ezekiel: Yeah, we just had this real strong feeling that He was coming. And so much so, like a kid running to a Christmas tree on Christmas morning. You know, couldn't wait to see Him, so we just took off - on foot. We thought we were gonna get to Him somehow, meet Him, cut Him off at the pass.

Clare: How many people were with you?

Ezekiel: Oh, gosh, probably all of ten or twelve people to start with, maybe. Maybe less than that.

Clare: Did you recognize who they were?

Ezekiel: Just some friends and a couple of people from a little local prayer group/family. And we knew it was coming from the East, so we started East. I remember it took a few days to make this trip. We didn't know where we were going to meet Him. In our mind we thought He was going to come "down", like...

Clare: You were driving, or...?

Ezekiel: No, we were still on foot. We thought He was gonna come "down", like down to us somehow. And even though we're gonna be caught up to meet Him in the air, I understand that now, but I didn't know anything about it then. We just went over hill and dale. I remember us walking along the sides of highways, up through into Oklahoma, just constantly... parts of Texas, heading from where we are, northern New Mexico, heading East. I remember sleeping in schools, on cafeteria tables. We didn't want to eat, we didn't want to sleep.

We just were so excited to see the Lord, we just kept on going. I do remember that some in our group - and the group began to grow, probably to twenty or thirty people along the way - some people in the group started looking back. There'd be like a large shopping center or shopping malls or something off to the side and a few people started looking, "Oh, look at the mall - look at this - look at that". And we were so caught up, the rest of us, in the Lord and Him coming back, all we knew was just to keep going, face forward, you know. But the people that started looking to the side and looking back, they left the line. They walked off to the side from where we were going and just walked over and into whatever town it might happen to be and they went, literally, to the mall, to the store, wherever. And they left us, turned back, you know, they turned off to the side. And then…

Clare: Did they come back?

Ezekiel: No. No, that was it. I mean, they peeled off, just left the group. It was like when they took that first look - they were hooked, you know. They just got pulled off.

Clare: I can relate to that.

Ezekiel: Yeah, just the money and the world and the trinkets and all that stuff, the excitement, I guess. By that time, after a few days, maybe they got bored. But, boy, I tell you - I still couldn't eat, sleep, think, or drink anything but "the Lord coming". And most of us couldn't. But the group began to dwindle back down again. And it was interesting that a few people along the way would be at the parking lots or the little towns, or whatever. And they'd come across a field or something, across a highway and literally leave everything and join up with us.

Clare: Wow.

Ezekiel: Yeah, just a handful of people along the way like that would actually join us.

Clare: Maybe that's kind of an allegory for, as we get the word out more and more, more and more people are responding, and waiting for the Lord, and repenting and changing their lives?

Ezekiel: Well, it would have to be the Holy Spirit, to pull you out of something like that. And most of these people seemed like they were just... sick and tired of being sick and tired, you know. Kind of like I was when I came to the Lord. They were tired of it all and they knew we were headed for something big. And they left everything, literally just left everything.

So we went on and we continued eastward, going through the different states. We had just entered into Missouri, we were going across into Missouri and we saw this yellow-like, golden light descending. It grew larger and brighter, I mean, we knew it was Him. We just couldn't believe it, we were so excited!

Clare: What did it look like? Was it a ball of light? Or a bank of clouds? How did it look?

Ezekiel: It started out like kind of a ball of light in the clouds, kind of a roundish shape coming down. And it was larger and brighter, and it was coming toward us. And I mean, this was within minutes, at this point. It had been days, hours, days. And now it was just within minutes. We saw it. We were excited. This light was coming on. It seemed to come on really just slow and gradually. But literally, it was within minutes. We could see Jesus coming on the clouds, like miles off in the distance, but coming toward us. Obviously, we weren't sure, you know... we just didn't care what was gonna happen next. All we could see was Jesus.

And, at some point, we ended up in front of Jesus, whether that's being "caught up" or whatever, but it was almost like we were...Well, if He's coming on the clouds of Heaven, what we were standing on seemed pretty solid because it was like a knoll, a hill or something, but it was a cloud we were on.

But a friend of mine, an older man, Joe Graves, who has two daughters that he was separated from for years, at that point, and had been praying to be reunited with them - he came up beside me. And just like everyone else, he was enamored by the Lord. And his children, his two daughters were with him, one on the left, one on the right. Then his ex-wife was kind of off to the side. And I thought that was kind of peculiar, because she had left him and the church and everything years earlier. But Joe had this anguished feeling in his face, you know. He looked really hopefully at the Lord. The Lord just shook His head, and He said, "She's not ready. She's just not ready." And he looked kind of sad, but then he was encouraged by the Lord's brightness and beauty, and his girls were with him, and you know he just walked right on up to the Lord.

It was interesting, because even though we were meeting the Lord, He would address and kind of go around to different people, and welcome each one of them personally. It was really, really neat.

Clare: Very personal, then. It wasn't just like, this huge crowd was being lifted up. It was more like a personal encounter as well.

Ezekiel: Yeah, it was like a gathering – He was welcoming us. Later on, I'll talk about…just His eyes, and how kind and normal and natural He was, even though He was brilliant and all these other magnificent things.

So, anyway, Jesus brought us up to Him – we thought He was coming down to us. And then I woke up. And I had all kinds of questions!

Clare: We had some kind of a distant, shadowy knowledge of what the Rapture was, and we'd heard people talk about it. But since the Church didn't believe in it, and didn't teach it, we didn't take it real seriously.

Ezekiel: Well, we just weren't in the circles of people that it was a part of their reality. We just didn't know.

Clare: So, how did you know that the dream was from the Lord and not just a "pizza" dream?

Ezekiel: I had an inner witness. I woke up and it had a profound effect on me. It was one of those things where you wake up and it's still there. And three or four years later, it's just as strong with me as it was the night I had it.

Clare: Well, I remember you woke up and told me about the dream – and it just rattled my world. It just turned my world upside down, really. I thought, 'Oh my goodness, if THIS is the case!!' We had both planned on being martyred in the Tribulation, we knew that we were coming into that period. We had already settled that we were going to be martyred.

Ezekiel: Remember the "Bye Bye Boxes"?

Clare: Oh, yeah! For our children – two of them knew the Lord and two didn't. We made, in case they didn't get Raptured, we made these big Tupperware boxes with all kinds of materials and notebooks with instructions, gifts, encouragement. Something that….well, we called them the Bye-Bye Boxes.

Ezekiel: Yes – "What happened, Why did it happen, Where were we?" answers to things like that.

Clare: "What's next?" You know… "What's next in the world?" It hit me profoundly, because I realized that at any moment there would be a decision whether the Lord would take me as His Bride. First I thought, being missionaries so to speak, in ministry and serving people, and leading a substantial prayer life, I thought, 'Well, I guess we're going to get Raptured.'

I remember asking, "Honey, was I in the dream?" And you said I was, so I felt better about it. But it did shake me up because I didn't feel real secure about my position of being able to be with the Lord. The Scriptures say, "Lord, we healed in your name and did this and did that in Your Name…but the Lord said, "I never knew you."

So, I wanted to be sure I was in a good place with Him, in good standing. And I knew there were some areas that I needed to change. I think understanding the Rapture, knowing that it could happen at any time, it really made me more seriously examine my conscience, examine my life and my behavior and get more serous about spots, wrinkles and blemishes.

Ezekiel: So, it wasn't like, "Oh, wow, cool – I'm just gonna get swept up and swift, click and slip - there I go and that's it."

Clare: Yeah, yeah…

Ezekiel: "I'm guaranteed and that's cool."

Clare: Well, and right after that time, right on the heels of that, I remember being in our little chapel and praying, and I was given a Scripture about the wise virgins – the 5 virgins that were ready and 5 weren't. And that really, really got my attention down deep in my spirit. I just felt that was addressed to me.

Ezekiel: hmm…it's interesting that the 5 that went to get the oil for their lamps and missed it. They showed up the first time, they were on schedule and on plan, and doing the right things. – but something changed and they still weren't ready.

Clare: Right – and I felt that. I felt like the Holy Spirit was telling me "you've got some work to do."

Ezekiel: Yeah. Me too.

Rapture Dreams from Ezekiel #2

September 30, 2015

Clare: You said you had three (dreams) in total that you recall – actually I think it's four. Share the next one with us.

Ezekiel: Well, the second one, you were simply walking up to a freight train in a freight yard.

Clare: It was not a passenger train?

Ezekiel: No, it was like a freight train, what I could see. – I just saw a boxcar. You got into this boxcar somehow. It was almost like I was a cameraman behind you; I could see what was going on from behind you. You walked into this boxcar – it was dusty, with some boxes and things. But there was a door at the end of it that looked like it opened up into a coach car. Which for some of us old enough to remember, it's a regular doorway into a passenger car. You walked through that.

At first there was just seating. As soon as you walked through the door, though - from outside you could see that there were seats – but when you walked through the door, instantly it just opened up into this whole Adventure Candy-Land place. I mean seriously, it sounds a little silly, but it was kinda like the little Christmas time Candy Land. Lemon drop trees and gumdrop this, and chocolate and ice cream. Just a fairy tale fantasy land. Some places were kind of whitish and pure and bright and fluffy and soft – but it wasn't cold. And other places were springtime looking – green and all the pretty colors.

Clare: So, it became more than just a boxcar.

Ezekiel: Oh, yes – that totally vanished. That was just a segue way – you just walked through this door and Boom! there you were. And YOU were like a little girl.

Clare: Yes, that's what I was going to say – the Lord always…well, much of the time, when He approaches me I see myself as a little girl in our communications together. And with God the Father, I remember getting up on His lap. Very often when I have a vision of Him, He invites me to come and cuddle with Him.

Ezekiel: You know, I'd never met anyone who even considered anything like that until you and I met. I didn't have any reality of being a child before the Lord. I had a real hard time with God the Father my first 20-something years. It's only been the last few years that I've gotten in touch with the Lord as a Father, because I had such an abusive, scary, hard father situation.

Clare: Yeah, you're childhood. When you first shared this with me, I knew it was about the Rapture. It had the signature of the Holy Spirit; I could feel it. I was a little disappointed, because I thought, "Candy Land??"

Ezekiel: (laughing) I'm sorry…He picks what He picks!

Clare: I mean, yeah, I like candy…but not THAT much!!

Ezekiel: I just found out today that you love lemon drops. I didn't know that…

Clare: Yeah, yeah I do. But the Candy Land image...well, on one hand I felt good that the Lord was saying I would be raptured. But on the other hand, I was a little disappointed about the Candy Land thing. But when I thought about it for a while, I think, very possibly it was an allegory for all of the wonder that is there for a child in Heaven – all the wonderful, beautiful things. The fresh life and everything – it's like a Candy Land, it's like walking into a candy store at six years old and all these different candies. I could relate to that after a while.

Ezekiel: I think there's a lot of healing for a lot of people when they go on to be with the Lord. When my older brother passed on, I kept having these kind of dreams, visions of him for sure, as a little boy - kind of like the little Debbie Kay girl on the box – they looked like his pictures as a little boy. I could see where the Lord could have taken him back to a time where things went off the tracks and made it difficult, where he had to be super responsible, grow up quick. Taking him back to a time where he could be a child again. That would be a beautiful thing for me; I'd love to be a kid again.

Clare: Yeah. Well, I think for us who've had difficult childhoods that we were bent in the wrong direction by those incidents. And I believe the Lord is going to heal all those things. Not only by His Grace, helping us to get over certain behaviors that we have that are a result of trying to protect ourselves, but just because, when we're in Heaven, I believe He's going to, from the bottom up remake us.

Ezekiel: Yeah, He knows what's in each heart and everybody's whole makeup and I guess you could say, well, we're changed in an instant, and just like the Lord and perfect. And that's probably true in the Rapture and the situation. But, I think He knows and tailor-makes everyone's little particular place. He's already said He's made a mansion for each of us. He knows what you're going to want or like or need, Your desires - every desire is met.

Rapture Dreams from Ezekiel #3

October 1, 2015

Clare: You had a third dream after that.

Ezekiel: I had an old bus dream. That's the best way I can describe it.

Clare: Like a city bus?

Ezekiel: Kind of like a renovated school bus. In fact, we traveled in this missionary bus across the states when our kids were small. So there were places to sit, and bunks and tables, also seating. So, there was a small group of us on the bus, and most of the people, including myself were kind of sickly and poor. But we were happy enough, we were on the bus, didn't know really where we were going, didn't care. All of a sudden, we noticed the bus was leaving the ground!

Clare: Wow...(laughing)

Ezekiel: Yeah, we were like, "What's up with that?" so we looked off to the side, and it was like in a jet, just going on up. We could see the ground leaving us. And I knew it was kind of a blustery day, but when we got up in the air it was really cloudy and cold outside. We were even bundled up inside of the bus.

Clare: Gee, Lord I wonder if that's a clue it's going to be a winter-time Rapture?

Ezekiel: Yeah, who knows? It's exactly what it felt like – one of those sleet/icy kind of days. So, we were banking up to the left, then veering to the right a little bit. And we looked off to the left, which at this point the bus had kind of veered going east towards southeast. We could look out the left window and we'd be looking straight East – and we see this far of light coming downward. And man, it was like the further up we went, the darker and the stormier the clouds got. Peals of thunder and lightening.

Clare: Was this during the daytime, or night?

Ezekiel: Probably early evening – in the winter it gets dark earlier, so maybe 5:00 or dusk. It got real dark and stormy but we could see that far-off light coming in. And all of a sudden out from behind this lit-up area in the clouds... The best way I can describe it was a sweeping comet like with a tail – only it wasn't a comet, it was a HUGE battle line. There was this vast, sweeping army that circled around and was coming down beyond the light and kind of off to our left – towards the southwest. But they were heading down toward the Earth.

Clare: When you say army, were they on horses, or vehicles? Or what did it look like?

Ezekiel: This thing was massive, like the Old Testament type guys... in some ways they almost looked like the Nordic type. Long hair, long beards...

Clare: Warriors!

Ezekiel: Warriors – that's exactly what they were. They were all men in warrior battle gear.

Clare: Mounted on horses or on foot.

Ezekiel: Mounted on horses, and they had all these weapons - the iron balls with the spikey things, they'd swing them around, spears, swords. It was interesting because this eerie reddish, orangish–reddish light – kind of glow began to appear off in the stormy clouds, off from this beautiful light that was coming from the back. And all these men and horses had a reddish, fiery glow to them. The whole thing just struck fear into you.

But they actually went past us and down from us, so we're ascending, and they're descending – they passed us, they just went around and below us and went straight down to the Earth at an angle. And then we noticed a large angel outside one of the windows that we could see out of at this point, out the left side of the bus. Here's this light getting closer, and there's this HUGE angel – it looked like he was just walking on air. Of course, WE were in the air, but he comes walking right around the bus and comes walking up into the bus door, literally. And I remember, he was so big he had to duck down to get in the door, to get in the bus.

Clare: Did he have wings?

Ezekiel: No, no he just had a simple white tunic and belt on, muscular, real beautiful copper-colored skin, blondish golden hair. But when he walked into the school bus, walked up the stairwell, and up to where you'd come down the center row. And I noticed back in the stairwell there were all these packages. They were just plain, white, tissue, tied with kind of a tannish off-colored string, very plain.

Clare: They were like presents?

Ezekiel: I didn't know what they were, they were just these packages. I thought maybe they were pillows or something.

Clare: Okay, about the size of a pillow.

Ezekiel: Yeah, about the size of a pillow, some kind of a duffle or something. So, he walks straight back to the middle of the bus, then he turns around and goes back towards the front. And there was a little old lady sitting in the front, front seat. He went to her first, and he got down, squatted down and looked up into her face with these big, beautiful eyes.

Clare: Awwww

Ezekiel: Kinda held her face in his hands, reassured her. Then he said, "Come on! Let's go!" And he walked her back to the middle of the bus, and a doorway – like a lot of older busses would have a doorway in the top…

Clare: A hatch?

Ezekiel: A hatch, yes, you could climb through.

Clare: Going right straight to the roof.

Ezekiel: That's exactly right. And he lifted her up through the roof and there were two other angels up on top – you could barely see. They were helping her up – they were already on top of the bus.

And it was like, "Whoa! What is THIS?" Just before he lifted her up, he said, "Wait, just a second." And he took a couple steps back, reached down into the stairwell, got a package, brought it back and gave it to her. "Be sure and take this with you." She said, "okay". They lifted her up through the hatch, she had her package with her.

I didn't know what was going on past that. Somebody else came up, and then somebody else. And he'd go to each one, reassure them, kind of welcome them and tell them, "Come on! We're gonna go!" And these again, keep in mind, a small group – they were, all of us were at least in our 50's or older, kind of middle aged. Maybe some of them a little younger. All poor, simple, plain, very simple, very humble souls. He'd give each one of them this plain wrapper bundle package to go up through. I thought, 'I guess this is it – I guess we're going up to Heaven from here.'

Well, when it was my turn, first of all, I remember as I got closer, and it was getting to be my turn, I heard this voice, I heard the Lord's voice and I couldn't believe it. I got goose bumps. It was so soft and sounded like a young man in his 30's. Maybe in his early 30's. Just a soft, masculine, kind, gentle, beautiful voice. I couldn't even understand what He was saying exactly, but they were words of welcome to the people, some interchange going on.

So then it really IS my turn, and I'm thinking, 'Man this is IT! This is IT!!' I just kept thinking. 'This is IT!!' So the angel said, "Are you ready?" And I said, "Yes!" – so he lifts me up under each arm and these two huge angels are up on top. They lift me up and you know, when you're kinda sickly, kinda achy and in pain, it's cold and everything…

Clare: Fibromyalgia…

Ezekiel: Yeah! And I wasn't in pain or anything at that point. They lift me up and out and in the background, off to the sides it all looked stormy. But as soon as I turn around…Man! Here's Jesus on a throne. I couldn't believe it – my knees buckled, my legs gave way and I almost fell back in the hatch! One of my legs slipped, and they're catching me, and I'm thinking, 'Oh no, I've messed up, and I've fallen, I'm gonna go back down and they're not going to let me go …'

No, they picked me up and motioned to me (he'd given me one of the packages) they motioned to put my package to the right where there were these packages the other people brought. They set them down. It was almost like a simple, little Christmas-like setting. Because, here were these little plain packages off to the right, against a fir tree type of thing…there was some kind of setting there.

And here's this throne and although He was absolutely King Jesus – stunning!! He's sitting on this very beautiful but simple, approachable throne. It looked like a captain's chair that you'd go up and see your Dad or Grandfather rather, or great Uncle. And yet with all the wisdom of the ages and everything else you could see in His face, and His hair seemed as white as snow.

Coming out from that was this persona was that of this beautiful Jesus with His chestnut colored hair and His youthful face. And He was so kind and so gentle and so welcoming. The throne was right in front of this hearth, almost a cozy fireplace setting, which I didn't expect at all. Wow. It totally took my breath away, so much so that my whole being just poured out with all the strength that I had left, that I could muster. Which wasn't anything, I was so taken by this whole thing.

Jesus! God! Jesus, My God, My Lord is right in front of me!! I remember pouring out His name from deep inside of me…JESUS!! And I woke up.

Clare: Whoo! That was quite a dream!

Ezekiel: You mentioned one other dream that I had a couple weeks ago.

Clare: Yeah – that's right. It was very, very short but it really got your attention and it had the signature of the Holy Spirit. We both felt the anointing on it.

Ezekiel: Let me mention here that we base everything, every move we make on the Scriptures. And if the Lord doesn't give us a second and third witness from the Scriptures, we don't make a move. And I know that I went to the Lord prayerfully, asking Him to give some kind of rhema or rhemas, some confirming words from Scripture. I've had dreams that weren't from Him, and I've gotten things about lying, and all kinds of yucky junk.

And then these dreams, one by one by one, I've gotten beautiful Scriptures about joy and Heaven and fulfillment, just the love of the Lord. And I'd just know. Sometimes it would be smack-on Scriptures of Holy Spirit, so I just knew it was from Him. Plus that deep, deep inner witness, and that strong feeling and sense that you're so moved with that it just lasts for years. It never goes away.

Rapture Dreams from Ezekiel #4

October 1, 2015

Clare: So what happened, in your dream.

Ezekiel: Well, we kiddingly call it Rapture Practice. I walked out in the back on this little artificial golf strip thing that my wife got me after I was recovering from a hospital stay. It points exactly east and west. And I go out and I'm standing on this thing, looking up through these massive Cottonwood trees they have out here in New Mexico. Up through the trees and I can see the stars and the moon and the skies– whether it's day or night, I'm just looking East all the time.

And I kid around - I've got this cable out there and I run and jump and practice some flying.

In this dream, I was out there on this little golf course thing, I was looking east – and I noticed the clouds started to turn almost...like they were icing up. It was weird. They were clouds, but they looked like they were turning into this plastic cellophane crunchy folds in them, like they were icing or glazing. And all of a sudden, they were taking a shape: a long line at one end, at the far end, and then two long lines coming toward me like a long table. Then two long side tables coming toward me.

Clare: Like a U-shaped banquet table?

Ezekiel: Yeah, that's exactly - like a horseshoe from the open side. There's the guest of honor and the Bride and Groom's table, and then these two side tables for the guests. And you came out and you were beside me, and I said, "Look, look! There's something..." And there were a couple other people there. We could all see that there was something in the clouds.

And we were like, "Wait a minute – You could see...Yeah, there's someone moving there." We could see people moving around the chairs and the table, which were becoming clearer and more distinct. Tables and plates and settings and candles and dinnerware...and it was kinda coming a little closer. And we were seeing all this stuff – and this beautiful movement going on.

All of a sudden, we could kind of feel ourselves drawn to that - maybe it was just our passion and desire. But as we were feeling that pull and draw – here came Jesus along the side, I guess to the right side. And He was just...He had on a white tunic with a reddish sash, like an over-robe. And he'd look at the table here, and walk down a little bit, talk to one of the servants, and once again – I didn't see wings, I didn't see angel's wings – these were table servers. Old time type, with tunic type things, robe type things. Simple servants. And they were checking. The table was magnificent, beautiful – satin, lacy white tablecloth, silver and gold candle and table settings. All that was rich. But the servers again just like the angels, plain white tunics and belt.

They were getting things ready and they were beginning to bring food out – and you just knew! I mean, it just dawned on me in the dream..."Wow! The Wedding Feast of the Lamb!!"

And again, boom! I woke up!

Clare: Oh no, I want to see more!!

Ezekiel: Yeah, I was ready to go and take my seat, you know. And I thought, 'Wow, that's weird that I had that dream – I don't ever think of the wedding feast or that time…'

Clare: You wrote a little song after that, didn't you? High Table. Beautiful. It's just has one word, that's all the song was.

Ezekiel: I couldn't get any lyrics going it…

Clare: Oh, but it was so beautiful!

Ezekiel: Just one thing "It was a high table" (singing) Then you hear these harmonies coming in…

Clare: Did you record that?

Ezekiel: No, not yet. Some things are just so precious, and just a few words you don't want to tamper or mess with it.

Clare: Well, I'm putting it on your list…please record it and I'll put it on Youtube along with this interview

Ezekiel: When the Holy Spirit gives me that, it'll be great. But in the meantime, that's exactly what it was. It was High and Lifted Up. It was a High Table. It was magnificent! And I was thinking, 'Why would I have a dream like that?' 'Cause I'm not really into weddings and feasts and gold and silver... I just want to get on with business, get on into Heaven and head for the Honeymoon Shack, so to speak.

I just want to love the Lord, be in His arms, and just BE there. Get on with beautiful life with Him in Heaven. But for whatever His reasons, He brought that. And the feeling that I woke up with and that stayed with me is, "This thing's for REAL. This is the REAL DEAL. There's a real table with real settings, it's really being prepared, He's checking on the preparations – He's ready to bring us UP!!"

Clare: I just put out a message, I guess, yesterday. It was what the Lord told me during my prayer time, He came to me during my prayer time and He told me **"Everything is ready and I'm at the door. But I'm waiting for the Father's word."** And I kinda chided Him, 'cause I know what the Scriptures say, that He didn't know the hour and the day…that "no man knows the hour and the day" but I kinda chided Him and said, "I just can't believe that You – Almighty God – don't know… anything? How can this be??"

He was very sweet with me, He said that the reason He doesn't know the hour and the day is because He is so close to His Bride, He's so attached and loves her so much and has so many expectations, that He doesn't...He can't back off from the whole picture to call the shot. And the Father is calling the shot and will tell Him when it's time. And He's relinquished His privilege of knowing the hour and the day and the time. But He's in readiness because He knows it could be at any moment.

Ezekiel: Yeah, He'd have to relinquish that because you'd think, well - He could call the shots or do anything – He's God. But If He chose to put that on hold and to…

Clare: Leave it in the hands of the Father, Who's in some ways more distant from the situation. I can understand it, totally understand.

Ezekiel: Well, I'm not sure what it all means or what the theological Scriptural implications are…all I know is, it gave me a different perspective when you brought that forward. And that is, I'm not begging and begging and begging the Lord to come back and rapture us out of here as much, because…He said it. No one knows the day and the Hour, not even the Son…only the Father.

And I'd been thinking all this time, 'Well surely by now YOU know, because you're God? But if He doesn't know, if that's still the way He said it was in the Scriptures, then it caused me to calm down a little bit, be more peaceful about it – not be tugging at His robe so much, beseeching Him…"Lord! Please, I just…!!"

But it also caused me to go to the Father all the more and tell Him, "Daddy." And that's who He is to me now. "Daddy, please, You know I love Jesus. I need Him, I want Him so much, I've got to have Him. I can't survive without being fully united with Him. I have got to have Him completely. I've got to be with Him completely, please." I begged Him a couple weeks ago out on that little golf course run, looking up in the sky. Stayed up all night with just passionate tears…All I could say is the desire was SO STRONG to just be with Him, finally, once and for all. But it's caused me to say, "Wow! So I guess, yeah – there are souls that still need to be saved, and You gave ME more time at one time."

And the Father's heart, I'm sure, is to save as many souls as will be saved. But there will, like the Lord said, right? There'll come a time when the Father says…

Clare: Okay, well that's what I was going to share with you, is that the Lord…last night when the Lord was talking to me about this, you could feel the anxiety in His heart over the whole situation. And basically what He was saying is that He's being ignored, His warnings are being ignored, people are still being married, given in marriage, running around shopping, buy and selling – they're still going about their business and they're not… Even though the Internet, for instance, has been flooded with all this information about dreams and visions about the Lord's returning – even though all that's going on, they're still not paying as much attention as all these gifts would warrant.

As a result of that, the Father knows what the balance is. He knows how long…just, He knows when to "push the button" so to speak. When to give the word, because He can see the balance of the ones that are trying to change and turning from sin and reforming their lives and listening to the Message – and the ones that aren't. What the Lord told me last night is simply that, it's getting to the point where not enough people were listening, and that therefore, this could happen at any time. At any moment, because there will come a moment when the Father will say, **"Enough!"**

Ezekiel: Yeah, that's what really caught me, my attention. That's really had an impression on me that "I won't contend with man forever."

Clare: Right. "There's a window of grace. It's been open a very long time, but I've got to bring it to a close now, we have to move on."

Ezekiel: I got the Scriptures yesterday in my prayer time about the one who had entered into the Wedding Feast not properly dressed, and how the Master came. **"My friend, how is it you came in not properly dressed?"**

I know the Lord has been pointing out to me, bringing up deep in my heart and my soul and my memories things that maybe I've either forgotten about or I just didn't pay that much attention to. And He's really, really been giving me a real grace to feel contrite, to feel repentant about things that I might never, ever repented of before.

But, things seem more serious now. There's no, "Well, that's just a little thing. That's just a little white lie."

Something about His presence, His majesty, His purity. His pristine integrity. In the light of that, boy you see EVERY spot and wrinkle on your wedding dress and you want it out! You don't want to show up in front of Him with that. And I think He's giving us an opportunity to clean house a little bit of these things.

Clare: Oh, Absolutely!

Ezekiel: Right the wrongs, say I'm sorry, ask for forgiveness... whatever we have to go back and right. Right some wrongs here.

Clare: Well, the next teaching that I'm working on is how to recognize the Bride. And the topic the Lord seems to really be stressing is humility. Of course, you know 'cause you've had to go through it with me, I'm recognizing my pride more than I ever have before, and I'm more disgusted with myself than I ever have been before. And yet the Lord is encouraging me that He's working with it.

I think the Bride is not going to be perfect until He perfects her. But if she's made the commitment to be perfect and is on the way – I think He receives that as the finished product, so to speak, 'cause He knows He's going to finish her off.

Ezekiel: Right. We can't do it on our own, but I think that He wants us to have a heart to be right before Him.

Clare: Well, thank you for sharing all this. Maybe sometime we'll be able to share our testimony. We've both had beautiful conversion experiences over 30 years ago, and at some point we'll share those too.

Ezekiel: Yeah, kinda slammed us into each other a few years after that. That's a whole other story.

Clare: I just want to thank you Youtube family for tuning in and if you like this, leave us a little thumbs up if you like, or leave a comment.

The Rapture and Nuclear War Dreams & Prophetic Word

November 3, 2014

The dream that I had of the nuclear annihilation of Miami and the message and the promise that came with this just a few days afterward.

I dreamt that I was on a white, sandy beach on a sub-tropical ocean and a fishing dory was nearby with fishing nets and primitive looking implements. It was obvious to me I was not in America. It was a sunny day, perhaps midmorning or early afternoon and I was occupied cleaning a fishing net when I turned and looked behind me, over my right shoulder across the ocean, and saw a first sized cloud on the distant horizon. It quickly began to swell, getting bigger and bigger and I realized that a city in the distance, though I could not see it, had just been struck with an atomic bomb.

I cried out, "Oh, my God!" and awoke from the dream.

Immediately, I knew the dream had been from Holy Spirit. All I could do was pray for mercy. Later I looked for the location of the city and determined that it was either Houston viewed from the eastern coast of the Baha, or Miami viewed from a Cuban beach. I'm pretty sure now, looking back on it, that I was looking northward, so it would have been Miami.

"Lord, I want to know more about what's going to happen in the world and what I can do to help. You know I did not want to pry into things that are far beyond me."

At that point, (this was during my prayer) before me was a beautiful white and sandy beach, edged with aquamarine waters. There's something strange, though. All the way down the beach, as far as the eye can see, large grey masses have been thrown up along the shoreline. As I looked more closely, I realized they were human bodies. It was so gruesome I dared not look any more closely.

I turned to the Lord and asked solemnly, "Where are we?"

He answered, **"Nassau in the Bahamas.**

"There will be carnage such as has never been seen. Do you remember the message you were given many years ago? 'Do not fear death, O' righteous inhabitants of Earth.'"

And I do, I remember that, and I will share it with you at the end of this message.

We were now suspended above Earth between the Bahamas and Miami. Jesus was weeping and I was in shock. It was one blackened mass. At once we could see up close and there was not a survivor stirring.

"Are you listening to Me?" Jesus asked.

Numbness engulfed my entire being and I simply could not comprehend what I was seeing.

He began again. **"You will still be on the Earth when this happens, but very quickly afterwards I will whisk you both away in the Rapture."**

I asked, "How soon after this happens will You take us, Lord?"

He answered, **"Within a week."**

"Seven days?"

"At maximum. There's no reason for you to be here past that point."

"Lord, I don't know what to say."

"Such carnage as this has never before fallen upon the Earth. Never was it possible for a man to inflict this kind of damage on My Creation. Were not the End soon approaching, I would intervene - but it must happen this way for the fulfillment of Scripture. Because you are leaving so quickly, you will finally understand: there's no need to store up anything. Nothing to worry about, no shortage or lack."

I think it's worth noting here that there's been a lot of confusion over when the Rapture would happen: before the Tribulation, after the Tribulation, mid-Tribulation. I think that it is noteworthy the Lord said about the coming of the Son of Man in the 29th verse of Matthew 24.

Matthew 24:29-31 But immediately after the tribulation of those days the sun shall be darkened, and the moon shall not give her light, and the stars shall fall from the sky, and the powers of the heavens shall be shaken: and then shall appear the sign of the Son of man in heaven: and all the tribes of the earth mourn, and they shall see the Son of man coming on the clouds of heaven with power and great glory. And he will send out his angels with a trumpet blast, and they shall gather together his elect from the four winds, from one end of the heavens to the other.

The point I'd like to make here is this series of events that fits this particular outlining here that the Lord gave is that, if you were to see the Earth from above and there was an exchange of nuclear missiles back and forth between the Middle East and US and Europe, it would be unprecedented chaos. And of course, from all of the release of pollutants from these bombs, the sun would be darkened and the moon wouldn't give it's light. That all fits that profile. And that the Lord sends out his angels to the four directions to gather His elect - that makes sense. And the trumpet blast - that makes sense that that would be the Rapture. So, it does indeed make sense that this atomic war would begin before the Rapture. That's not to say this is the Tribulation, this is something different. This is a war, a nuclear exchange that will wreak havoc on the planet and perhaps throw things off course in the heavens and certainly obscure the sun and the Moon.

I take this prophecy, this word from the Lord very seriously and it explains a lot to me as to how all this could come about and still be a pre-Tribulation Rapture.

And as an aside here, this is very interesting to me. I was starting to, well you know we have a food bank, I was ordering extra food to store up and the Lord rebuked me for doing that.

He said, **"No, I don't want you to do that."** and so I gave all that food away and stopped doing it. I couldn't understand why, but He explained it to me here. I'd like to leave food for other people, but out of obedience I'm not going to do it.

One thing is certain – the Scriptures must be fulfilled. Mercy leaves boundless room for God to intervene but certain things must take place. It is in His hands and in the prayers of our hearts to see to it that the greatest mercy possible could be shed on the world and the souls of those involved in these events. Especially the grace of conversion to these souls that don't know him.

Another thing in this message, in the timing of the Rapture being right after nuclear war on our soil that caught my attention, is that there will be a tremendous amount of grieving and repentance that will take place amongst the Christians in this country and in the world. A tremendous amount of looking at their lives and repenting.

And I think this is probably going to be the finishing touch on the Bride's garment – the things that have just been hanging there, and hanging and hanging for so long. And the enormity of the situation things are going to just fall right off, just gonna be blasted right off of the garment because the real priorities of life – loving God, loving our neighbor, eternity and the last things – these are going to come up and they're going to be very strongly in our minds at this time. And I believe that that's going to be one of the forces that will help to prepare the Bride.

I still think there's great possibility in this message and great merit that He's coming for His Bride in a time of unbelievable turmoil and agony in society.

Later on in this vision He continues:

"Tell them for Me, those who are destined for the sword, if you are caught in the midst of these events and are innocent of the sins of this culture, are repentant and reformed in Me, you will wear a martyr's crown and great glory will be yours in Heaven, because you survived with your soul intact, and remained faithful to Me in a wanton, reckless ungodly, generation. You have suffered for your faith, everything from ridicule to exclusion. I have been present with you each time you suffered reproach for My Name's sake and your recompense is on the way.

"Understand that once this time of unparalleled suffering begins, the living will envy the dead. For at that time, there will be great Tribulation such has not been since the beginning of the world until now nor ever will there be. There's great Joy awaiting you and your reception into Heaven will be the occasion of feasting and merriment. Your time of exile is almost at an end."

So, several years ago, (going into the message that He gave me) several years ago I was on a mission trip in South America and I beheld the vault of the deep blue sky as if from a space shuttle. The Earth was clearly before me and there were missiles being launched from one continent to another. They seemed to originate in the Middle East and land in America. When they hit, smoky gray clouds hovered over the area and spontaneously something like fourth of July fireworks shot up into the heavens all the way to the Throne of God. The fireworks ascending to the Throne of God were the souls of the just.

I heard this: *"Do not fear death, O righteous inhabitants of the Earth."*

Then the Lord began to speak. **"See, I will bring devastation on this Earth, not by My design but by your own, O wicked men among mankind. You who have perverted the truth and robbed the poor: you, too, shall lament and wail; for what you have engineered to destroy others shall be your own undoing.**

"Truly it is written of you: ***"Those who have dug the pit shall be the ones who fall into it. And those who set the snare shall themselves be caught in it." Proverbs 26:27***

"Woe, Woe, Woe to you wicked amongst mankind. For the hour of your great undoing is upon you, but my righteous shall shine like the stars in the firmament. Fear not the hour of your death, for that day you shall be with Me in Paradise, and inherit your eternal reward - for to you I have given a crown of Victory."

"For those who have had a hand in planning the demise of the poor and helpless of the world, while making arrangements to save themselves, it is written: *Isaiah 28:15-18 Because you say, "We have made a covenant with death, and with the nether world are we have made a pact; when the overwhelming scourge passes, it will not reach to us; for we have made lies our refuge, and in falsehood we have found a hiding place." therefore thus says the Lord God, "See, I am laying a stone in Zion, a stone that has been tested, a precious corner-stone as a sure foundation: he who puts his faith in it shall not be shaken. I will make a right measuring line of justice: a level. Hail shall sweep away the refuge of lies, waters shall flood the hiding-place. Your covenant with death shall be cancelled, and your pact with the netherworld shall not stand; when the overwhelming scourge passes, you shall be trampled down by it."*

And that was the end of His message.

So, it's an encouragement to believers and a warning to those who've planned all these things. Without going into the details, it's all over the Internet – the kind of intrigue and plots and planning that have happened in order to prepare us for this time, prepare themselves for this time and to wipe out and annihilate so much of America and so much of the world population.

But the Lord shall take those who are righteous and they mount up into Heaven like stars ascending to the Throne.

Pacific Ring of Fire Earthquake and Wyoming Nuclear Event

November 23, 2014

We have lots of dreams, but very few carry the signature of the Holy Spirit. It is a certain kind of knowing and urgency we feel deep in our gut...and many times they may just be warning dreams so we can pray that the events will be mitigated or not even happen at all.

Wyoming Nuclear Event Prophetic Dream

This is another dream that I had about an atomic blast in Wyoming. It's very short.

I found myself in a desert clearing where there was very little vegetation. It was a large parking lot at a crossroads. There were press and media trucks, cameras, and newsmen scattered around in a general atmosphere of panic.

There had just been a nuclear explosion in Wyoming. It had devastated a very large area, which was now restricted from anyone entering. Even the newsman who was preparing himself to go on the air was at risk from radiation poisoning. I remember in this dream that the skies were very dark and it seemed to be sometime in the winter.

As I look back on this dream, I think a lot about Yellowstone and the possibility of an eruption there, but I have to say that when I went to check the details of this dream, it very specifically said that there was some kind of nuclear event that happened in Wyoming. I know that there are quite a few silos that have not been decommission in Wyoming, so I don't know if it had anything to do with that or not.

This dream was on April 5th in 2007. You want to keep the people of Wyoming and pray for mercy that the Lord will have mercy and prevent things like this from happening because of our prayers.

Pacific Ring of Fire Earthquake Prophetic Dream

This is a dream that took place on December 31st 2006: a devastating earthquake. The Ring of Fire swayed back and forth like a bowl full of jelly. A deep heaviness fell upon my soul in prayer and I saw what appeared to be a very rough, bowl-shaped depression in the Earth filled with liquid swaying back and forth, from side to side. I recognized this formation as the Ring of Fire in the Pacific Ocean as the Lord lifted me up in the spirit above the Earth.

Below me was the city of San Francisco in rubble. I saw a man walking out of it dazed and injured. To the south, where Los Angeles had been, a dingy was floating past a pointed object protruding from the water. I recognized it as the very top of the skyscraper. It slowly sank further down into the water until it could be seen no more. I saw a volcano far to the north along the coast. The whole right side (southeast) facing of the mountain had spilled out and collapsed. The entire west coast had a different shape I did not recognize.

The spirit within me began grieving as I cried out "Mercy, Lord, mercy" over and over again. And then a new prayer echoed forth,

“Repentance, Conversion”

“Repentance, Conversion.”

“Mercy, Lord, mercy.”

State of Each Soul Revealed: Prophetic Dream

December 15, 2014

This is another prophetic dream from Ezekiel that occurred in the winter of 2001. At that time we were living in a high mountain retreat in cabin, no water, electricity, very primitive.

I had just finished feeding our horses and getting wood in for the night. As I was very tired, I went to sleep early and during the night I was transported to a large football stadium. There was a professional game well underway and cheering thousands filled the stands. I was sitting on the south side of the field when I noticed a commercial airliner flying low over the stadium lights.

Suddenly, everything instantly stopped as if frozen in time. The plane was so low that I could see the passengers through the lighted windows. During a span of about three minutes, every spectator, player and air passenger along with pilots, coaches, assistants and workers, each and every person was transparently illuminated from the inside out. Each soul was immediately visible in perfect detail.

Many of those were absolutely beautiful and had a pearlescent kind of sheen. Others were horribly grotesque. And some looked charred in black and very thin. Still others looked to be wretched and moldy green. They were more creature than human.

The beautiful souls lifted up their hands high rejoicing and praising God. The black-charred souls fell to their knees and wept bitterly, begging for forgiveness with sincere repentance. The greenish creatures shook their fist in angry defiance at God.

In the blink of an eye, everything resumed as normal. The jet roared by overhead, players snapped back into motion. It was like everything just picked up where it had stopped.

However, many people quickly paused. Many were totally bewildered at what had just happened.

Some began to cry tears of joy knowing they had been forgiven. The beautiful souls lingered in an ecstatic afterglow. Unfortunately, others began to shake their heads and shrug their shoulders dismissing it all as nothing. They simply stood to their feet and walked away.

I felt such a sense of heaviness and grief over those who were so arrogantly going their own way, knowing that they had so willfully and scornfully rejected such a merciful grace from the Lord as His last and final help for their salvation. And that's the end of the dream.

Let us continually pray for so many souls who with full knowledge will run headlong over the edge of the abyss into hell with such prideful contempt for His love and kindness. Let's pray that somehow, someway their hardened hearts will be softened and touched in these last hours.

NWO & Russian Troupes & North Korean Snipers on American Soil, Prophetic Dream

December 21, 2014

I had some very dark dreams a few nights ago. This one was two nights ago – the 17th of December, 2014. I've had a lot of dreams like this in the last year or two, and I kind of wrote them off to pizza – but after talking to my husband about it, I began to understand that the Lord was showing me things that are going to come. For that reason I'm going to share this dream with you, and as I can remember other ones I'll bring them up, too.

A lot of those dreams I never wrote down. Part of the problem is they were so dark, you just didn't want to remember.

But this was a New World Order dream and it was during the Tribulation. The New World Order was in complete control. It seemed to me that everything had fallen into place for them. The people were upwardly mobile, healthy and beautiful. They were engaged in every area of the world, controlling all that went on.

There was no way for me to get food. I didn't have the Mark. I couldn't put gas in my truck and go to the mountain where we had our cabins, our retreat and hermitage. I thought to myself, 'Even if we DID get up there, there's no food. But then, maybe I can hitch a ride up there and find something to eat.'

It was like we were totally trapped: no food, no gas, no way to get up there. It felt very dismal and desperate.

Well, in this dream I was in town somewhere – and I was visiting a lady, a poor woman who was living in a trailer park. I could see a disc satellite dish out in a vacant field about two streets over. It was on a busy street like a boulevard in an industrial area with high-powered electric lines. I had the understanding that they were tracking devices in the store-bought items in the house, even in the food like the cereal and canned goods. It made me angry and I knew that satellite dish was tracking us, so I did something - and for the life of me, guys; I don't remember what it was I did. It was probably something in the Name of Jesus. Don't know what it was but the dish fell over and started rolling until it just came to a stop. Totally disabled.

There was a young woman who was from the New World Order that came into the trailer. She and I kind of hit loggerheads with each other. And she said, "Do you want me to call for back up?" She called before I could even answer her and a van pulled up outside the trailer with five big guys who got out.

They came into the trailer – and actually they were pretty well mannered, they weren't real bullying. They came into the trailer the way the police would come into a non-threatening situation, kind of to check out what was going on.

One of the men in his 20's sat down with me on the couch and began asking me questions. I could soon tell that something else was on his mind – not sure what. But I began telling him, "You don't really believe these people you are working for are on the up and up with you, do you?" He looked at me with interest.

I continued, "They're going to use you until you are no longer useful, then they'll do away with you. Probably leave you and your buddies locked out when a neutron bomb hits or lock you out of their underground cities and let you die of the plague. In any case, they are being used by the aliens, who are really demons sent to destroy the Earth – and you are being used by them. In the end, they will get what they have sown to others as well."

And the dream ended there. Wish I had more to share but that's where it ended.

Okay now, here is another dream that's very, very short, so I'm going to tag it in onto this message. This was November 11, 2014.

I was alone at the southern border of the United States, probably towards east Texas. Russia had occupied troops throughout the whole area. And it was cloudy; I remember it was very cloudy and dark outside. They were well established with boots on the ground, buildings, vehicles and everything they needed to occupy our country.

I watched two high-ranking officers talking together and making more plans to move deeper in to the country, take more ground. Somehow they didn't pay any attention to me and I managed to slip away. I left undetected and began moving north from the Mississippi Delta area. I believe I got as far as northern Arkansas. Deep in the forest, I began to see North Korean snipers in the trees. They were covert forces, peppering the deep woods. And that was the end of that dream.

Now, I do remember a dream – I haven't got it written down, but a dream from 20 years ago where we saw Russian tanks on the freeways in Texas in Dallas. Russian tanks and Russian vehicles, army vehicles moving into America from the Mexican border around Dallas. That was years and years and years ago.

Anyway, that's all I have to share with you on dreams right now. The Lord willing, we will have more to share with you later. God bless you Youtube family. Thank you so much for listening.

Russian Fighters over Nebraska, Prophetic Dream

December 28, 2014

Good evening, precious Youtube family. Had a little break here for the holidays and doing a little bit more work with music and writing songs, So…been away, but the Lord kind of brought me back with a snap!

This morning I had a very powerful dream, which I want to share with you. It began somewhere, I would say, in the Midwest – or at least in an area that looked very much like the Midwest. It was in America, in the United States. It's about Russian fighters and drones that were flying over our air space and attacking us. So, I'll go ahead and begin the dream.

I'm not sure of the exact location but seemed to be somewhere like Nebraska, outside of a major city, about 20 miles or so. It was open land, farmland in vast tracts. Modern houses about a mile or two apart were scattered here and there - obviously these folks were comfortable financially – they had SUVS, and ATV's and you name it.

The two places where I was at, there were two houses side by side. I was visiting a family with young children. The house was kind of modern and newly built, and they had young children. They were having a small, casual meeting with their neighbors in the living room, and the subject was the Russian invasion of America, which seemed imminent.

Now, I remember the mother was putting together dinner, and she showed me some kind of gourmet meat roll with artichoke hearts that she was going to prepare. The kids were home, and I believe it was mid-to-late summer time, because some of the things in her garden were ready for harvest.

I noticed her talking about her neighbors, I noticed a bit of rivalry in her voice over her neighbor's cooking and it seemed like there was some petty jealousies between the two women, in the two families. So, I decided to take a short stroll over to her neighbor's house to meet her.

Their houses were very similar, and both families' children were playing outside and just having fun. The woman was very cordial and showed me what she was preparing for dinner.

I'm not sure when it all began, but suddenly we heard low-flying fighter jets approaching. We all went outside to see what is was, and someone recognized them as Russian.

Now, the first time that we saw them, they were headed from south to north – like they were coming back from some kind of sortie, and going back to their source. Because from that point on, every fighter that flew over us was coming from the north. Off in the distance we began to see smoke and one plane exploded in the air some miles away. More Russian fighter jets came in from the north, but this time they were accompanied by drones, you know those big grey drones with the kind of dolphin heads on them? It was that kind of a drone. And while I didn't see any explosions or bullets strafing the ground, I knew that they were attacking us.

There was a calm for a short while, and we went outside to look. We saw smoke off in the distance, and someone said that the smoke was from farmers who had set the edge of their field on fire deliberately to impair visibility.

Off in the distance, another Russian fighter exploded, then they started coming in again: one fighter, with a drone trailing closely beside it. We all ran for cover under a picnic table tarp set up in the back yard. This turned out to be a foolish choice, because in came a helicopter, and I saw it's landing skid touch the ground behind us. And he was right on top of us. I thought, 'Oh, this was a bad choice! They're going to land right on top of us and we're going to get crushed!'

And then I woke up. And that was the end of the dream.

When I told Ezekiel about the dream, he quoted the Scripture in Luke: Just as it was in days of Noah, so it will be in the day of the coming of the Lord. For men were eating and drinking, marrying and being given in marriage until the day Noah entered the ark and the flood came and destroyed them all.

Well, obviously this is fulfillment of the Lord's talk about wars and rumors of wars that have been going on before the Rapture. And what is to say they're not going to be going on in America before the Rapture? Absolutely nothing. That's just part of the world condition. Wars and rumors of wars, and we were entering into a war with the Russians in this dream.

Now, this does seem to apply the Scripture to the situation, because the women were involved in petty disputes and gourmet meals. I asked about bomb shelters and they said they had none. The men were not in crisis mode, they were sitting comfortably in their armchairs talking things over. Then it hit. And there they were: sitting ducks in a shooting gallery, totally defenseless.

So, lets pray on these things, pray for the best outcome. I really do believe that this dream had the signature of the Holy Spirit. All we can do is pray for God's mercy, that those who need to be prepared will be prepared. And as I said before, the Lord promised us wars and rumors of wars. There're wars going on all over the world, and America is no different than any other nation. Well, I shouldn't say that – because we've had our very good points as well as our very bad points. We're just as vulnerable to wars as anyone else.

The Lord bless you, and let's pray for each other.

Prophetic Dream of an Apocalyptic Event in the U.S.

February 11, 2015

My husband, Ezekiel, had a dream last night, or this morning actually, of apocalyptic proportions. The dream itself was not long and it didn't show a lot of things, but what it did show, I think was fairly significant. So, I'm going to go ahead and get right down to business here and relate the dream to you.

Ezekiel: I was walking down a boulevard that seemed to be inland quite a ways from the ocean, when sheets and waves of wind and water began to fall from the sky. News crews were milling around and showing up at different places, and I wondered what could be happening. Parts of buildings were falling off, and cars were turned on their sides.

I ran into a gas station to take cover under the canopy and just as I was going to ask someone what was happening, 3 jellyfish-looking creatures came flying through the air and attached themselves to a sign.

I looked around and there were people lying on the ground - maybe four of five, here and there. These creatures seemed to be on them, also. Some other creatures were dead, lying in clusters. Many of them were very traumatized and terribly disoriented, almost in some sort of shock as they were flailing around, grasping anything they could get a hold on.

Waves and sheets of water were coming down from the sky carrying these creatures from high up in the air. There seemed to be other species and I saw some small stingrays, but I couldn't identify all of them. They were nothing bigger than a large sea turtle.

The overhead structure of the gas station was beginning to fall apart and I noticed more and more groups of these sea creatures had already attached themselves to other buildings and cars. As I walked further and looked closer, winding my way to news crews and police officers, there were many people staggering in shock. I could see more clearly that these were actual creatures from the ocean. Completely out of their element. Not only jellyfish, but clusters of horseshoe crabs were also being blown in by the wind and attaching themselves everywhere to people and buildings and cars.

I turned to walk back out to the boulevard and the traffic was beginning to back up, with cars veering off to the side of the road. I took a closer look to see what was causing the problem and there were sea turtles completely out of their element - they were struggling to get across the road, in many places. They were being blown in by the rain in clusters and bunched up throughout the area. Kinda like small herds of sea turtles.

Many people were down, there was a lot of screaming - they were just trying to get away from these things coming down from the sky and landing on them. I didn't know what to say, as it seemed these creatures were all being blown in by the storm - but it wasn't rain. It was sheets of water.

At that point, I woke up and I told my wife about the dream. And her first question was, "What could cause creatures from the ocean to go flying through the air, carried by the wind, ending up on dry land?" And I deduced that there must have been a massive disturbance in the ocean. I don't know if it was caused by a meteor, a tsunami…but my first impression was that it was some kind of massive bomb or missile that had exploded off-shore with such an impact that it nearly emptied a coastal basin area, since this seemed to be further inland. I say massive, because the area where this took place did not seem to be on the coast at all, but far inland. BIG question mark.

And that's the end of the narration of the dream. That's pretty amazing stuff. I mean, it could be the meteor that people are talking about, many meteors that we've talked about. It could be something…a little "gift" from Russia. Who knows? There're so many different things it could have been. The Lord at that time didn't reveal the source of it, but the scene itself was terrifying. The creatures from the sea just coming flying through the air in sheets of water and landing everywhere – it was really, really scary.

We prayed over this and we went to our Scriptures about it and we feel Holy Spirit has put His signature on this dream or we wouldn't be sharing it with you. It certainly is bizarre.

So, the Lord bless you, Youtube channel and thank you for tuning in to this channel.

Prophetic Dream from Ezekiel - Magnetic Pole Shift, Rocks Fall From the Sky, Hybrid Carnivores

February 24, 2015

Clare: My husband Ezekiel had a dream in the wee small hours of the morning that I'm going to relate to you.

Ezekiel: I seem to be somewhere in Montana, on the southwestern side of the foothills, in a broad valley just below the pine-forested mountains. I was with a group of about 10-12 forestry workers with different toolboxes and instruments, clipboards and antennae's. I was a volunteer – an auxiliary helper.

We had all spread out in a crooked line from northwest to southeast and were slowly walking across the field away from the tree line. I kept hearing a lot of noise in the tree line area: people yelling to one another, trucks and cars also, as there was an access road in the area. Then I noticed some civilians coming out of the trees in different areas, and running out into the field towards the southwest, away from the tree line.

Many of the men on the crew were beginning to hesitate, and look back over their shoulders at the trees. Simultaneously the crew leader, who was beside me, turned and said, "Come on, come one! Let's GO!"

We started to run towards the southwest away from the trees and foothills. I turned around and looked behind us and to the left uphill, just in time to see large rocks raining down from above. The stones were not on fire, they were just one and two foot rocks and boulders the color of sandstone. But they were hurtling in from such a distance high up in the sky into the field just behind us. Then they began to overtake us and land even further beyond us. I thought it was by the grace of God that we weren't hit.

Then I noticed herds of elk, buffalo, bears and other animals coming out of the woods and the trees everywhere – and running down hill in a panic. Unfortunately, these stones and even larger ones that began to fall, started hitting many of them, killing them instantly.

I began to run towards the animals, and the crew chief began to yell, "Don't run that way! Don't run that way!"

I looked downhill to the right and saw huge, amphibian-looking creatures coming up the wide valley towards us. They were in the shape of salamanders, tending towards a whale shape – with huge mouths and very large, sharp teeth. They were greyish-black with off-white bellies, about 30 feet long and 20 feet high. Their skin looked moist and their feet had mutated – they looked stubby, even though there were fins there. Somehow, what they had allowed them to walk on the land.

They were far ahead of us down the valley, yet moving up towards us and as soon as the buffalo and other animals met them, they opened their gaping jaws with huge teeth and completely engulfed and ate many of the fleeing animals in one sweeping move – one by one. It was almost as if they were just coming up the hill, and the animals were running right into their mouths.

I remember the crew chief yelling back, "Don't go that way – don't go that way!" So we veered off to the left, slightly.

The scene changed and we were at a triage unit that had been set up to care for the wounded. A very strange thing began to happen. (Yeah, as if the other thing wasn't strange – that was pretty weird!)

The Earth's gravity began to reverse itself slightly, and anything lightweight – such as grass, debris, etc. began to float up in the air. And you could feel the strange sensation in your body, like all your body fluids were rising up with a bit of vertigo.

I heard two doctors saying, "Put him down. Put him upside down!" I looked to see a man on some kind of respiration device, and the liquid vapor treatment kept rising up to the top of the container and wouldn't go through the tube. And they had to turn the man upside down and put the container below his head, so that the vapor would rise up and go into the tube and get to him, so he could breathe.

Then I heard a man yelling behind me. I turned to see a grown man, beating his 12-year-old son with his fists, mercilessly in the face. He had him up against a car. Four of the other rangers and myself circled around and forcibly took the man off the child, but before we could even catch our breath, other fights began to break out between many different people: couples, men and women and even children.

At that point, there were a couple of police dogs at the guard station – and they began to viciously attack each other. As we were still in a relatively wooded area, two deer came in close to the station and began to attack each other aggressively with hooves and antlers. It was as if suddenly, something had changed the whole pattern of behavior for people and animals alike. Even the birds were attacking each other.

In that moment, I had four questions. Number one: What would cause boulders to be displaced and thrown to a high altitude, causing them to cascade down onto the Earth?

My second question was: What would cause gravity to begin to shift – not substantially, but slightly? Obviously, something had taken place of cataclysmic proportions to unearth these rocks and cause gravity to shift.

Number 3: Where did these bizarre creatures come from? What could have caused such mutations in creatures like that?

Lastly: what would cause such a dramatic and instantaneous behavior modification, causing both humans and creatures to become dangerously aggressive towards one another?"

And that was the end of the dream.

Clare: When he woke up, he picked up his Scriptures and opened to *"Call Me and I will answer you, and tell you great and hidden things you have not known." Jeremiah 33:3*. And *"The Lord does nothing without revealing His plans to His servants the prophets." Amos 3:7* And using that for just a bit of a test, I could only conclude that this was a prophetic dream from the Holy Spirit. In fact, he opened his Bible Promises book to "Holy Spirit" when he asked about that dream.

So, strange things, Youtube family – really strange. But then, the Lord said there would be many strange things. Our only preparation is to be right with the Lord, to love Him with all our hearts and to obey Him. And to pray and repent daily of our shortcomings, and really ask the Holy Spirit, "Please, Holy Spirit, show me. Show me what I'm doing with my life: if I'm sinning, if I'm falling short. Reveal these things to me. I don't want to find out at the last minute. I want to be pleasing to the Lord."

So, on that note, God bless you, Youtube family. I hope the Lord touches your heart and strengthens you for what is ahead with His love and His peace. Amen.

Prophetic Dream: Aliens Disguised

March 9, 2015

Well, here we are again, Youtube family. And this is all about a dream that Ezekiel had this last night. My husband is a very cautious man and has many times uncovered hidden and spiritual things, keeping us from falling into error.

After I was given the part 6 messages, the one preceding this one, he was very concerned because he knows from experience how much the Lord hates to talk about aliens and things that seem out of this world to most people. So he had a serious check about the veracity of this message.

Given that, he went into serious prayer. Well, during the making of that message, a Scripture verse from a site that gives out random Rhemas just happened to pop up...you know, just "happened to"!

And it said, He who believes in Me, as the Scripture has said, *"From his innermost being will flow rivers of living water." It's John 7:38*

So, I knew when I was finalizing the message, that it truly was the Lord. Because I had some doubts, too, since the nature of the material's pretty far out.

Even though I had that confirmation, and I had an inner sense that truly it was from the Lord, I still would not publish a message that my husband was not comfortable with. Because I totally honor and believe in his discernment and it could very well be that I was making a mistake - so I was willing to put it on hold here.

Interestingly enough, after prayer for several hours in seeking our Lord, my husband opened the Scriptures to the very same Scripture, He who believes in me from his innermost being will flow rivers of living waters. And he felt fairly safe in saying that was a good confirmation.

Then we asked a sister in the Lord who is very well seasoned, to pray on these things, and she came back with: "It is from the Lord and accurate in details."

So, my husband listened to it a few more times and he decided, you know, it's not the kind of thing that he would like to hear about or say but he really believed that this is from the Lord. So, just in case, I prayed and said, "Jesus would you please give him a dream, just in case he has any leftover doubts?" And then he went to bed.

Well, several hours later he woke up from a dream that confirms some of content in the message.

So here's the dream.

(And I want to say, the Lord's whole purpose in giving us these messages is to prepare the ones left behind, so they know that Jesus prophesied that this was going to happen before the Church was raptured. So, there's no need to despair, God IS in control. NO doubt about it.)

And the dream begins:

Ezekiel: I was in a large, open, park field. I noticed a man in a uniform with a ball and bat, and what seemed to be his little daughter - she was running across the field and he would hit the ball to her. I looked around and several young high school boys were beginning to come out and practice the game together; within a few minutes there were several groups of young men practicing baseball in different places.

I thought to myself, 'Oh, great! Spring talent training. This place will be full.' As I noticed other adults bringing lawn chairs to watch, I found a seat and sat next to an older man watching the practice game. A woman walked up to my right – whom I assumed was his daughter. She seemed like a normal, 30-year-old housewife and mother, but she had the most piercing eyes and smile. There was something extremely magnetic about her.

I turned my attention back to the boys on the field, casually conversing with the man next to me. I didn't realize it, but she had sat down to the right of me. As I conversed with the man, he asked what my occupation was, and I responded that I was a missionary. Before he could say another word, we were both distracted by a flock of large, black birds flying to the west overhead. This was a very unusual kind of bird that I'd never seen before. They seemed like large, black leaves floating in the wind. In fact, rather than flying, they seemed to be just carried along by the current.

More and more groups flew over us and there were so many it took about five minutes for them to pass. I said to the gentleman next to me, "I've been all over the world and I've never seen that kind of bird - ever."

He didn't seem too concerned and said that birds like that had been seen in the area before. But they were so strange. They seemed like some sort of harbinger. Their wings took no specific patterns but looked more like large, black leaves and their beaks were curved and hooked inward. Very strange.

Within minutes after the birds passed, I saw a gleaming copper-colored ship – an airship that looked like one of our stealth fighters flying overhead. However, it was flying in a strange pattern, like the birds. Then several other ships began to appear in the sky, and just like the birds they seemed more to be floating rather than flying, as if they were being carried along the airstream.

Since the birds had not gotten his attention, I exclaimed to the man, "Look! Look overhead! Do you see that?" At this point, I noticed the woman beside me - and all of us, in fact, craning their necks looking up to behold this spectacle. Just as there was something so magnetic about this woman, there was something very magnetic as well about these aircraft, the way they gleamed and floated.

Spontaneously, the whole field full of people began to walk towards the west in the direction of the planes and we could see that they were touching down not far away. Many began running, as most of us walked hurriedly in that direction.

Soon we found ourselves standing before what looked to be a large university complex of some sort. At the front of the campus was a large welcoming center and various staff members began to come out and greet all of us. They welcomed us in and we all followed eagerly as our curiosity was so heightened by this.

As we were walking in, the older man I was with had veered off to the left side. I was standing at the intersection of two buildings, so the woman and I walked over to him. As we got closer, we could see a strange, plasma-like substance on the wall, and all over him. It seemed to be an opaque, light grayish color.

She said, "Are you okay?"

He turned, wiping the slime off of him saying, "Those blankity, blank, blank, blank greys. I knew this was them. I never trusted them anyway. They've done this before and I hate it. I don't want to have anything to do with it." He simply threw up his hands and walked away in disgust.

Meanwhile, one of the greeters motioned for us to proceed into the building, which we did.

(Now taking an aside here, the grays are aliens - demon aliens.)

We looked up and could see more of these copper-colored craft flying overhead and also small white pod ships with actual civilians like ourselves flying them. A smartly dressed middle-age woman met us and said, "Do you want to be flying or grounded?"

I immediately responded, "Flying." Because I've always had a great interest and desire to fly.

The woman beside me that I had assumed was the man's daughter didn't seem to respond. Nor did the woman address her at all. She simply seated us at the front of a large auditorium. Two men came in orange coverall uniforms and came up to the woman next to me, who I had already suspected might be some kind of alien herself, though I didn't really believe in such things.

They helped her up from her chair and instantly she transformed into a large organism floating aloft between them. It seemed to have the shape of an upside-down teardrop of sorts, but with cells and vessels pumping some sort of fluid throughout. It seemed almost like a larger-than-life amoeba or parasite of some sort and it simply floated away between the two men.

Obviously, I was taken aback by this, as it was very bizarre. But the drama and curiosity, the pull on my desire to be airborne was so strong, I quickly shifted my focus back to the greeter administrator. Seeing that she was the instructor, I was disheartened at the thought of so many hours of instruction and ground school as I knew these things took a long period of time to learn. She must have read my thoughts, because she told me, "Oh, no – this won't take any time at all. The capsule's very user-friendly and it simply will do whatever you want to do just by your thought patterns. It's very intuitive that way."

In my excitement, I got up from my seat and began to walk towards one of the pods to get a closer look. And as I did, a personage of some sort about 15 feet in front of me with its back to me whirled around to face me. At that moment, I could see it was an angel in gleaming armor who looked intently into my eyes and said, "Stop! Do not go there. Don't do it."

At this point I began to awaken slightly from the dream and reached for my Bible to ask the Lord if it was from Him. Before I could pick up my glasses to read, from the head of the bed I heard a voice say, "Faithful and True" and then slip back into the dream. I saw Jesus standing in front of me with the most beautiful countenance and kindest eyes saying, "Faithful and True." I turned to a Scripture about Honesty and Truth. I can't even tell you which one it was, but I began to slip back into the dream.

And I saw Jesus standing in front of me. "I am Faithful and True. You can trust what I give you because it is honest."

I just asked the Lord if it was truly Him and I got the Scripture about Honesty...and here's Jesus back in the dream looking at me, telling me that He is Faithful and True and Honest.

Then I awoke and that's the end of this dream episode.

Clare: So, there are elements in this dream that really parallel some of the things the Lord had given me in Part 6 of His messages: What Is To Come. And it was a real confirmation for him that – even though it's something He doesn't like to talk about, but it's something He needs to talk about right now – and that was a confirmation.

So, the Lord bless you, Youtube Family. I hope that these dreams and these messages are something that you hang on to, especially pass on to your loved ones that you know are not going to be Raptured. Because there's going to be so much confusion that will start happening, that it will be absolutely priceless for them to know that the Lord foretold all of this before we were Raptured.

God bless you, Youtube Family. Keep us in prayer please. Thank you!

President Putin Takes Aim, Prophetic Message & Vision from Jesus

March 20, 2015

Hi, Youtube family. It's been a few days since we've posted. The Lord has had us in intercession. Last night I did receive a vision and a word, basically.

Last night in prayer, the Lord invited me to dance with Him – as He usually does - in a large ballroom filled with brides. And I saw that I was in my bridal gown.

A few minutes after that, I saw President Putin loading a revolver, bullet by bullet, putting bullets in the chamber. And then he lifted it up and he aimed at the heart of the Statue of Liberty. And there was an American flag flying in front of the statue. I didn't see anything beyond that – that's exactly what I saw.

I asked the Lord, "Lord, how can you be here in this beautiful and joyous setting, dancing and enjoying Your Bride when the terrors of war are approaching?"

And this is something that I really haven't understood for a while – so it was a nice opportunity for me to ask Him about this.

He looked deeply into my eyes, so there was no mistaking who I was dancing with or talking to, and He said,

"Because I am undiminished. I can be fully present in both places because I am not diminished in any way, ever. I am in the fullness of My Godhead dancing with you and in the fullness of My Godhead preparing for war." And that was the extent of His spoken message.

Certainly, we are finite human creatures, we really can't understand how this could happen. I guess you could say God "multi-tasks." He has the capability to do everything, and have His full attention on everything – and to be fully engaged in everything that He's doing. Because He's omnipotent – everywhere all at once without being undiminished in any way.

So, He didn't give me any timing on any of this – that was the extent of the vision. And in the meantime, I pray that the Lord keeps your heart and mind in Peace. Be Ready! Because we don't know the day or the hour. But I am believing, continue to believe in the previous words that there will be an incident in Miami. There will be a nuclear event in Miami and that will be the signaling of the Day of the Rapture.

Just to make one thing clear: we don't know the day or the hour – I don't think the enemy even knows the day or the hour of the incident in Miami – because that can change from second to second.

I do want to share with you the Scripture the Lord gave me, because I did go to a Scripture in my Bible, asking Him for verification of message. And of course, my husband went through it thoroughly.

Not one of all the oracles shall be unfulfilled. Everything shall take place in the time appointed for it. For I know and believe, that whatever God has spoken, it will be accomplished. It shall happen, and not a single word of the prophecies shall prove false. Tobit 14:4 From the New Jerusalem Bible (I really enjoy that version.)

So, the Lord bless you all. Please pray for us. We do need your prayers, that we can stay on target and stay accurate. The reason it took me a few days to get this out is, I was under correction for something – living situations and what have you. I've got my faults, just like everyone else, and He tends not to talk to me when I'm doing something that isn't pleasing to Him, to get my attention.

So, I've repented, I've been restored and this is the message. So...if you want to hear uninterrupted messages...I DO need your prayers!

The Lord bless you and keep you in His perfect peace until that Day.

Dome of the Rock Dream

September 7, 2015

The Lord bless each one of you, precious Heartdwellers. Thank you so much for tuning in to our channel.

I had a dream just before I woke up which had the signature of the Holy Spirit. So, I'm going to share it with you.

I was on a ship out at sea. Not far from us was the enemy's ship. The high-ranking commander of the ship was there with his little boy. Within eyesight, I saw the enemy ship and the commander of that vessel had come to visit ours. There seemed to be a very strong attraction the little boy had to this man. I could not make out exactly the significance except that the little boy turned out to be the son of the enemy commander, who was a Muslim, and he didn't know it. Yet, the boy was supposed to be the son of the American commander, officially. That's what everyone thought, anyway. In other words it was thought that the child was the son of the American commander, but in actuality, he was the son of the enemy's ship commander, the Muslim commander.

It seemed like they were all friends; even though they were thought of as enemies, yet behind the scenes they were working together. There was supposed to be an event that was to occur soon and the Muslim commander invited the American commander to come and look. We were in Israel, we were in the City of Jerusalem, and the Muslim commander was walking down a long corridor. He said to the other commander, "Come look, over here, this is a really good view – this is a perfect view." As he motioned for him to come closer, I thought to myself, 'What is it they're looking at?' No sooner did I get that thought through my mind than I caught a glimpse of the top of the Dome of the Rock.

In the meantime, the ships were still out at sea. The Muslim ship was about to fire a plasma ball, but three times the equipment stalled and the very large plasma ball had gone down to one-third of its original size, when it finally fired.

Going back to where the two men were watching the Dome of the Rock, it was obvious they were waiting for it to be blown up. And finally, after quite a long while, the Muslim commander said, "Something's gone wrong. It has misfired, or something has gone wrong." I heard in my own mind, 'Or God has intercepted it; it will never be seen again.'

Then I awoke, because someone was knocking on our door. I think the Lord sent them to knock so I'd wake up and remember this dream.

I sought the Lord for the meaning of this dream and I heard Him say, "Joel 2". So, I got out the Bible and started reading it. And I thought it was very interesting, because this whole second chapter of Joel is about the repentance of the people turning God's judgment away.

Now, about Joel 2. Literally speaking, I don't believe it had to do with this situation, I think it was figuratively. I think the Lord was showing me the dynamic behind why the plasma ball was intercepted. And, there have been a few people who've asked me about a meteor that's coming to destroy the world, or whatever – the Lord hasn't spoken about it to me at all.

But the plasma ball in this dream, they do resemble meteors. And I don't know if you can even tell them apart when they are burning. I don't know that it's possible to tell them apart. It's been speculated that what happened in the Soviet Union was a plasma ball, and not a meteor, and that there were a lot of plasma balls being shot off at that time. So, it's really hard to say what was going on, except in this dream, it was definitely a plasma ball that was going to be fired on the Dome of the Rock by the Muslim ship.

So, after seeking Him for the meaning of the dream, and reading Joel 2 – the two things I took out of it, which I felt were indicative of the dynamics, were:

1. Let all who live in the land tremble, for the day of the Lord is coming. It is close at hand. 2 A day of darkness and gloom, a day of clouds and blackness. Like dawn spreading across the mountains a large and mighty army comes, such as never was in ancient times nor ever will be in ages to come...12 "Even now," declares the Lord, "return to me with all your heart, with fasting and weeping and mourning." 13 Rend your heart and not your garments. Return to the Lord your God, for he is gracious and compassionate, slow to anger and abounding in love, and he relents from sending calamity. 14 Who knows? He may turn and relent and leave behind a blessing.

And then the Lord began speaking to me again, and He said, **"The meaning should be obvious to you, My Love. I have delayed the event that would have set things in motion."**

Remember, guys? He talked about He was waiting for a certain event to take place before everything would go into motion?

So I asked Him, "The destruction of the Dome of the Rock?"

"That's right."

"Is this the event you were waiting for back in the Spring?"

"It is. It was all set to go off like clockwork. But once again, We relented because of the prayers and fasting of many around the world, especially Australia. That was a landmark prayer event that had much to do with the repentance of those in this nation. You see, I raise up my Vessels unto Honor to stand in the gap and Australia had much to do with the delay in the judgment. For this, every American should be very grateful.

"Now, since I have relented and stayed off the execution that was planned back in June, things have changed. Priorities have shifted and I have once again delayed the well-orchestrated plans of the nations to annihilate two-thirds of the world's population.

"This poses new problems for My People and new remedies as well. And, I will move forward with My saintly army of souls to fight the advancing darkness. It will redound to My Glory, for great shall be the victories. Make no mistake about it; the Rapture was about to happen in June.

"This is why I have been preparing you all to stand and take up your positions. It is not time to sit and wait; it is time to swing into action. This is why I spoke to you about assuming your positions; your effectiveness in serving Me during this extension of time will have a direct effect on how long I can stave off the events leading to the Rapture.

"Yes, I know, I hear it already - many of you want to sit down and cry, giving up your labors for Me. But may I say to you, the rewards for your faithfulness now far out weigh anything."

"Lord, I am thinking years...are you delaying it by years?"

"No, I am thinking months.

"In the meantime, I am also giving My Brides-to-be another chance. The Brides that would not have gone in June, I am giving them another chance to wake up and take new territory for Me. I am asking them to swing into action and commit themselves to a direction that will bring forth fruit for the Kingdom, not just sitting around waiting. Many have spoiled the plans I had for them with this kind of thinking. They, too, are getting another chance. Oh, this is so important Clare, over half of those who thought they had it all together in June were still falling far short of what I had expected of them. Their preoccupation with themselves disqualified them.

“Since then, many have had a change of heart and are finding ways to serve and have become much more serious about making better use of their time. I have seen much improvement and will have much mercy. But for those stragglers who are still biding their time, I say to you, ‘Wake Up! Do not waste another day of your lives thinking about yourself. My Brides must be about My business, not their own.’"

“Lord, is there really a meteor or is this hype?”

"You stay with what I have given you and let the world follow its prophets. If it were important for you to know, I would have told you. Is that good enough for you, My Love?"

“Yes, Lord.”

"I tell you what is important for you to know. I don't speculate, I bring what is truly necessary and leave the rest. So many people right now are highly agitated and don't know what to do with themselves. They are tied in knots. They are tied in knots from all these prophecies: this prophecy, that prophecy. Once they hear something, they throw it in with all the other things. Once they hear another prophecy, they throw it in with everything else they've heard and become profoundly disturbed, to the point of not being rational.

"That is why I have taught the souls that hearken to My Voice on this channel to stay away from all the speculations in the media. It does nothing to edify and build up, but plenty to undermine and sabotage the things I had for them to do. This is deliberate on Satan's part to take their attention off Me and onto their own survival. Some have even made themselves sick from worry. When you come away from a channel feeling panicked, that is not good fruit, unless of course you misinterpret what is being said.

"Many have listening disabilities and tend to fly into a panic without listening very carefully to what I have said. The demons are also very fond of exaggerating and twisting what's been said to the point where it no longer resembles the original word. Therefore, My Precious ones, always listen very carefully and listen again if you begin to feel panicked.

"Well, all in all, My entire message tonight is to make your time here count. Don't grow lax or lazy, rather rise up, put your hand to the plow and don't turn to look back, or grow weary in well doing. When you begin to grow weary, change the balance of prayer and work - get more prayer, less work. In this way, you will be constantly rejuvenated for the next round.

"I am with you all, even at your right hand, strengthening you at communion, refreshing you in worship, protecting you all day long and singing love songs over you.

"Listen for My sweet voice; receive all that I wish to give you with no guilt or condemnation. We are doing this together; you are truly My Helpmates. How then can I leave you to languish on your own? No, I am right here by your side, ploughing with you.

"My blessing of hope is upon you all. Amen."

What Happened to All the Animals?

Your Pets Will Be Taken in the Rapture

March 27, 2015

Tonight, I have some interesting news for you. I really believe the Lord has put an anointed vision in my hands from a woman by the name of Sheila. She had a vision when she was 13 years old – she was not a Christian, there was really nothing Christian at her house except for a picture of praying hands and her parents never went to church. When she was 13, she experienced a very vivid vision, definitely a supernatural move of the Lord. And the vision, I believe, was of the Rapture.

So, I'm going to include the vision at the end of the video. It's not going to be a very long video, the Lord was not on a real good place to talk to me tonight. He wasn't feeling "well", in the sense there was a lot on His heart and mind.

One thing I wanted to mention to you tonight, when I came into worship with the Lord and I saw Him, He held me very tenderly, but He had tears just rolling off of His eyelashes, just streaming out of His eyes and down the side of His face. I didn't stay in worship for very long – He wanted to stop and talk to me. So, I did stop and we began to talk. What's coming is just so unbelievably painful for Him, and I could feel it tonight, at the end of the message you'll see. Also, that He didn't want to carry on a conversation any longer – He just couldn't.

He began the message tonight with these words:

"The vision was highly accurate – it's going to happen just the way she saw it. ALL men will see Me coming on the clouds – not just Christians. ALL will see Me. Just as she was shown, I'm coming that way.

"Children and pets will also be taken. I will not leave the dear ones down here to suffer – they shall be taken with you. Try not to be apprehensive, My Love, I know you're not used to seeing Me this way. Please, do get used to it. This was the way I first appeared to you, when you first became a Christian, remember?"

"I do, Lord."

As an aside on this, the picture I'm using for the Youtube is the way that I've been seeing Him of late, and I think that the artist did a really good job on this. It's from the Shroud of Turin. He did a great job of accurately portraying His face, and there is some softness to His face. I think the pictures that I've been using capture more of His Spirit and sense of Love and Tenderness. That's more what I'm used to, even though I know those pictures could never be accurate of Who – what the Lord REALLY looks like, objectively. I think He's preparing me to see Him the way He truly is, so I'm half struggling about that. We've had a few little talks about that.

He continued, **"I know you're nervous and scared. Try to hold Me close to your heart and I will steady you. It will be glorious – more glorious than you can ever imagine. And terrible and frightening, too. But, you will be brought up in such an ecstasy that you will remember nothing about Earth, only the Glory transforming your body and lifting you up. It will be perfect. Is anything that I do LESS than that? No. My Bride deserves this.**

"Do not weep for those left behind – this was the course of their lives, the course they must take. This will be the refining process that brings them into perfection...in ME.

"Yes, you may tell all that I am taking their animals as well: horses, cats, dogs, birds, loved ones – family – to all of you. May I say that I would never abandon these poor, innocent creatures at the very worst time of history, when they've brought you so much comfort."

When He said 'loved ones and family to all of you' He was referring to the fact that the animals are all like family to us.

"Over and over again, I have used them to minister to you. A look in their eye, a touch, a nudge. Such joy they have experienced in your sweet embrace. They love you – and I shall not abandon them to neglect and suffering.

"Your grandchildren, as well. Some of you have suffered such alienation from your children that they've deprived you of your right to see your grand-children. This will be the time of restoration for you as these little ones are removed and taken to Heaven.

"Many of My ministers have no knowledge of the extent of My Mercy to creatures. They do not understand the true role that animals on this Earth have played. Adam had fellowship with the creatures as well. But, despite his closeness to the animals, none proved to be a suitable companion until I created Woman.

"Nonetheless, do not underestimate your relationship with animals and pets. I love them dearly. Not one sparrow falls to the ground that I do not embrace it and bring it back to Heaven.

"In Heaven, you will communicate freely with them, and most of your interactions will be times of love and play. You will swim with dolphins, tumble with lions, glide with otters, float with polar bears and tuck into the giant paws of grizzlies. They will welcome you with Love. All things in Heaven are saturated with Love. Even the bees will express their appreciation of you."

"Oh, yes, Lord! I remember that. I remember how the bees made a heart shape as they grouped together, lifted off the hive, dipped your hands into the honey and brought some out for us. And, I can't wait to eat those plum- sized raspberries!"

"So many delights, My Precious Bride! So many joys – on your left, on your right. Beneath and above you. You will find delight in My Creation, as I have made it a reflection of Love for you. How many ways can I say I love you? Seeing is believing...so many ways. Only just experience them and you'll understand."

At that point, I remembered something I needed to write to my children – about routes out of the city, keeping gas in the tank and things like that. So, I took a few minutes and did that – the Lord released me to do that. Then I came back to Him, and He was silent.

And I said to Him, "Jesus?"

His head was down and He said to me, **"It's hard for Me to talk."**

I could feel that He was choked up.

"That's enough for tonight, My Love. Stay close. Don't let Me out of your sight. Watch and wait with Me."

"Jesus, will You watch with me when I fall asleep?"

"I'm always by your side – always."

That was the end of the message tonight, of our exchange.

Here is a transcript of the Dream I spoke about in the beginning of this message:

My Vision of the Return of Jesus Christ

I have heard the saying that young men have visions and old men have dreams. I was a young girl when I had a vision from God. I was 13 years old when it happened and it hasn't happened again since that hot July day in 1976. I'm 49 years old now, but not one detail of that vision has ever left me. It was profound and life altering, yet as a young girl I didn't know what it meant or recognize what a significance it would prove to be in my life and others.

I pondered it for a while and eventually I just got on with life, and though I put it aside, it never went away. For the past five years, this vision has been in my thoughts constantly, pressing me to write it down and share with the world. God won't leave me alone about it; I have to do it. I can't sleep at night for thinking about it; I feel like a grape in a wine press. The need to do this is pressing and oppressive and urgent.

I find it ironic that I grew up in the middle of the Bible Belt, yet I had not been to church more than two or three times in my life and that was limited to Sunday school when I was a much younger girl. I had no idea of the symbolism or what these strange things that I would see would mean to me or anyone else. Church, God and the Bible were not a part of my family or our lives.

My Mom was taken to church as a child and baptized, as were all good Southern Baptists in her day. I don't recall that she ever went to church as an adult, nor do I ever recall seeing a Bible in our home. I do remember the plaque with praying hands in the den that hung there for many years as it did in many southern homes. We were never taught how to pray or worship or praise God and as an adult, this is something that I am just now learning. I do have to add that when my sisters and I were very young, I remember Mamma teaching us how to say our prayers at night. You know, "Now I lay me down to sleep..."

Oh, yes, then there was the print over my bed, the one with the little boy and girl crossing a broken and crumbling bridge, and a beautiful guardian angel in a pink dress was helping them safely across. That was the extent of my Biblical teaching.

Nothing that I learned in our home prepared me for what God would show me. I remember that, right before I had this vision, I was fond of telling everyone that I was an atheist. Never mind that I really didn't know what that meant, let alone the ramifications of what I was saying. I think I was doing it for the shock value, like all teenagers in the 70's. But, God heard me loud and clear and saw past my smart mouth. He knew the disobedient

path that my life would take and he knew it wasn't going to be pretty. I guess he figured I needed a visual aid to bring me back to him. It only took me 30 years or so to come back Home.

My family had finished Sunday dinner, which is lunch to those who aren't from the South. Everyone decided to go down to the river for a swim and fishing, but – for some reason, I did not want to go. I felt tired and I just wanted to lay down for a nap, so my Mamma allowed me to stay home alone for the first time ever.

It was like any other dry, sultry, boring day in mid-July in south Georgia. We lived out in the country in the middle of dusty plowed fields, dirt roads and woods. Everything looked kind of brown and crispy, like it needed rain bad. As soon as everyone left, I went to my bedroom, which faced out the front side of the house and looked out onto our front yard, which had a semi-circular dirt driveway and beside the left entrance was an old dogwood tree, which had to be at least a hundred years old. Highway 341 ran from east to west in front of our house, which faced north, and the cornfield I spoke of earlier was on the other side of the highway. There was a slight rise in the middle of this field and you could not see the trees on the other side, so it looked like an ocean of corn that went off into the horizon.

As I lay across my bed looking out the window, contemplating what I saw before me, I began to hear music in the distance. I specifically heard it in my right ear and the direction from which it came made me think of the high school band which practiced several miles southeast from where I lived. When conditions were right, we could hear the band playing, but usually only heard the faint beat of drums. This sounded like trumpets and as I was thinking this, I began to notice the music getting louder and louder, coming closer and closer very quickly.

Within a few seconds, the sound wasn't just something that was exterior, but it was inside my head as well, reverberating throughout my entire body. It was so loud and it sounded like lightning crashed directly over my head and, in that split second, the trumpet sound thundered throughout my body and throughout the entire world.

In a flash, I was no longer lying on my bed, but I was standing outside my bedroom and I beheld the scene in front of me with tremendous awe. It was still my front yard, only now everything was different. The trumpets continued to sound and I saw that the blue, sunny sky had turned black and the clouds churned and the wind blew with a violence that I had never experienced.

The cornfield was now a sea of wheat that was golden brown and ripe for harvest and I could see every stalk of wheat individually, billions of them. And I watched as the wind thrashed the wheat until it was beaten down, yet straining against it. I now know that the Bible speaks several times about, in the time when the wheat is ripe for harvest, how the wheat will be separated from the tares.

Then I noticed the dogwood tree. It was mid-July, so of course I know there should not have been any blossoms on it, but the tree was in full bloom. I had never seen anything like this. You couldn't see any leaves on the tree because of the thousands of dogwood blossoms. It looked as if it were lit from within by a glowing white neon light and it glowed gloriously against the darkened sky.

Now, I know the Bible says no man knows the day nor hour that Jesus will return, but if we watch for the signs, we can know the season. I have always felt that He might come back in the spring when the dogwood trees are in bloom. Of all the things that could have been highlighted in this vision, why the dogwood tree? I believe there is a special message there.

Just as I was taking all of this in, lightning filled the sky and the trumpets thundered over head again and in an instant there appeared two angels. They were dressed in white robes, facing each other up in the air and blowing golden trumpets. They were huge and filled the sky in front of me and I knew that the entire world must be seeing this as well. I didn't think the trumpets could get any louder, but they grew louder still, building to a great crescendo. And I heard a great shout that was louder than anything that you could imagine. And with that shout, the black, violent clouds began to roll back onto themselves from the center of the sky and I saw light in the distance.

It was more a combination of light and clearing of the clouds in the distance that got my attention. As I looked up at this shaft of light and clearing sky, I saw what seemed to be fluttering and movement in the distance. As it came into view, I saw Jesus on a white horse and behind him were millions of angels or saints (I could not see this clearly) on white horses. It was at this moment, when I realized what I was seeing, that it disappeared and I was back in my room lying on my bed. Everything was back to normal and I was again looking out at a bright, sunny day.

As a 13 year old girl, I had no idea what I had just experienced. I had no frame of reference; I didn't even know what a vision was. I'd never heard of such things. I certainly didn't tell anyone about it. I didn't know how, and I didn't want my family to think I was crazy, but – to be honest, I was starting to think I was.

Time passed and I filed it away in the back of my mind where it gathered cob webs for many years. Every once in a while I would think about it, but always re-filed it as an unsolved mystery. After all the years of pondering about it, I finally picked up a Bible about 5 or 6 years ago that had a concordance and looked up the word "trumpet".

The first Scripture it sent me to was *Matthew 24:30-31: And then shall appear the sign of the Son of man in Heaven: and then shall all the tribes of the Earth mourn, and they shall see the Son of Man coming in the clouds of Heaven with power and great Glory. And he shall send his angels with a great sound of a trumpet, and they shall gather together his elect from the four winds, from one end of Heaven to the other.*

The next Scripture I was lead to was *I Thessalonians 4:16-17 For the Lord Himself shall descend from Heaven with a shout, with the voice of the Archangel, and with the trump of God: an the dead in Christ shall rise first, then we which are alive and remain shall be caught up together with them in the clouds, to meet the Lord in the air. And so shall we ever be with the Lord.*

I know that what I was shown was from God Himself and since that day, I have known that I would see Jesus come for us in my lifetime. The time is urgent and God has really pressed upon me to share this with you. If you are a Christian, I hope this blesses you and gives you reassurance and that you will share this with others. If you're not a Christian, I beg you to repent now and ask Jesus to forgive you and be the Lord of your life, because our time is very short.

The one question people always ask is why I feel this urgency now. The only way I know how to explain it is that I remember how I felt when I had the vision. I didn't feel like I was seeing it through 13 year old eyes. I remember how I felt emotionally and physically and spiritually. I felt then like I feel now and that's the only way I know how to articulate it.

Whether you believe this was a vision of the Second Coming of Jesus Christ or – if like me – you believe this was a glimpse of the Rapture to come, just know that it was real and every word of this is truth. For some reason, God chose me to deliver this message to you at this time.

I'm not a preacher, nor a teacher, nor a prophet. I am the least likely person to be chosen to deliver such an important message. I have pondered and prayed about this and I feel God gave me the following analogy: You have two clay pots. One is perfect, the other full of holes and cracks. Which one lets the most light shine through?

I try to send this message to 50-100 people a week randomly. I have prayed that God will lead me to send this to those who need it most and that they would be able to discern the truth in it. People wonder what reason I had for sending it to them in particular. Many are going through things in their lives now that make them question, make them hungry for something tangible in this crazy time we live. People need something real to believe in now, when everything is totally not what it seems.

I have learned that I can't do anything on my own, I need the Lord's guidance. I lived a life of sin and debauchery most of my adult life and I didn't think that God could even like me, much less love me. There is not a sin that I have not committed, including murder. I had an abortion in 1989 and after that I just knew I was going to hell anyhow, so I really lived as if I had nothing to lose. I never thought I would live to see 30, but now I am 49 and I'm just learning that I didn't have to do anything to change except love Jesus and let Him love me.

When I finally opened the door for Him, He did all the work. He changed my heart, my mind, my thoughts, my actions, my feelings. Everything changed when I took that step and I realized that He had ben there all along, leading, guiding, waiting. I have peace and joy and kindness and preciousness in my life that I never knew was possible.

I have had this vision in my heart for 36 years now and I only shared it with a few people over the years. But, I realized that what I was given was unique and special and to be shared with others. God urged me to write this last October. It just sat there until mid-February. Every day He put in my heart to share it but I could not figure out how. On Tuesday morning, I woke up and the first thought I had was to send it on Facebook, Youtube and email to all my friends.

When I was done, I sat back and felt Him urge me to send it to their friends as well, and so on. That's how you got this. Let me make something clear: God does not speak to me in an audible voice. But He speaks through urging and prompting and pushing and even nagging sometimes. I had doubts about sending it; people are funny about their beliefs, but I have gotten dozens of emails that encourage me to keep going because this has made such a difference to them.

One young man I sent it to professed his faith as wiccan and said that he doesn't believe in a Supreme Being. The night that I sent this to him, he had a dream that God told him that a woman he did not know was trying to bring him the light of God. He dismissed this as a silly dream until he woke up in the morning and my email was the first thing he saw. He said he no longer doubts God's reality. And, after hearing this, I no longer had any doubts about what I was doing. I knew it was inspired by the Lord.

I also feel that the way I was living my life was designed by Satan himself. He knew that the day would come when I would share this vision with others, and I think he did everything he could to make sure that did not happen.

He lost.

Love and Blessings to you, friend. I'm no Morpheus, I'm just a mamma and a grandma who's lived and learned.

One more thing: I think one way that Satan creeps into our lives is by accusing us and making us feel guilty and condemned. He wants to separate us from the Source of Love and forgiveness and grace and faith. He wants us to believe we could never be good enough, that we could never deserve it. Well, he's right – we can't be good enough and we cannot earn or deserve it. All these things were given freely on the Cross of Calvary. We only need to accept this free gift and it is ours.

The ones who are forgiven much…love much.

Just because we become Christians and love God and Jesus does not mean we become perfect people. We will never be without sin, but – we have already been forgiven for it. People who are not Christians say that if God really keeps on forgiving, what's the point of changing – just do what you want to. I used to feel this way, too.

But now I know that when Jesus comes into your heart, you don't want to do evil things anymore, you want to please Him, not hurt Him. The Word says that we are saved by Grace through our faith, which is a gift from God Himself.

SECTION THREE

Messages For the Left Behind:
Jesus Speaks

Jesus Speaks On: What Is To Come After the Rapture Order of Events - part 1

March 2, 2015

Lord, we ask You to impart courage and strength to us. And for those listening after the Rapture especially: Courage, Peace and Trust in the Lord. He has wonderful plans for us.

Well, this is a really different message tonight. The Lord has shifted gears – He's talking more about what is going to happen AFTER the Rapture, and He's talking about the things that He's going to allow to happen to America and to our continent, and the things He's NOT going to allow to happen. And what He has in store for America after the Tribulation.

So, just a little background on this, I really have been yearning to know more about the sequence of events and to have an understanding of how all the puzzle pieces fit together. And it finally came to a head yesterday when I cried out to the Lord, and I said, "Lord, please...please. Have mercy on us and share with us what Your plans are." And He did. And it was rather funny the way it all started, so I'm just going to begin reading it to you.

I had a Communion service and afterwards, when I had received communion, the Lord said, **"I will instruct you about these things."** The Scripture that came to mind was, *"This poor woman cried aloud and the Lord heard her."*

"But I have done nothing to deserve this knowledge, Lord." You know, like…fasting for weeks…all the things that prophets are supposed to do, right? I haven't done anything like that. So, I don't deserve this knowledge, but I sure would like to have it anyway!

Anyway, He said, **"Do you think, for one moment, this depends on your righteousness?"**

And I thought for a moment, and I said, "Well I guess maybe I do."

"Well, you are wrong. All depends on My Mercy. My Love. And I have chosen to be merciful to you tonight."

"Lord, you are merciful to me every night."

"True. But why do you suppose you want to know all these things?"

And I thought for a minute, and I said, "Because You put the desire there?"

"How did you guess that?" He said smiling.

"Oh dear, God, please help me hear clearly and accurately and to believe. "

"A very wise prayer My Love."

"The Destroyer – the planet Nibiru - will not come until the end. The things you have been shown are to happen after you are taken. This will be a record for some that they not lose hope but see clearly that I am in control, they can take Me at My word, and it is not hopeless.

"I want mankind to have confidence in Me and My Mercy. That is why I have foretold these events...at least in part. To have some kind of roadmap that will give them security, they can see things unfolding and will know I foretold and am in control. I already said that, didn't I?"

"Yes, Lord. You did."

"Well, I am repeating it because it is so important that men not fall into despair. The temptation to fall into despair will be very powerful and by this the Devil will snatch many away in his grip.

"You must know, Remnant of Earth, there will be an end to the tragedy and the day will come when all is restored in pristine purity and evil is harnessed. In those times, whatever evil emerges will be from the hearts of men, not demons. And there will be a baptism by fire to cleanse the Earth and the hearts of men. It will never be forgotten by those remaining alive.

"And yet as time goes by, men will forget as they did at the waters of Meribah and again I shall be forced to purify the evil from Earth - this time for good.

"The Destroyer (The planet Nibiru) will not come until you are removed, My Brides. There will be a season of chaos directly after you leave in which nations will conquer nations and Marshall Law will be installed under Sharia principals. All that do not renounce Me will be slain. All that take the Mark of the Beast, they will perish. Know that My Mercy shall know no boundaries for those who call to Me in these times."

I want to say something just aside here. There is a technology now, that if you take that Mark, they can actually affect your thinking. They can deprive you of thoughts about God and cause you to think more logically, and to have scorn and contempt to reject Him, simply by stimulating parts of the brain electronically. They can also instruct you electronically to go into a mad frenzy and to kill whatever's in front of you – to fight and to kill.

There're so many things that can be done now, the technology is way, way, way advanced. And anyone who takes that Mark is going to lose their mind, literally. Their mind is going to be in the hands of the government, and whatever the government wants...well. That's what you'll be doing, because you'll be stimulated in that way.

The other thing is, that it is written in Revelation (in the Bible) that those who take the Mark are going to suffer terribly – pain, like the sting of the scorpion for many months. And they'll want to be dead, they'll look for many ways to die, but they won't be able to. This is written in Revelation.

And for those of you who didn't believe the Rapture was real…well, it WAS real. And the next thing is the Mark – that's real. And that suffering from having the Mark is real, plus you'll never be able to repent and receive the Lord – it'll be the end.

So **DON'T TAKE THE MARK!!**

Continuing on with His Message: **"Rise up, My People and call unto Me, and I will save you. Trust Me, trust Me, even with your heads. What you suffer on Earth will be nothing compared to those with the Mark.**

"The beasts you questioned Me about are being bred inside the Earth. They, too, will come forth to wreak havoc at the appropriate time."

What He's referencing there is the strange giants in Ezekiel's dream that I just posted a couple days ago. And I thought about it for a minute, and I thought, 'Oh my God! The animals! How they are going to suffer!'

And the Lord picked up on my thought, and He said, **"The living will envy the dead. This goes for every species, not just man. Do I not love each and every creature with tenderness and devotion? Do I not provide for them every day: water to swim in, food to eat, sun to warm... My providence for them abounds. But, they will come to Me during the worst part, as many already have and are happily with Me in Heaven.**

"Clare, I love all creatures. I know how to ease their suffering. Trust Me."

"Lord, I cannot imagine how much pain it will cause You to look upon their estate in those times."

"All of creation is suffering for this sinful generation. All. It is the consummation and pinnacle of evil from the very beginning.

"Things are going to gradually deteriorate as the planet gets closer and Satan will be in a hurry to impose his agenda on mankind. There will be desperate attempts to force the Mark and the suffering of those with families will be devastating. But, I will be with them to give them strength - only just endure to the end, for the Crown of Victory awaits you.

"When people have gotten to the point where they believe there is no more hope, that is when I will come and restore all things. Right then, at the very darkest hour, I will come. As in Ezekiel's dream, there will remain remnants of technology that functions."

I'm going to take a break here and insert just a couple things. I've been looking into the Three Days of Darkness and praying about it. And, it really seems to be correct that the 3 days of Darkness will be at the very end, when the planet Nibiru comes closest to the Earth, and the poles begin to shift dramatically.

According to the dream Ezekiel had a few nights ago that I posted – about those strange creatures and the man that had to be turned upside down for the breathing apparatus to work, 'cause the fluids had to go in the opposite direction, there's going to come a time in the 3 days of darkness, and the flipping of the poles that will be... well, demons and terror will just abound on the Earth.

But the very moment the Lord sets His foot on Mount Zion, that will be the end of those demons. His angels will go throughout the Earth and the air and He'll destroy – they'll destroy every demon. Or bind it. As the Scriptures say, Bound for 1,000 years. That is definitely going to happen.

But that will happen after the three days of darkness, which will be ended by the Lord coming with His angels. That's what I believe.

So, a lot of people wonder, "Well, what kind of technology is going to be left after all this devastation?" So, that's where I'm going to pick up on this. And Ezekiel's dream.

"There will remain remnants of technology that will function. I have protected this because there will be a need for communication. I will continue to use the Internet, radio and other media to reach My People with a message of hope. All will not disintegrate, as you suppose. And I have not allowed for the E-bomb that fries all technology."

"I really wondered about that, Lord."

"No, it is much more like the movie you saw." (10.5 Apocalypse)

And in that movie, guys, the continent of America was being divided in half – there was a helicopter flying overhead, observing the whole thing.

"The Rapture will be the beginning of the End. All are waiting for that. Not only Christians, but the evil ones as well. They will take advantage to install their system because of the disappearance of many. Yet it will take time. There will be intervals of peace.

"Your country will not be completely destroyed - land masses, earthquakes, the separation of the continent will not happen until the end. In the meantime, there will be war on your soil. I have told you about Miami. Do not listen to other voices. What I told you is accurate."

What He said about Miami is that, when a nuclear weapon is used on the city of Miami – He will be rapturing us within that day. Or week, possibly – but I'm pretty sure it's within that day, the same day. And this really fits with the other dreams that He's given us.

For instance, when Ezekiel was taken up in a bus during the Rapture, he observed thousands and thousands of warriors descending down on the Earth. And the Earth was in chaos – there was smoke rising from the Earth.

So, what's He's basically saying is, there's going to be a nuclear event – or several nuclear events – and we will be taken from the Earth right after that. So, He's repeating that 'cause, you know, I'm human and I think to myself, 'Was that word really secure? There're so many different scenarios out there, Lord. Was that really You telling me that?' And He's confirmed several times that Miami is going to be the key.

And, for folks who think, 'Well, it's written: no one knows the day or the hour.' Well – no one knows the day or the hour that Miami is going to be bombed! The Russians could plan it for one time, but technology could fail and it wouldn't work, so they'd have to pick another time. Or a bunch of different things could happen to thwart them from knowing exactly the day and the hour that that's going to happen.

But He's saying that that's a sign to you – **"lift up your heads because your Redemption draws nigh."**

That also fits with Matthew's rendition, 24th chapter of Matthew, that after this time of extreme chaos, the Lord will come.

"Lord, I'm sorry for giving in to other ideas and being weak. Please help me to have complete trust and confidence in You. Please."

"Your confession moves My heart to tears. (And I did see tears streaming down His cheeks.) **You are not alone, you know. What I mean to say is, that the forces are working against you to cause doubt and scruples. But I have heard your cry, My Love and I will help you.**

"Clare, look at Me."

And just at that moment I went from looking at my computer screen to looking at Him. He was right behind it, sitting right behind it looking at me. And His face became SO visible I could almost touch it. And His eyes were SO tender, I said, " Lord, you are so beautiful."

"I'm beautiful for you, My Bride. And for My Brides. I love and cherish you all. Despite your many flaws and weaknesses, your heart is for Me alone. And for that I am eternally grateful, for never will I forsake you."

And then He addressed my "wishy-washiness", or sometimes my doubting.

"Sometimes you make an error in your own mind. But most of the time, almost all the time, you are hearing Me correctly. I want you to rest in that. I know you are trying very, very hard not to insert your own agendas, your own thoughts, or ideas, scenarios or what you've heard from others. You have tried to keep it pure. I will honor that. I will give you details that are highly accurate."

Then He continued on with the instruction:

"Even now Russia is planning to strike your country. Even now they are seriously stalking the American continent. They have many in place here in America. Weapons are hidden in the forests. Underground entrances will be opened up on American soil and artillery and other weapons will emerge. It will be for the most part a conventional war."

Well, what He is talking about is after the initial nuclear things that we see happening - Miami especially was the nuclear event. And it seemed like there were other nuclear events, too, in several of the visions I had. What He is saying is, they're going to move in on our soil, and there's going to be conventional war here on our soil.

"Yes, I have been so confused about NYC – is it going to be nuked or flooded by tsunamis?"

"It's going to be nuked."

"But what about all these ideas of tsunamis and quakes, that other people are having?

"What will be left will go down underwater, it will actually happen simultaneously with the bombs. It will be both."

"Oh, Jesus. I feel so badly for all the innocents!"

"Yes, My Love. All the innocents. But, remember, Clare - I love them more than you can possibly imagine. I will take them quickly and mercifully. It will be for those who remain a hell-on-earth scenario."

When I talk about "innocents" I'm talking about the children that are born after the Rapture, the animals. People in wheelchairs or mentally handicapped - you know. These people are innocent.

"You saw the Koreans and Russians. They will be in many areas, as well as American Muslim recruits - that will be treacherous. People will lose faith in humanity because of the betrayals of their own kind.

"These recruits have been convinced they are doing a good thing by killing every man woman and child in the name of Allah. They will find a vent for their anger at mankind and the hard lives they lived because of the selfishness of many - the inequality, being rejected and looked down upon. They will be dazed with blood lust. And there will be no stopping them without lethal force.

"Yet, I will have My pockets of survivors, those who have not bent the knee to Baal. I will protect them, but they will suffer much. They will be tried by fire and when I come - be found worthy. This will be a very small percentage of mankind. Your family will be among those survivors. Much of what you taught them growing up was preparation for this time. There will be much brokenness and repentance among them.

"What you left behind for them will be a goldmine of instruction, but My Spirit will be with them and much that they do will be because they learned it from you growing up. They will be healed of their bitterness and judgments as the realization dawns on them that you were both right."

"Thank you, Lord. Thank you so much."

And as a note on that, we get a lot of scorn and contempt for believing in the Rapture, the New World Order and the whole thing. And our children are no different. One thing I taught my children growing up was to rely on the Lord and to pray in every situation and to count on His help. And that may be what He's talking about. Plus, we lived in out-of-the-way places; we lived in the wilderness quite a bit.

"Most of these things you have known as I have spoken to you along the way. Much of what you think are your thoughts - are Mine. They are weighed and balanced with much consideration of truth. Truth is your plumb line and as long as you hold to that you will not err."

"Lord, what about Yellowstone? It has the capacity to destroy America."

And here I want to say something very quickly before I get into what He said – because I forgot about this until just now. After I saw the movie about Yellowstone – the super volcano movie, I was very shaken. I really wondered what REALLY is going to happen. And I went to the Lord in prayer, and the answer He gave was that He would have Mercy – there would be Mercy. And I'm not just talking Mercy for those who are not annihilated because of the huge area it's going to effect. He's talking about...He's going to do something. He's going to intervene with Yellowstone so that it will not be as bad as it's predicted to be. Not anywhere near as bad. And this is what He said:

"There is a pattern in Yellowstone. The main caldera will erupt, but it will be on a much smaller scale than is anticipated. This will be My doing. My Mercy. However, there will be many new outlets for the magma, much like Kilauea. The magma will bubble up from underground for many miles, just as you have seen in the vision."

What He's talking about here with "the vision" - I kept seeing an eruption in Wyoming but on a much smaller scale than what has been shown as the 'super volcano'. After the eruption – kind of like Mount Saint Helens, but in the surroundings it was miles and miles of streams of lava, just like what's been happening in Kilauea for decades. That's a far more tame response than what we're expecting from that volcano.

"I still have plans for America. I will break and humble her, but I will also restore. I wound and I bind up. Yes, this land is corrupt and has led many into heinous crimes, but still there is a remnant of goodness, which I shall increase. I will not totally destroy her, only severely break and reorder her thinking.

"Yes, there are groups of militants that will fight for liberty. They will be much like My people when they conquered enemy territory in the Promised Land. I will be with them. I will fight with them and protect them supernaturally, because of what they stand for. They will be the backbone of this country when she is restored. There will be many heroes and saints among them."

"But, Lord, I thought You viewed this whole thing like the Mission movie, where you just allow yourself to die rather than take up arms?"

"Not so. I will empower these men and be with them. Again, for what they stand for. There will be skirmishes and wars round about. I have some very talented warriors planted among them. They will rise up at the appropriate time. They will be endowed with supernatural wisdom because they will rely on Me, not on their own devices.

"The cities will not be safe. The wilderness will be much safer. Yet, there have been prepared creatures that will seek out humans and hunt them down in the forests and ravines. This is where great wisdom is called for. Many will use My Name to defend themselves from these creatures and I will work on their behalf. Monstrosities of nature, bred and tailored to seek out and destroy."

So, I want to break away from the message for a moment, and tell you about a real life episode of two young men that were in a young adult group in Montana, when I was there with my children. The one man had just been saved the day before. He and his brother were going for a walk in Glacier National Park. It was Springtime, early, early Spring.

They just rounded a bend when they heard the unmistakable sound of a grizzly sow, who they assumed was protecting her cubs. As they looked, she was at a full charge only about 40 feet away.

They said, "All we knew to do was call on the Name of Jesus, so in that moment we both simultaneously said, 'In the Name of Jesus, STOP.' And in that moment, she halted immediately, throwing up a cloud of dust. Then she grunted and lumbered off in the direction she had come from.

So use the Name of Jesus. I have seen so many miracles using the Name of Jesus – things that you cannot control in any other way. Use the Name of Jesus – it's POWERFUL.

So, after He had shared those things with me, He reached out His hand and placed it over mine tenderly. **"That's all for now, Clare, this is only a start. There will be more."**

"Thank You Lord, Thank you for coming to my aid and rescuing me from all these converging thoughts that were bringing only confusion."

"You are welcome, My Love."

We discerned this message, we studied it, we prayed about it and we believe that this is a prophecy from the Lord.

So, God bless you Youtube family. Keep us in prayer as we pray for you.

Jesus Speaks On: What is To Come After the Rapture Restructuring - part 2

March 4, 2015

This is the next segment in "What is To Come". It was given to me some days ago, but due some insecurities of mine, I held it aside, wanting to know for sure that it truly was the Lord. And after many confirmations – here we are!

So, I'm going to go on with what He told me at that point.

One thing I'd like to begin with is, one of the confirmations that came – you'll probably notice that it is posted on the same page with the first set of instructions of "What is to Come". And that is that, a very dear friend of ours, who has been in the Lord for over 50 years and been receiving messages from Him for that long just had a dream last night. She saw streams of lava around Yellowstone, rather than this gigantic eruption that everyone is expecting and that the Lord told me would NOT happen, because He would intervene. She also saw streams of lava, which is what I saw – I shared that with you in the last video. Just streams of lava everywhere – and the lava was pouring out peacefully, so people had time to prepare and it would not cause a "nuclear winter" kind of scenario for our country.

I'm going to move on now to the instructions that were given to me the day after the first set of instructions on "What is to Come". It's very short, due to some difficulties that I was having that day. So I'm going to give you the short version, (I'm calling this Instructions 1 ½) then go into Instructions #2.

"Lets talk about Nibiru. Yes, what you've heard about the headquarters of demonic powers is correct. Yes, that is another reason for the Vatican telescope. So when they say it is to discover life on other planets, that is reasonable and not a lie. However, they know well the nature of this "life" and what it will do to Earth.

"In anticipation, they have dug their hidden cities and provided them with all they think they will need to survive. This, in My eyes, is utterly ridiculous! As if I will allow them to escape the conflagration! In no way will they escape – they will die in the graves they have dug for themselves, while I will preserve many of the righteous still on the surface of the Earth.

"There's still much debate among the ruling class that these so-called "helpers" (meaning demons posing as ET's - 'benign ET's') are only using them to gain access to the planet – and that they will be traitors and harbingers of destruction. Which is quite correct, I might add. But in their lust for power and technology – the "ruling elite" of the Earth – they press on into a scheme that is to be their undoing."

I replied to Him, "Kinda messed up, like – if you DO, you're messed up. And if you DON'T, you're messed up?"

"Exactly. They are caught in a trap because of their lust for power."

Here I want to say that, I believe in my own mind anyway, that these demons are capable of destroying the Earth easily. But I believe the Lord has held their hand back. You know, demons are on a leash. They're like rabid dogs – they're chained and can't go any further than God will allow them to go, and He won't allow them to destroy the Earth.

Although…the demons have used mankind to destroy the Earth, and to destroy many things. So, it's our own undoing, in a sense.

"Yet, what is missing in their thinking is ME. They are so educated and so informed that they can't relate to God being in control."

Kind of like the joke: the most intelligent man in the world who bailed out of a plane with a Hippie's back-pack (I don't know if you guys have heard that?)

"It's laughable, really. The Scriptures declare that 'The One enthroned in Heaven laughs; the Lord scoffs at them.'"

I'm going to read this to you, because it's really beautiful:

Why do the nations conspire and the peoples plot in vain? The kings of the earth rise up and the rulers band together against the Lord and against his anointed, saying, "Let us break their chains and throw off their shackles." The One enthroned in heaven laughs; the Lord scoffs at them. He rebukes them in his anger and terrifies them in his wrath, saying, "I have installed my king on Zion, my holy mountain."

That's Psalm 2:1-6 And also Revelation 6:15 Then the kings of the earth, the princes, the generals, the rich, the mighty, and everyone else, both slave and free, hid in caves and among the rocks of the mountains.

So, I continued with the Lord – I asked Him a question:

"So, Satan being cast down to Earth will happen with Nibiru?"

"It's all part of the same event," the Lord continued. **"So much unfolds in layers, but this is the final and definitive layer to descend on Earth. The most destructive one. I know this is a lot for you to comprehend, My Love."**

"Jesus, would you please give me a vision – please?"

"I will." He said. And I beheld a red planet that came into proximity to Earth, something like fire descended into Jerusalem, and Satan – who took over the body of antichrist – stood boldly in the Holy of Holies and struck the ground with his staff. Rings of fire radiated out from that point that covered the whole Earth, much like you would see if a droplet of water fell into a pool of still water.

The Lord continued: **"This is the final scene of destruction – the End is come.**

"There is Hope. These instructions I'm giving you are meant to bring people out of a nosedive of despair. They are important to Me. There will come a time when they are invaluable. Don't discount My motives – I do know what I am doing, My Love. I think you've figured that out by now, huh?"

"Yes, Lord…my bad…"

"Yes – your bad," He said. **"Let's move on."**

Okay – so now I'm going to move right on into the second message:

I get curious and I mess around and do foolish things...and I caught someone on Youtube who was talking about Yellowstone. They had a vision about Yellowstone. So, I took the bait and started listening. And then I realized, "This isn't the Lord – what am I doing?? Why am I listening to what other people have to say, when I have the Lord speaking directly to me and telling me what He's going to do? This is foolishness on my part!

So, I closed it down and repented. I said, "No, I'm going to believe my Lord – I'm not going to believe what ANYONE else has to say." And I turned it off.

Well, when I came into prayer to begin to listen for Him, for His instructions, He said:

"It was so good to hear you say that. I will never, never give up on working with you. Never. Rest assured, He who has begun the GOOD work, will continue to its completion."

You know, I believe He said that because He was intercepting my thoughts – and my thoughts were at that moment, 'Oh, Lord! How do you put UP with me?? Why didn't you pick someone else for this job? Someone You could really count on, and that wouldn't doubt You and wouldn't wobble like I wobble!'

And being compassionate and sweet and loving, and knowing that I had a little bit of fear that He would reject me, because I'm not qualified for this job. He stopped me for a moment and He told me that He would never give up on me. See how gentle and beautiful He is? And for all you guys out there that are "wobbly" like me, there's so much HOPE for you! He'll fill in all the blanks, don't worry about it. Just repent, and trust in His Mercy and obey Him. And He'll complete the good work He has begun in you.

"And yes, I do believe the word about Yellowstone is important to share."

At this point, I was thinking, 'Am I supposed to share this or not?' I was waiting to see, after the second and third message, if they were consistent and if this truly was the Lord. That was our discernment – that they were consistent and this was the Lord. So that's why I posted number one.

Then the Lord began to speak again. He said:

"People are expecting the worst and given the circumstances, I can say that is logical. What they are not counting on is My Love for America and the Mercy I will show her. Yes, among all the nations, She is one I love and still have great plans for, after she has been humbled completely and restored. Then, again I will use her.

"She is very much like My Bride and even as I exiled My people to Babylon, never did I plan on completely abandoning them. And so it is with America. Never were My plans to reduce her to nothing, without the hope of future glory. She will be used by Me again.

"One thing that truly has not dawned on the people of this country is her beginnings. Many of the founding fathers were Masons and spiritually corrupted. The entire estate of Washington (District of Columbia) was laid out on pagan principals and now these principles have come to fruition - she is reaping what she has sown. I will destroy what has been and is corrupted about her and restore to her the true heritage of her God, and she will once again be a force for the good in the world.

"Clare, when I come to rule there will be equality and justice around the world. Never again will I allow governments to repress and denigrate a human being of any race, color or creed. Although the knowledge of Me will fill the Earth and it will be her glory, still the selfishness of man will arise to take the liberties of others for the sake of greed.

"I will not allow this and it will be the turning point ... greed will be the hinge from which the good will turn to evil. But, until that time, (He's talking about the end of the Millennium here.) you have much beauty and peace to look forward to. The generations will flourish in an atmosphere of good will. The true faith that I intended for mankind will bring all into the light of My Glory and living for Me will be as easy as breathing. Joy will abound within families, villages and even cities, because the knowledge of Me and My Love for mankind will be readily available and openly professed.

"The Western United States will remain for the most part intact. And from this place will the new government arise. This is one reason why I will spare Yellowstone, that it not completely destroy the West and Southwest. Both farming and technology will arise based strictly on Godly principles and enforced by My Angels and those entrusted with governing - those who have proven themselves worthy and fit to care for all without selfish ambition and underhanded motives.

"This so contrasts what you have today springing from the occult motives instilled in Rome from the beginning. When I speak of Rome I speak of the government, not the Church.

"The restructuring of My Church will arise very organically from those chosen to lead in every village and township. They will be kept small except for the exceptional gatherings I, Myself, shall attend, to impart new understandings, revelations and ways of living in peace and love with one another. And yet, from the onset there will be those who will shy away and search for alternatives to what I have established. These will be the seed of discontent that cannot bend the knee. They will be the forefathers of those who will incite the rebellion. (at the end of the Millennium) Greed and Pride will always exist, Clare, until I remove the evil from within.

"I want to impart to you the Hope for the Future that I have. It will be a long, dark, bloody road until My Kingdom comes on this Earth, and I want all to know it will come. It will come.

"There is great hope for the generations yet to come. Peace will be established in mutual brotherly love and though nations shall retain their own identities, their own cultures, there will be no quarreling or squabbling for resources or power. It simply will not be allowed. Much in the nature of man continues to tend in that direction but I will enforce true liberty and justice for all. No one will be overlooked. Not one, not even the littlest one, for My Spirit will search the Earth and see to it that wrongs are righted and justice is done to the poor, the little, and the marginalized.

"You will be part of this, My Spouse. I will have so much joyful work for you to do. Your happiness will stretch from sea to sea."

And here I thought, 'But the country will be divided…?'

"Yes, the country will be divided. Yes, it will be quite a distance from one side to the other, not something you can take a ferry to cross. There will be distinctly different climates, culture and industry. There will be trade between the two halves of the country. Never again will men squabble over petroleum, for the new energy system will be installed almost immediately after the purification."

Wow! I'm really looking forward to that one – no more electric bills, guys! No more gasoline bills!

"Communication will be simpler than ever. Pollution will be a thing of the past. No one will be allowed to carry on operations destructive to My Creation or to humanity. Yet, in their foolishness, men will toy with over-throwing the beautiful lives they live, and I will allow them to accumulate and band together that they may be no more on the face of the Earth."

This again He's referring to the last Armageddon, the end of the Millennium.

"Lord, I really want to understand the whole Alien agenda and how You are going to deal with it."

"The technology they possess and have developed is deviant and cruel in the most grotesque ways. All is motivated by greed, hatred, lust for power and complete disregard for all that is good. I will totally destroy and wipe out every single one. There will be no more influence from these treacherous demons and their perverted technologies that vie with Me and declare they are capable of creating life. They are only capable of destroying life. Period.

"What your government has bought into will cost them irreparably: their lives, their souls, their offspring. And never again will they rise to power. The whole world will be turned upside down and emptied of all evil. This I will see to when I come. The three days of darkness will come just before I do. This is when all men will be on the brink of despair that there is no longer any hope at all. This is when I shall dispatch My angels to bind and destroy every wicked agent and agenda of terror and destruction.

"Life will be so new at the end of that period that it will seem that Eden has been restored to the whole Earth and the brightness of those days will declare My Mercy and Glory. And spontaneous regeneration will occur in many places on the Earth. It will truly be a new dawn where wickedness reigns no more. People will look for violence and wickedness, but all will be put to rest – they will not find it."

"But what about adulterers, liars, thieves...etc. that cannot enter the holy city?"

"There will be massive attempts to rehabilitate those with twisted lives. My love, My kindness and My Mercy will cleanse those who are willing and they shall be healed. I will spare no resource to help them into a new life. But sadly, many will still hold to their old ways of doing things and eventually be punished. I cannot allow evil men to reproduce evil in My Kingdom. They will be stopped before they can corrupt those who are following what is right and good."

That is, with the exception of what He allows at the very end of the Millennium and the final purification of the souls of the Earth.

"Transportation will not be only for the rich anymore. All will have an equal right to the things needful to fulfill their own destinies. Those who have succeeded in the past and hold to My Laws, they will be put in the position of raising up others who will rise to fulfill the very thing they were born to do.

"There will be no hindrances, no politics, no favoritism, no bribery - nothing of the sort will be allowed to exist in My Kingdom. All will have their share and what is needful for a happy life. You see, communism had these ideas as well, but because of the corrupted nature of man, it was bound to fail. Nothing of the sort can thrive, grow, and last without My Law and Order. Man will always tend towards selfishness and those who are succeeding will be trampled down by others who are stronger and want to steal what they have built up.

"OK, that's enough for tonight. Agreed?"

"Yes, agreed. Thank you Lord."

"Thank you, My love, for listening and writing. These are important things I want to tell many to help them persevere in the darkest hours of humanity."

And that's the end of the message. Thank you, Youtube family for listening, and the Lord bless you and keep you, and please keep us in prayer as we do this important work for the Lord. You just wouldn't BELIEVE the opposition we've been getting! But the Lord is faithful – He overcomes everything.

Jesus Speaks On: What is to Come, How to Stay Under God - parts 3 & 4

March 4, 2014

Part 3:

"I have been listening to your heart and you are dealing with many forms of demons posing as E.Ts. And Clare, I must tell you to stand convinced, not one of them is good. They are all fallen angels working against Me and humanity. Some put up the facade of being good, but don't be fooled - their agendas are just as wicked. They just manage to get more deeply entrenched because they are disarming.

"They are far more dangerous than the grays. Oh, how I hate this subject. Nonetheless, I do not want you to remain ignorant."

He really does hate this subject, guys. When I start poking around on the Internet, wanting to learn more about these despicable creatures, He is so grieved. I have to stop what I'm doing because it's just disgusting to Him.

"Every single one of them are extremely evil. There is not one good thing about them except that I can use them to make My people more holy and stronger. They actually are My vassals. Thinking they are doing things independently, they are carrying out what has been planned from the beginning of time."

I had to look up Vassal, guys: a person or country in a subordinate position to another "a much stronger nation can also turn a weaker one into a vassal state." In other words, the Lord is using them for His own purposes.

"They come in different shapes and sizes as well as ships that are different from one another. You were thinking the ship that was sighted over Phoenix and Arizona came from Nibiru to look around on Earth. That's not so. That was a government exercise, that's why the military didn't get involved even though there was so much time in which for them to act.

"Are you with Me, My Love?"

"Lord, I'm wobbly, feeling insecure about discernment. Is it really You, Lord?"

I told Ezekiel and he said that I need to push through, that the Lord was talking with me.

"He's right. You need to push through. When you are finished and go back to read this, it will make more sense to you. I love you, and I'm sorry this is so hard, but part of it is your over stimulated emotions.

"I have wanted to talk to you this way for a long time."

"But..."

"You weren't ready and I knew it would be difficult to convince you it is Me. But I have taken you to task because I need you.

"I could have chosen someone else you know."

“Yes, Lord, I know very, very well and I don't know what to say except I'm a piece of work.”

"OK. Back to work.

"The people are still misinformed about what they are dealing with. They (demons disguised as ET's) are very crafty and able to take advantage of people's weaknesses. They blithely invite them in not realizing that they are a force to be reckoned with. And putting a few ‘grays’ down to impress them is nothing, except the opportunity to pull the wool over their eyes and convince them that they are benign."

“Lord, I'm tired. Can I rest my eyes?”

"Clare, let's proceed."

“OK.”

"Part of this 'tired' is unbelief and laziness."

“Ouch.”

"Well, at least you are persevering. I'll give you credit for that."

“You know I can't take credit for what you do, Beloved.”

"You're a smart one." He chided. **"But actually, it's your love for me and obedience that is keeping you here."**

“Awwww...”

"I'm only speaking the truth. So let's move on together, OK?"

“I'm all ears.”

"Much of the mass confusion that is going to fall on the Earth will be the newness of all these different breeds of clones.

"The confusion they sow, by being many and varied, they will take advantage of. And yes, they do have the capability of destroying planet Earth. But remember, they are dogs on a chain and permission will not be granted. I love the Earth, Clare. She is beautiful, a masterpiece - and I will not allow her to be destroyed."

“But what is that about a new Heaven and a new Earth?”

"I will make them new and what was once will no longer exist or be remembered.

"It will change instantaneously according to the vision in My Heart. And all men shall see the Glory of the Lord. What was will be no more, all things will be made new."

“What about the sea creatures?”

"There will be lakes, everywhere. No more need for violence, no more violence in the atmosphere, because there is no more rebellion of man. Everything will be a pristine Garden of Eden.

"Men will mine the Earth, but not in a destructive way. On the Earth every metal and substance necessary will be available to man. All hearts and all projects will be directed to glorifying Me.”

Okay, that’s the end of Three.

Part 4:

Things were a little bit sketchy this evening, static-y…

"Lord, it is a full moon, I feel a lot of resistance and static. It took me longer than usual to be in the right place and receive Your words in faith tonight."

"You are going to have to listen more carefully."

"I'm sorry."

"Well, now that I have your attention let's go on, shall we?"

"Oh, Jesus thank You so much for that confirmation on Yellowstone! Wow, thank You!"

And I think I might have mentioned that in the last video, guys? A good friend of ours had a dream about Yellowstone, and in the dream there were rivulets of lava – streams of lave flowing out of Yellowstone. It didn't blow up the way it was supposed to, because the Lord intervened.

"You are going to come to believe Me more and more as these months go by. You will be shocked by how clearly you have been hearing Me but didn't realize it. A little more repentance goes a long way, but mostly MY Love, more confidence in Me."

I'm going to stop here to say that when He said, "As these MONTHS go by…" I was not a happy camper! Like everyone else, I was expecting the Rapture to happen maybe this Easter. On the other hand, while I was editing this just now, it occurred to me that "months" could refer to us seeing it from Heaven, as the "great cloud of witnesses." So, that still doesn't pin the Rapture down, really…

"Alright, so Yellowstone is just one instance of My Mercy at work. The prayers of the Christian people have mitigated much that Satan wanted to do to completely annihilate the Earth. Not only that, but they have had an effect on those who are going to be taken and saved. Silence is deadly right now, it is time to shout out from the rooftops, 'Your King is coming, your King is coming!!!'

"By the time planet X becomes visible, it will be too late for mankind to do anything about it. They will be at the complete mercy of happenstance (something that happens by chance) and of course My Mercy, which most will not engage.

"Those who shall survive in the rocks, crevices and ravines, I will supernaturally protect and provide for. Their spiritual growth will blossom exponentially because all that they do will be reliant on My Provision.

"There will be multiplication of food, healings, water and all manner of protection for those who turn completely to Me. By the time I come and it is over with, they will truly be purified like gold and silver shining in My kingdom as saints. I have chosen them for this hour and most have a premonition that something much bigger than their lives have been is coming for them.

"Some have prepared, others are just awaiting circumstances. Most are not as yet Christians; they do not know Me, although they have heard My voice in their hearts. The legalisms of churches have kept them from Me, along with their fondness for freedom from laws and rules.

"But all that will change when I come for you. There will be searing conviction amongst the relatives and especially the children and spouses of those I take. It will go deep, deep into the depths of their hearts and divide bone and marrow. Then, as the purification of Earth advances, more and more will have a passionate love for Me and righteousness - it will blossom and overtake them on the way.

"Many will cease to care about living and be ready to die to be with Me. They will be envious of those who have been raptured. But not for the common motive of escaping suffering, rather for the burning fire of love they feel for Me. Yet, they will persevere in what is laid out before them.

"The more My children rely on Me during this time, the more miracles they will see. The more they rely on their own flesh, the more in danger they will be. I operate best with total faith. It causes a vacuum that only I can fill, whereas providing for themselves will weaken My ability to intervene. More and more they are going to rely only on Me. More and more things will become more desperate and they will have little choice. The sooner they come to terms with that, the better it will go for them.

"I will not give them over to defeat, rather I will be with them as I was with David when he fought Goliath. As they pour over the Old Testament, they will find example after example of battles where My people were outnumbered 10 to 1 and yet My right arm won them the victory. And as they confide their trust in Me, I will bring it to pass.

"There will be traitors among them. They must learn to know one another by the Spirit. Many will attempt to join their ranks. But I warn them now: do not accept anyone I do not approve, no matter how dire or urgently they present their request.

"You see, they will use good will against them, to pry open the group. Then, because they are not of like mind, they will undermine everything that they do. Do not allow anyone into your ranks that I have not approved of. Use the system of lots and pray Holy Spirit to choose, put your confidence in your flesh completely to death. Put your confidence in Me totally. I alone know the hearts and motives of men and women and even children.

"The Devil is underhanded, he will use your goodness against you. Rely on Me and not your own human reasoning.

"There will be times when you will look at each other and say, 'We're going to die.' And yet, because you put your hope and trust in Me, I will move on your behalf and rescue you. I will make you invisible to the enemy, and fearful to the beasts that will be bent on destroying you.

“Remember always to use My Name. There will be times when the enemy is combing the forest looking for you and they will walk right over you and not even know it. I will make you invisible to them. There will be times when I will cause panic in the ranks of the enemy and completely turn them off your trail.

“I have many ways, My children, of saving you. Many, many ways. There will even be times when the ground will open up to hide you.

“Never give up, trust in Me and My love for you, for I will be with you. The power of the Blood...plead My Blood, *‘The Blood of Jesus cover and protect us, make us invisible to the enemy.’”*

I sense here He is talking about heat sensitive drones seeking you out – calling upon the Blood to cover you and protect you so that you aren’t seen.

I remember when my oldest son had to have emergency surgery at six months old. His small intestine telescoped into the large intestine and he wasn’t able to eat or drink anything without violent vomiting. While he was in surgery, I was praying and I saw a red demon hovering over his little body. I heard, "Raging infection" and so I pleaded the Blood of Jesus over his little body, and try as he might, that demon could not enter the body - it kept hitting a clear polymer-type shield and bouncing off. Thank the Lord, the operation was a success with no complications of infection. The Blood is powerful! Use it.

"Those who are well equipped and prepared will have no advantage over those who have put their total trust in Me. This is one reason why I have not allowed you, Clare, to lay up for the future. I will provide everything necessary. Only listen very carefully for My voice.

"There will be times when I will prompt you to do something that seems out of order, but it will be your salvation. Prayer will be your weapon, a weapon that no one and nothing can defeat. Pray in tongues. Much wisdom will infuse your minds and bypass your intellects, which have been trained in the thoughts of the world. My ways are not your ways, My ways are not the world's ways.

"Prayer will be your greatest weapon. Pray and listen very carefully. Expect Me to instruct you, give you visions, answers, understanding. Expect it and learn to discern it early. The sooner you embrace this wisdom, the safer you will be. I will lead you and teach you the way you should go.

"Use the Bible for Rhemas – that's the anointed Word of God. Listen for Scriptures that float into your mind. I will be speaking to you in so many ways – even songs will come into your mind to warn or advise you. Only be alert and pay attention. Do not allow anything to escape your notice. I will send you signs and images to alert you of danger ahead.

"My children, I love you dearly and if I could have taken you with your loved ones, I would have. But for your own reasons you resisted Me. Now you must learn to open your hearts and minds to receive Me without resistance, without doubt, in total trust.

"When it seems that nothing is going to work say, 'Jesus, I trust in You.' Say it over and over again, visualize Me as you say it to Me, so it fills your inner man with confidence that I will act and spurs Me on to act because of your faith in Me.

"Remember, when you have no other recourse, you have ME. Remember, also, that you with the Father, Myself, and Holy Spirit are greater than any force on Earth. You and I are a majority. There will be times when you see angels protecting you. I will open your eyes.

"Believe."

Thank you for listening Youtube family. And I would ask you please to download this message and save it for your children and your loved ones. This whole series is designed for those who are left behind. I know that it's satisfying a lot of curiosity and questions that we've all had, but more important than that, it's for those are left behind and have been resisting this time. It's like...the Fast Track initiation to the Lord's ways – quickly. Although your families have had the opportunity to see you operate in the Spirit, they are well acquainted with what you do in certain situations – still they're going to need a lot of confidence and a lot of trust. I really believe these videos are going to help them.

So, please consider downloading them – it's very easy to do. All you have to do is find ClipGrab on the Internet – it's a free program. Download that, and then you can download these and make them into MP3's, or into MP4's if you want.

The Lord bless and keep you – pray for us as we pray for you.

Jesus Speaks On: After the Rapture
Who I Can Protect and Who I Cannot Protect - part 5

March 6, 2015

It began when I was feeling very responsible to be sure that people would be in the right place of heart and mind to be protected by the Lord, to be led by the Lord. And I was just musing on that, and told the Lord:

"Lord, I feel responsible to talk about who You will protect and who You cannot protect."

"You have brought up a good point...and where do you suppose that came from... hmmm?"

"Really?"

"Yes, really."

I thought, 'Well – thank the Lord, it was His idea."

"Humility, self-control, honesty, and charity are absolutely essential if you want Me to walk with you. If you are used to leading and getting your own way, you won't do very well as a leader. If you are unsure of yourself and know that you need Me more than ever, you will excel as a leader.

"My children, the ways of the world that you have learned are totally inappropriate here. I protect those who humble themselves before Me. If you are prancing around proudly with all the answers, you are bound for destruction.

"I am counting on your breaking when you realize all you've been taught by friends and family has just come to pass before your very eyes. I am counting on you face flat on the floor begging forgiveness for your pride and arrogance. I am laying the groundwork for you to survive the trials that are now at your door, both body and soul.

"If you humble yourself before Me, I will most certainly be with you. Even if you are in a long-standing habit of pride and arrogance, and are aware of your sin and want to be delivered, I will work with you. But if you insist on your own wisdom, I can do little for you.

"It is of the utmost importance that you put others before yourself. When I came into the world, I did not lord it over others. No, I bent the knee and humbled Myself, washing the feet of My disciples. The lowliest job in the house – left for the lowliest servant. That is what a leader does – he, or she, looks after the interests of others.

"Some of you have come from very humble families and have seen what I am talking about. Others will have a struggle because they have not have good examples. Don't let that discourage you. I am dedicated to you and your make-over. I will not abandon you to your arrogance; rather I will instruct and lead you as you come to Me sincerely, wanting to change.

"Much, even in your survival and the survival of your loved ones, will depend on your total reliance on Me and My ways. I will always, always provide a way out for those who have humbled themselves and relied totally on Me.

"Though the mountains shake and the seas roar, I will be with you and never abandon you. You will know them by their love and humility. You will recognize those who are sincere by whether or not they are authentically humble. Anger, back biting, strife, insisting on your ways, those are the ticket to defeat. That is NOT humble behavior.

"Above all, preserve your souls by giving your life to Me. The very first step in the ladder of humility that leads to Heaven is recognizing you have failed with your life. You have sinned, you have hurt others, made foolish and immature decisions, and neglected those you owed respect and support to. And those who you should have listened to, you discounted, especially your elders.

"So, having made a mess out of your life, you need to give it to Me, unconditionally. 'Lord I have sinned, and sinned, and sinned. I am not worthy of You, but I beg your forgiveness. I repent of the selfish and arrogant life I have led, forgive me. Wash me clean with Your Blood, deliver me from the evil within. I want to be born again: fresh, new, and in Your Image. I give You my life, unconditionally. Receive me, lead me, save me.'

"Along with that pray the Our Father I have taught and expect Me to make immediate adjustments to your character."

Our Father, Who is in Heaven,
Holy is Your Name;
Your Kingdom come, Your will be done,
on Earth as it is in Heaven.
Give us this day our daily bread,
and forgive us our sins,

as we forgive those who sin against us;
and lead us not into temptation,
but deliver us from evil. Amen.

"Learn of Me, for I am meek and humble of heart. I have left you innumerable love letters - read them, believe them, allow them to take root in your heart. There is no joy that is compared to knowing and loving Me. This knowledge of Me and My love for you, unworthy as you are, will sustain you through every trial. No matter what you go through, I will be there on your right, holding your hand, speaking to you, comforting you. Nothing can separate you from My Love.

"NOTHING.

"Not anything on the Earth or above the Earth, not aliens, not death, not even when you fall - still I am by your side to pick you back up. Nothing can separate you from My Love.

'So, don't be afraid when you fail. Expect that you are going to make mistakes along the way, expect that you will fail, and know that I will lift you back up again. Do not run when you fail, turn to Me. Do not run away, rather run to Me. I will take you into My arms in a full embrace and wipe away your tears. I do not condemn you, I am not a man that I should judge you. No, I love you. I know before you even fail that you will fail and I already have a provision to raise you back up.

"Know, understand in full knowledge, that I never, ever will forsake you. Even when you cannot feel Me, I am there supporting you, ready to come to your aid, to forgive and restore. With this knowledge, I want you to go forward now in total reliance on Me. From this day forth, your life is not your own - it is Mine to cherish, guide and bring to glory with Me in Heaven.

"Fear nothing, for I am with you always. And where I am, you too shall be, for I have gone ahead of you to prepare a place for you. A place uniquely your own, where we will be together forever. I am not a man that I should love you as a man.

"I am your God, and never will you find the limit to My Love for you, because there is none. I am eternally yours and you are now eternally Mine."

Jesus Speaks On: After the Rapture
Demons, Aliens, Volcanoes and Hell Expanded - part 6

March 7, 2015

"Let's talk about volcanoes."

"OK"

"Recently Yellowstone has become more active and what is anticipated is the destruction of much of America. And yet I have told you I will moderate this outpouring so that it is not catastrophic. Not many believe or will believe this, for much of the world still relies on what is sensational and the worst possible scenario, simply because they don't believe in God or what I can do to save your country, which is also Mine... for it is My country, too, you know."

"Even though they've rejected You, Lord?"

"It is only the foolish. But in America there are many, many Christians and though they haven't completely come to terms with their Masonic capitol, My Spirit is with them and on their hearts. Especially as things begin to heat up, many more will return to Me wholeheartedly."

I was thinking about the revival that is supposed to happen, that so many prophets have prophesied that there was going to be a revival before that Rapture. I looked at the Lord, and He shook His head back and forth in the negative. I flinched and thought, 'But everyone says that, good prophets say there's going to be a revival...'

"Clare, it's not going to happen. You hesitate because of the embarrassment it might cause you if you are wrong. May I say that if you are wrong in hearing Me, a revival would totally obscure your negative prophecy. That is: 'There is no revival coming to America until the Rapture.'"

What He means is, until AFTER the Rapture.

"I'm sorry, that's the way it is going to be, that is My agenda."

"Who can argue with God?"

"You, My Love. All the time, as a matter of fact." He said wryly.

I laughed. "Yeah…I guess I'm guilty as charged."

"You are a stiff necked one, you are."

"Is that why my neck hurts, Lord?"

"Undoubtedly."

"OK, but this is not a laughing matter. Many prophets have said there would be a revival before the Rapture, but I've always felt a check in my spirit, and now I wonder about..."

"The destiny of those who would have repented?"

"Yes."

"I have given ample opportunity for turn-arounds in this country - ample opportunity. I will not have My revivals met with scorn and contempt again. Something must soften the hardened hearts in this country, those who have made materialism their God. That is why I am waiting."

"What about the economic collapse?"

"That will be coming after the Rapture as well."

"Wow."

"Yes, Wow! A time of unparalleled suffering. But this will break the backs of those who have nothing but scorn and contempt for the Bible. For Prophecy. For the little ones, the simple ones, those who's God means everything to them. And they do not live for what they can get - they live for Me, because getting Me means everything to them.

"And so I am not about to make life more miserable for them. I will wait until they are up and gone, then the hammer will fall."

"Hammer?"

"Yes, the hammer of judgment on this nation. It will come all at once. Which, by the way, fits in with the agendas of the ruling elite. They will have more control when there is no recourse for people to get food, other than the government. You have noticed, slowly the squeeze is being put on the little food banks, those not in step with the government. The alternative groups, the ones that are more independent."

"Yes, I've wondered about that."

"I do fill you in, you know."

"I'm beginning to see just how much!"

"Getting back to volcanoes. I have targeted the areas of the world that deal in human trafficking, drug running, and gross injustices against mankind. Earthquakes and volcanoes will take many lives and destroy much. It is not My wish to see any suffering in humanity, but you have no idea the atrocities against mankind these areas are involved in. The blood of their slain cries out to Me from the Earth. I will not delay; I will bring justice.

"Also these volcanoes are entrances to the underworld, direct channels to the bowels of Hell, and as Hell fills up, the Earth expands. This is no private thought of yours; I know you've had this thought before. I have given you this understanding, it came from Me."

"Oh, Lord that is horrible!"

"There is also an increase in activity before demon aliens make their public entrance on the Earth. Everything is orchestrated to bring forward the last kingdom that will rule the entire world, synchronistically.

"Demon aliens will be enlisted by that government to search out and destroy communities of resisters, along with clones that will come forth from every corner of the Earth. Even now, small pods of such creatures inhabit even the most remote areas of the world, waiting for the word to come forth to search and destroy resisters. This new government would not be possible were it not for the help of these clones."

I want to take a break here for a minute. The Lord permitted us to watch the X-files for a while. I don't think I've ever watched anything darker and more morose in my life than those X-files.

But I remember one particular episode, where the star of the program was looking for his sister. It was up in Montana, I think – on the flats of Montana. He saw a little girl who was raising bees with a bunch of other girls and boys. And she looked exactly like his sister, the last time that he saw her.

They were in a very remote area – I remember the scene where they were with these bees that they kept. There was a man working on the telephone lines, and the bees killed the man, and they just stood there and watched. No emotions, no nothing. That was pretty grotesque, that was really bad.

"The skies will be so full of demon aliens that people will be beside themselves with shock and awe. In the very beginning, they will be led to believe they are benign. Then without warning, the supposed evil ones will 'invade' and a war in the heavens will break out. This is only a staged even to galvanize all the countries into one government."

"Lord, may I have a vision of this?"

I was expecting a multicolored scene, but the skies, somewhat polluted, were filled as far as the eye could see with discs and other vehicles of strange proportions and shapes, all very monotone and metallic. Although the sun didn't gleam off of any of them, it seemed to be a rather hazy day. Maybe that's why.

"It is no coincidence that volcanoes and sin are in proximity to one another. There are connections to demonic activity, increased in an area where the portals are open. This is also a fact in Hawaii.

"Oh, My Love. There is so much you are ignorant of, stop trying to make it fit in your logical mind and just type what you hear. Will you?"

"Uh oh, ouch!" And that's what was happening. He was telling me all these different things, and they were getting more and more bizarre to me and my mind and intellect were resisting Him – and He finally called me on it.

"I'm sorry, Lord." I hung my head.

He lifted my chin and said, **"I love you?"** with a lilting tone of voice.

I smiled, "I know I'm a piece of work."

"Indeed you are, and I never tire of working the work. So, don't crumble under My rebuke. Those who God loves, He chastens..."

"I love you?" He said again in that lilted tone of voice.

"OK, Lord... really, with Your help... assume I'm going to stick to Your facts."

"THANK YOU! I guess now you are getting to see just how much pride and human intellect is in control of your thinking, huh?"

"Umm. Way more than I imagined."

"Yes, I've hidden that from you. May I say that is what has hindered you from hearing from Me all these years?"

"Really?"

"Well, in point of fact, yes. And other things, such as cultivating more virtue so you could be trusted and wouldn't buckle under pressure.

"Well, that's enough explaining you for now. I'm not finished yet."

"Oh, I'm so glad, Lord. I want to hear more!"

"You're a funny one alright, one moment you're balking, the next you're pushing? Who can understand you?"

"YOU can, thank you Lord."

"OK. So, there is a correlation between the volcanoes and demonic activity, that is 'sin.'"

Okay, now – because of this little interruption here I wanted to go back to the thing about Hawaii, because that's where it started to balk. He said, **"There are connections to demonic activity, increased in an area where the portals are open. This is also a fact in Hawaii."** And I was thinking, "huh, really?" And that's when He called me on my unbelief.

"Also superstition and strange rituals, almost always involving human sacrifice are in these areas. Those movies you saw as a child were not just movies - they were based on fact. And you can be sure that where human sacrifice is involved, Satan is right there with them, under the guise of their local deity."

"Yes, I remember the Incas, and the Polynesians in those movies."

"Every culture has their own brand of Satanism. All, however, lead back to him."

"Oh, Lord, that is so gross, what I am thinking." I was trying to figure out how they managed to get life or get a body. And He began explaining that to me, and I said, "That is so gross…what I am thinking."

What I was thinking was, the life in the sperm is taken when it is not discharged properly, and implanted in the egg of an abducted woman or in an incubator.

"This is SO sci-fi!"

"But you are right on target. You've seen just enough on the Internet to know how they create life."

"But what about a soul?"

"They are soul-less, occupied by demon entities. They only take the seed. Demons have a similar pattern to angels and humans."

And what we are talking about here is the Uncreated Light. And there's someone on the Internet who has done some research about this. The Uncreated Light is something that the Russian and Greek Orthodox church have found – it's a phenomena, where there'll be an orb of light with kind of a hazy pattern to it. It's not a demon, it's actually an angel or one of those saints in Heaven.

“The uncreated light is a characteristic of life being present. Whether it is demonic or angelic or human, it is a life form.”

“But doesn't the soul come from You when the egg and sperm are united?”

“Indeed they do. But I have not given them a soul. I prevent it. Rather, they have hundreds of thousands of demons waiting for a body.”

At that I was picturing what the process was like.

"Yes, Yes..."

“So the demons take form when they are given a vacant body?”

“That's correct.”

“But what about the inter-dimensionality of these creatures. Is it like a glorified body? God forbid...”

“It is inter-dimensional, that is, it can take form in different dimensions without losing its substance.”

“Wow! That's over my poor little head, Lord.”

"I know, and you are blessed because you are following Me without editing anything to suit your human understanding. You see this is how inventors work, as well. I put ideas in their heads, they work them out and a new discovery of science comes forth. All has been done and allowed to bring humanity to this climax you are approaching now. This is the critical hour.”

“Whew!!!”

"Yes, I know. You see, that is why demons cannot be destroyed, only bound. And in the end, all will be fed into the Lake of Fire for eternity - that is, forever, and ever, and ever. Do you see? Life cannot be destroyed, but it can be confined. The bodies they inhabit can be destroyed, but not the demon within. At least I have not provided for that option.

"There will be so many lessons to learn. You've heard of tough love in the penitentiary, right?"

"Yes."

"Well, there will be visitations to behold the lake of fire for the sake of understanding the destiny of those who choose evil."

And the smoke of their torment will rise forever and ever. There will be no rest day or night for those who worship the beast and its image, or for anyone who receives the mark of its name." Revelation 14:11.

"I guess with that comes another question. After the millennium, there will no longer exist evil. So, why would tough love be necessary?"

"All things spoken by Me shall be fulfilled. The Earth will be full of the Glory of the Lord. No longer shall evil have any place to inhabit; all will be regenerated according to My eternal design.

"That's enough for tonight, My Love. I know there are some that will scoff at this, but don't trouble yourself about them and I won't either."

I laughed.

"In their own time, their eyes shall be opened. What I am giving you is for those who can receive it with understanding, that in the end they will see that Good shall triumph and there is much to look forward to.

"These records are being given to you that others not fall into despair. Had the church been doing her job, this would not be necessary. But due to political pressures, much has been suppressed - but now is the time for them to be revealed."

I heard this Scripture in my spirit: *"Go your way, Daniel, for these words are concealed and sealed up until the end time. 10 Many will be purged, purified and refined, but the wicked will act wickedly; and none of the wicked will understand, but those who have insight will understand." Daniel 12:9*

Jesus Speaks On: After the Rapture The World Will Mourn - part 7

March 11, 2015

Well, dear Family, this is a message full of surprises – certainly surprises to me. Tonight as I was in worship, things started out as they usually do, I was dancing with the Lord. And I noticed I had on a black dress – an evening gown, a black evening gown with sequins that reflected light. He also was wearing black. We were dancing in kind of a formal ball setting. I was really questioning why I was wearing black, as that is a sign of mourning, yet we were dancing. I was a little confused on that. So I began:

"Lord, I don't understand why I am wearing a black sequined evening gown and yet dancing so gracefully with You as if we were at a ball or celebration of some kind."

"Because the whole world shall mourn and you shall mourn with them, but have deep inner joy, which the world cannot take away from you.

"We will dance through the times to come, as My judgment falls upon this nation and the world. We will behold it with one eye, while beholding Heaven with the other.

"As things come to a close here in America and around the globe, you will draw closer and closer to your Heavenly homeland.

"I know, Clare, you sense in your spirit that time is short - and indeed it is, My Love. Soon, I will be taking you away with Me forever and ever and ever. I will lavish on you all My gifts of Love and we will live happily ever after."

And I thought to myself, 'In THIS world, NOBODY lives happily ever after…'

"Oh, Lord - that is so precious and exciting and my inner man trembles in hopes that it truly is You and truly this will come to pass soon."

"What have I told you about doubting? And trusting?"

"I guess I have no experience to compare it with, to hold on to... it is so far away from my reality. It's almost too good to be true."

He smiled, **"Yes, My Love, I know well how you feel... but it is true, Clare, just as surely as I AM. It is true. And I know it's beyond what you can imagine - and that delights Me even more because I love to see you surprised and overwhelmed with My loving provision for you."**

"So, the world will mourn but we will have one eye in Heaven and one on Earth?"

"That's right."

"Lord, how can I be happy knowing what mankind is suffering on this Earth and how You suffer with them? I really question this, as well as..."

"...Coming back to help?"

"YES! I mean, there's so many rumors about us being trained and coming back to help during the Tribulation."

"You are going to enter into My Rest - you have labored and now you are going to rest. I have not called My Bride to be any part of this judgment that is coming. I am not removing you so you can watch from Heaven and suffer. Is that clear?"

"Oh."

"Well, I'm not. Your job is done here until I return. I will come to you for comfort, but I will not expose you to the horrors of Earth. I cannot and I will not."

"Lord, can I question Your wisdom on this?"

"Why not, you always do! Why should today be different from another day, hmmm?"

"Well, this is no laughing matter but you are making me laugh."

"We can have fun together sometimes, even when it is hard and heart wrenching for us both.

"In My Divine plan, I have limits to what each one must undergo. I have purposes and I have limits. My love, do not question. Just accept. Just receive the gift of freedom from the alienation and troubles of this world."

"Lord, my gut feels funny."

"That's Unbelief, Clare."

So, I rebuked it. And strangely…it went away.

"My Love, many think it's heroic virtue to come back and be present for the chastisement. They don't know what they are talking about. My angels have been prepared for what is to come, they alone will be a part of what is to happen."

"But what about our prayers from Heaven when we see You praying...surely we will pray too? Our children! How can we not respond to that?"

"There will be times when you will pray for them, but your knowledge will be so far above what it is now, that even then, what you pray will be for their best. No longer will you be dramatically tied into them, rather you will see them as I see them - as a part of humanity that must be purified from sin. It will not lessen your affection but it will change your perspective to one of seeing from Heaven."

"So, I won't be pulled into an emotional whirlwind, like I am when they go through dramas now?"

"Exactly. You will love them...from a distance and yet, as their mother. It will all make sense to you then, My Love. It truly will."

"So, we will not be returning during the Tribulation or get to see all the things going on here on the Earth?"

"No. You will not. You will touch in from time to time, to give them courage but you will not be a part of the drama...rather more like an apparition that speaks encouragement, but not engaged in the painful realities.

"You see, your reality is going to be so much more different. In a sense, it will be impossible for you to get emotionally involved on the same level you are on now, in your body, on Earth. Your whole world and reality will be so different.

"I know it is hard for you to grasp this concept...although I do see a little light breaking through."

He smiled. **"You see, things are so different in Heaven, even now you cannot compute how you will react or see Earth from Heaven. It is the true reality. What you are in now is only a mist. When you've been distanced from it... well, there's just no way for Me to explain it, you have to experience it, My Love. But, you can take My word for it. Will you?"**

"Well, I do have a peace about it now that I rebuked that unbelief. I have a deep peace, Jesus, that You are speaking the truth to me, and that it shall be as You have said."

"Moving on. There are many who will be disappointed that they cannot come back and be a part of the drama. To you I say: Please, take My word for it, you would only get in the way. You would suffer what was intended for the reprobate. You have proven your love for Me and I will not have you go through these things with those who have shown scorn and contempt for Me.

"However, you will get your chance when we return together. Then you will have your assignments and all will be new, full of expectations and opportunities for you to use your gifts. Oh, the plans I have for you, My Bride - they are so exciting! So wonderful! And you will be fully equipped to do all that is in your heart that you have longed to do.

"Yes, you will be perfectly equipped. Your music will flourish, your playing will be nothing less than perfection, and the anointing will bring hearts to Me, to heal and restore. You see, that is what you are all expecting - you're just getting ahead of Me by thinking it will be during the chastisement.

"You will all have the opportunity to do everything that is in your heart and so, so much more that I have planned for you. No longer will you labor and see no results because of the hardness of hearts. No, hearts will be wide open to receive all that you have to give.

"Oh, REJOICE MY BRIDES!! Rejoice! Great is your reward, and great shall be your assignments. Rejoice! Look forward to this. Yes indeed, you will dance in the black dress, one eye on Heaven and one on the Earth, but your reality shall be in My Arms, not in sackcloth and ashes.

"Well, are you satisfied now, My Love?"

"Oh, yes Lord, I believe I am. I believe in You, Jesus. You speak only the truth and I have come to understand that You truly are preparing us for what is to occur very quickly."

"Thank you My Love, thank you for receiving. My heart leaps for joy that finally you have settled this question in your heart, and you truly have heard the voice of your Shepherd.

"And I have told you I will never cease to work in you to bring you into the reality of My faithful voice. It is I who will do these things, and all that I need from you is what you just gave Me.

“Thank you My Love, thank you ever so much for believing in Me. I adore you, Clare, and I have spoken My words through you and I will continue to speak them until the day you come Home with Me."

Maranatha Lord!!! Come quickly!

Jesus Speaks On: After the Rapture
The Day the Bombs Fall - part 8

March 12, 2015

I have a rather solemn message for you – I'm a little bit numb right now... I'm going to share with you what the Lord discussed with me this evening.

I've been having issues about Timing...like, what's new about that – everybody has them. But I've been having issues about timing, because the Lord had told me that I was going to accomplish everything He had put in my heart, that I would have peace about it. He didn't say what the time frame would be, but I assumed it was before the Rapture. So, I was a little bit surprised this evening, because I was bringing this up to Him.

"This is bothering me, Lord."

"Can we talk about it?"

"Yes, that would help me immensely."

"I never told you the time frame in which you would get this done. I just told you that you would complete everything I'd given you to do. But I didn't say when."

"Lord, You inferred before the Rapture. And also, You've told me that You had thrown up obstacles to give Your Bride more time. Now I am very, very confused. Because I can sense that things are ramping up."

"Let me clear the clutter for you. First of all, I did promise that all would be accomplished. I know you thought it would be before the Rapture, but I didn't give you any time frame."

"Oh... Help me Lord, you can see I'm falling into an Unbelief trap."

"Steady as she goes, My Love. Hold on. You must be patient. There's going to come a time when everything you have wanted to do which I have put in your heart, is going to be completed. After the Rapture."

"After?"

"Yes, after."

"But You said you were giving Your Bride more time?"

"I just did give her more time."

"But, I sensed or felt that you meant years - like a couple of years or three years."

"Well, I never clarified that for you because I am still waiting for My Father's word. There is timing involved, acute timing involved."

"Okay, well…I'm a little stumped."

"There goes that unbelief again."

"Yep, guilty as charged. Oh, help me Jesus!"

At this point, I needed to make a fire and heat dinner up for Ezekiel, and it was a welcomed break. I knew that if I went to him he would help me out of my confusion. Am I being toyed with or is this truly Jesus?

I'm back. It is Jesus.

"Well, are you satisfied and at peace?"

"Yes, Lord."

"You asked Me to help you. He is My mouth piece and protection for you, Sweet Bride."

"Oh, Jesus - how can you call me sweet when I question You so much?"

"I'm not offended. Your irascibility only gives Me the opportunity to display My meekness and humility for My children. In other words, if I can be meek and humble with Clare, surely you can be meek and humble with one another.

"You see, I make good use of your stubbornness."

"Truly, Lord, You are gentle and forgiving. Thank you for being so patient with me."

"It wasn't difficult. I love you and I understand your struggles – which, by the way, are universal to all men. But now that we've settled that, I need to fill you in."

"I'm here, Lord."

He kissed my forehead.

"Well, because the time is short, I have you both on the fast track to wrap up these messages and prepare yourselves for that day. Only in prayer and steadfastness will you weather the terrific storm that is about to hit America and the world.

"Each day, I want the two of you to make sure you are solid and prepared at any moment."

“How will we know that we are prepared?”

"You're going to feel a deep peace. It's been edging up on both of you, just continue to keep your focus and understand there's no time to waste. Please, buckle down and work hard to organize your messages and leave behind what I have given you.

"Clare, are you listening?"

“Lord, I'm foggy.”

"It's that sugar you ate."

“Whoops.”

"Just bear with Me.

"There is going to be a limited nuclear exchange, enough to throw the world into a panic and set the stage for Obama to take the reins of peace and be declared as the hero.

"Your country will be in pandemonium and communications will be knocked out temporarily. But in order to enforce Martial Law, communication will be necessary. After all, how can the victor enjoy his victory without broadcasting it all over the world? Your country will recover from this devastation more quickly than anyone would expect, because everything is in place with full knowledge of what is coming.

"Your country will no longer be a world power. She will have massive issues of reconstruction and contamination to deal with. Make no mistake, those underground cities will contain the important people, while everyone else struggles on the surface. Law and order will be out of control, criminals will take full advantage to rape and pillage. Life will be a mess.

"But the VERY DAY that the bombs fall, that's the Day I am coming for you. Lift up your heads and watch the sky. I am coming for you that same day.

"Let Me repeat Myself: LIFT UP YOUR HEADS – I AM COMING FOR YOU THAT SAME DAY!

"Do not fall into despair, do not panic. I have warned you over and over again, your redemption draws nigh. This is the moment of eternity you've been waiting for."

"Lord, I'm speechless."

"Well, it's coming. As surely as I AM, it is coming.

"Do not give in to fear. Stand your ground, raise your eyes to the Heavens. I'm coming."

"Lord, help us."

"I've already placed my angels to help you, you will not stumble or fall, all is in place."

"Thank you, Lord. Thank You so much."

"You see, I have wanted to confirm this to you, but I had to wait until you were secure in our communications."

"Jesus, I am really numb."

"I know, I know. It's a lot to take in. But I have prepared you well, and you'll pass in flying colors."

"Is that all, Jesus?"

"For now, yes."

And that's the end of the message…

Jesus Speaks On: After the Rapture Prepare Packages of Hope - part 9

March 13, 2015

We had an interesting situation today - the Internet was down. I don't know if it was the fiber-optic wire got cut or whatever – that's usually what happens when construction was going down. It was down all day, and of course the telephone is connected to the Internet, so that was down also.

I began to feel the frustration and isolation that comes with not being able to communicate with people you normally communicate with. Then I began thinking about how others will feel when the Internet is not running: how isolated, fearful and confused they will be, too. That was heavy on my heart when I came to prayer.

"It is very important for you to leave behind prepared packets for your loved ones. This thought is not from you, Clare, it's been on My heart all day, and the communication outage pinpointed it very well.

"Dear Children, if these messages have ministered to you, I would like you make copies and put them where they will be found by loved ones when you are gone. This is only a precaution, because the sites you visit may no longer exist after the Rapture.

"Those in a position of power have made note of who is a danger to their agendas. When you find something that touches you and gives you an enlarged viewpoint that secures your peace, download it and keep it where it will be found."

“Should we make CD's or DVD's?”

"Whatever is more stable and convenient. Even two copies would not be excessive in case something happens to the first one. The devils will be in a hurry to destroy anything holy and instructional so they can isolate those left behind."

“Well, we do have PDF's available that can be printed.”

"Yes, printed is best, easy to read and useful when there are power outages and the internet is gone, which it will be for quite some time until facilities are rebuilt. These packages should be accompanied by a very loving letter. Stay away from causing guilt, which will either make them mad or lead them into despair. Be constructive, be positive, be hopeful. But especially be loving.

“They know very well they missed it, you don't have to rub it in. Rather you need to strengthen them because their knees will barely support them.

"Leave behind a will of some sort, or list of how things are to be given away. This will help to prevent arguing. Be fair in the distribution; be especially kind to those who don't deserve it.

“Your whole attention right now should be on their salvation. I am a loving God, but with My Wrath on mankind, it will be difficult to convince many of this. But remember, those I predestined, I also foreknew.

"Be plain in your speech to forgive them. Ask for forgiveness, and recount how you have sinned against them and let them down. Ask for pardon. They will need these graces to cleanse the past and leap into the future. Believe Me it will be a leap. The most difficult transition anyone could ever imagine will be this change, but I will be with them.

"Encourage them to have soaking or dwelling prayer and to reach out for My hand, to grasp. I will lead them skillfully and comfort them lovingly. But they must enter into an approachable prayer. Yes, praying on your knees in supplication is very effective, but much better to have a personal, intimate, holding-God's-hand relationship...then all the rest follows naturally.

"I want them to know that I love them, I'm approachable, I'm with them, they have a future. Whether they die now or live through the Tribulation, they still have a beautiful future. I want them to know that all is not lost, all is not ended. No, their lives are just beginning. And though it is a journey fraught with dangers, it will be deeply rewarding as they draw closer to Me, see My miracles, and experience the depth of My love for them.

"This is something they've been skating through all their lives and been avoiding. But now is the time for them to recognize that I am real. That I DO love them, and that I am with them.

"All the things they should have been doing these years, but weren't, will have to be done now, in this season.

Those who lose their lives shall find them, those who grasp theirs tightly will lose them. It is a paradox that revolves around faith and trust. Hopefully the fulfillment of the signs and Scriptures from the Bible will turn them 180 degrees around.

"But sadly, some will choose - in full knowledge of impending consequences - to go ahead their own way. They have lessons to learn and some day you will see the true depths of their rebellion, and fully understand why consequences had to be so dire."

"Lord, will we ever see what happened during the Tribulation?"

"There will come a time for 'reviews' - in other words, you will be shown what is necessary for you to understand. Towards the end - the climax before we return - you will be shown much and prepared for going back to rule and reign with Me. But before any of that, there will be a time of great orientation, training, equipping and preparation for your stations on Earth.

"What you think of now as unbearable, from Heaven will look much different in its context. Nonetheless, there will be a Honeymoon and I will not spoil it by bringing in the sufferings of mankind on Earth."

At that point, I started to have some more questions – like I usually do, and I said, "Forgive me Lord." 'Cause I knew He could read my thoughts…

"Go ahead, every night it is something...but I do understand."

“I find it so very difficult to imagine that we won't be able to see and help our families. This is a real sticking point for me.”

"That's because you are too attached and do not understand the road of sanctification each soul must travel. That is why I told you last night you would only get in the way. Do you think your presence in their lives is more useful to them than Mine?"

“Oh no! But I would think that both...would be nice...”

"Do you see why I will not allow that?"

“I can only imagine how much trouble I would be if I were with them.”

"Clare, there will be times when you are allowed to touch in with them for courage, but no more than that. I have to do this My way."

“Lord, I accept Your way, but I need to wrap myself around it. Please help me.”

"It's already on the way. And in Heaven, My Love, you will be a very busy woman indeed. That will help to quell your fears."

“This may be a silly question but can the enemy affect your thinking in Heaven?”

"No. He is not allowed. And you will experience such freedom in thought in Heaven, that you will come to understand the horrendous pressure you were under from the dark forces in your life on Earth."

"So, whatever disordered thinking comes up in Heaven is entirely our own?"

"Clare, in Heaven, there IS NO disordered thinking. Only truth and clarity. It has to be experienced to be believed, so don't even try to imagine it."

"OK."

"I don't want you to fret or worry, everything is going to unfold very naturally. All has been prepared and made ready for your new life in eternity."

"Is there anything else, Lord?"

"Tell your listeners there is not much more time. They need to prepare their packages for their loved ones. And for those who do not have a loved one, make packages up for those around you. Not that you need this kind of incentive...but much grace will be dispensed by thinking of others and preparing them for what is to come. By this act of kindness you will keep many from the brink of despair. And they will later thank you for being their one point of sanity in all the confusion."

"Please be faithful. Please prepare.

"I love you. More tomorrow."

"I love You, too, Lord. Stay close."

"I am."

Song: He's Real, He's Coming, Please Listen

Ezekiel Du Bois

Don't you know He's real, He's coming, please listen.

Don't you know He's real, He's coming, please listen.

You know He's there for you, every moment of the day,

through each and every night time.

You know He cares for you, you gotta know it's true,

He's been there through your whole lifetime.

Don't you know He's real, He's coming, please listen.

Don't you know He's real, He's coming, please listen.

It's not that hard, open up your heart and let His

love come in.

Just call upon His Name, you'll never be the same,

there's a real forever life to win.

Don't you know He's real, He's coming, please listen.

Don't you know He's real, He's coming, please listen.

Jesus Speaks On: After the Rapture
Troubled Waters - part 10

March 15, 2015

Moving on from the message of the 14th. And the Lord began this message:

"Troubled waters.

"Your country is entering troubled waters, as we speak. Arrangements are already in place for the actions to take place, after an assault on your land. Appointments have already been made. Trainees are waiting in the wings to be called upon and what is ahead is going to be a very well orchestrated set of events to bring this nation down to its knees.

"Many who have not wanted to listen to any 'bad news' are going to be caught completely off guard and blind-sided. Many have no idea just how corrupt the leadership is and they consider those who blame the NYC (911) debacle on your own government to be kooks and conspiracy mongers. They will be among the most confused and blind-sided because their life revolved around comforts and maintaining the status quo. Never in a million years would they believe what is actually being done to them, while their attention is totally off what is really moving forward at an alarming pace.

"There will be mass confusion and mass panic as the bombs fall. The disappearance of so many family members will cause some of them fatal heart attacks and suicides.

“However, there will be a remnant that will finally get off the fence and stand up to defend their rights. Too late. Their rights have already been taken away. What needs to be done now is to secure their future in Heaven: their salvation, their repentance and their total reliance on Me. Those who take up arms with a mind to do it on their own without My help will fail. Only those men and women who knew all along and belong to Me, are called by Me to defend what is right in this country, only they will succeed against all odds.

"So, if you are thinking about going it alone, you are sadly mistaken. Come under authority and work with those who have been prepared."

“Lord, if those who have been chosen to defend this country You say are Yours, why weren't they Raptured?”

"That is a very good question. Do you understand the character of My Bride?"

“I think I do.”

"Is she war-like?"

“Not at all. She's like the priest in the movie The Mission who walked straight into the mercenaries that were firing away and killing everyone in sight, and were mowed down.”

"That's correct. Those were My Brides coming to meet Me. And that is the character of My Bride. She is a lover, not a warrior. The only war she makes is on her own sins."

“But in an earlier message You talked about those who are chosen to fight.”

"My Love, that is the character of their soul. Were that soul that is a fighter to become a lover, he/she would be Raptured as well. But some souls are very, very strong in the warrior instinct and they, too, have a part to play and a place in My kingdom. In the end, they will understand the way of love. My angels understand well the ways of love, but they of necessity have risen up to defend My honor and My kingdom, and when this is all over, and I do mean ALL over, they shall cease to fight, for there will no longer be anything to defend. But that time is a long way off."

"Lord, I don't understand something. Why didn't you do all this after the last cycle of destruction with Atlantis, and the dinosaurs and all that?"

"For you My Love, this is not necessary information right now. But in Heaven all will be understood clearly, OK?"

"You, Lord, are so sweet to ask me if it's OK..."

"You are also My little girl, and I don't in any way want to discourage your questions, as you are growing up. So, back to the plan."

"The plan?"

"Yes, the nefarious plans of the ones skilled in intrigue and selfishness, their conscience seared shut, and wholly eaten up with corruption and greed. What they fear shall come upon them. In no way will they escape the conflagration of what is yet to come.

"In their ignorance and self-sufficiency they believe the scenario will play out as planned. They have no concept of how far off they are from the truth. They have no idea of what awaits them as plan after plan backfires and brings the dire consequences of their near-sighted greed and atrocious sins against humanity, against those I created in My very own image. Sad will be the day.

"Mostly, My Love, I want to warn those left behind that to act on their own, to take up arms and strike out on their own will have dire consequences for them and their families. But for now, I want to say that this will be a time of banding together, praying together, and encouraging one another in the face of all that is to come.

"It is a time of banding together in hope, love and security and yet there will be traitors. Only by the Spirit will souls be known to one another - the flesh lies and deceives, but the Spirit bears witness to the truth. That is why it is of absolute importance for them to pray and have a relationship with Me.

"DO NOTHING WITHOUT FIRST CONSULTING ME!

"Accept no one without first consulting with Me, for I will expose what is hidden in the hearts of men, their evil agendas.

I just want to take a moment here and say lots work very well for discernment. Lots were used in the Bible for the choice of who was to replace Judas; they were used in the situation with Jonah to find out why the storm was so severe, why the ship was sinking. We use a book called Bible Promises and pray and ask the Holy Spirit to give us a reading. We'll ask the Lord a question and very often we'll get Scriptures like Lying, Lust in the Flesh, Jealousy, Joy, Holy Spirit – and that will tell us about the character of certain situations or a plan of action. You can also use Lots to discern. You know, pieces of paper with names on them to discern who should be a part of what you're doing and who shouldn't.

Here the Lord returns to what He was saying:

"So, to sum this message up: band together, put prayer in its foremost place, for without it you will be groping in the dark. Do not rely on human wisdom, lean on Me and My Spirit will instruct you. Not a mighty wind but a still small voice, gently prodding you on in the right direction.

"Remember: it is not important if you lose your body, that is but a temporary and fleeting event. But your soul determines your eternity - whether you will see your children or parents again, your animals, and innocent ones ever again. Whether you will be tortured in the fires of torment I created, (not for you, but for the rebellious angels), or whether you will settle in the Land of Milk and Honey, Promise and Joy for all of eternity. Be not mistaken, what you have lived for on Earth is nothing compared to what you will live for in for eternity.

"NOTHING, absolutely NOTHING is worth the loss of your soul to eternal damnation."

Jesus Speaks On: After the Rapture Why Revelation Must Be Fulfilled - part 11

March 16, 2015

Well, Youtube family – I have a message from the Lord tonight about why the book of Revelation must be fulfilled. It's difficult – it's really heart-rending.

As I came into time with the Lord, a really beautiful song that goes on and on and on, and I always get lost in this song with the Lord dancing, and He was so present to me tonight. It was so sweet and intimate and so tender and real – He was so real tonight to me. I believe the name of the song is "Jesus, Holy Jesus" by Terry MacAlmon. And this is what the chorus sounds like:

Jesus, (Jesus) Jesus (Jesus) Jesus my Lord.

I really encourage you to press in with the Lord, because He wants that intimacy with every one of you. That's what our channel's all about. If you go back to the very beginning of our channel, I have teachings on Dwelling Prayer, as I call it, and getting intimate with the Lord is prayer. Because that's my heart's desire, to see you all get connected to Him in the way that it is in Heaven! As it is in Heaven, let it be on Earth – right now!

Anyway – getting back to the message. He was so present tonight, and after a short while He asked me to turn the music off. And I've been going through some ups and downs the last few days. Why…you know, a feeling that the Rapture was very, very soon – and then all of a sudden, losing that sense of urgency, and not feeling like it was going to be very soon. Kind of like, "Oh, well. Business as usual."

And it's strange, you know. I don't know if He energizes us with the quickness of His coming to keep us going, and then kind of draws back a little to let us rest in that while things are developing. Or, if He energizes us and encourages us in such a way because it IS going to be very, very soon. That's what I believe in my heart of hearts, but I don't have all the answers.

So, I asked Him tonight and said:

"Oh Lord, what is it? Sometimes I feel it so strongly that you're coming any moment, then other days it fades off into the distance and it's business as usual?"

"It's human nature."

"But, I don't like it. It's painful not knowing when really painful."

"It is painful for Me knowing what I have to. I do not want the book of Revelation to be fulfilled, but it has to be so that I can come and rule the Earth. It is not My will but My Father's will that must be done, even though I fully realize the necessity for it all.

"Nonetheless, it is so very deeply painful to Me that these things must come to pass. But they are not meant for your eyes, My Love, you don't need to be convinced the way the rest of the world does. My Brides have already gathered to My side awaiting My coming for them. It is the obstinate ones, full of pride, arrogance and self-reliance and self-satisfaction, blinded by various desires and lusts - they are the ones for which Revelation must be fulfilled."

Let me just take a moment here and say, there's an issue with the world that I have, partially with my children. I didn't raise them all the way, my former husband did. And it wasn't like we had a sacramental marriage, a marriage where we were both equally yoked. The world was very strong in him. My children…the world is strong in them too – except for maybe one of them. It's very difficult to explain to them why the Lord did so many things that people consider terrible. Like killing whole communities of men, women and children. And very often that's used as an excuse by people who sin, "Well, God did this, and God did that. I can't believe in God because if God is love and God is good, He wouldn't do things like that."

I can't tell you how many times I've had to listen to that. And I've answered them, very much like the Lord answered me tonight on this issue. So, for those of you who think that God is cruel, or that it couldn't be God controlling the world, well – you're right about one thing. He doesn't "control" everything. He allows and doesn't allow – so in a sense that's true. But Satan is the one who gets things going, and Man – the will of man. To push the button or not to push the button. It's man's will. Even, to build the bomb or not build the bomb. It's the will of Man.

So, I know the Lord has intervened many times on the brink of disaster for us. Even overriding men's will by circumstance, but it's getting to the point now where the book of Revelation needs to be fulfilled, so that the Lord CAN return and come and reign. This is what He's going to talk about a little bit tonight.

So, those of you who think God is cruel and don't understand His ways, maybe this will help you to understand. What the Lord is saying here is that, for His Brides, He doesn't have to fulfill Revelation to get their attention, because they've already gathered to His side and are ready to be obedient to Him. But for the rest of the world, the controlling world, the ruling elite and what have you – the obstinate ones full of pride and self-reliance. They have to see the results of their selfishness and the results of their own thinking. I'll continue on now.

"Wow, Lord they must be serious hard cases for all you have to go through to convince them." (Speaking of the events of Revelation.)

"Anyone who would use the bowels of the Earth to breed dreadful animals, plagues and pestilences such as they have done for control of the world, well, yes... they need serious attitude adjustments. Nothing short of what I have planned will work for them.

"Don't you think that the Father and I have pondered all the different options and come up with the least damaging? The least hurtful? The least injurious?"

"Yes, I suppose so, because that is Your nature. Although being God, you don't have to ponder..."

"Yes, well... we do have conversations, we truly do. There are so many things to take into consideration. Looking at just one: I gave them clean technology decades ago - but rather, they chose something they could fight over.

"Selfish ambition is so strong in them, they are totally blind to even their own good and the good of their children. So many of the world's problems revolve around the energy source, and they couldn't accept a gift of free energy. No, they had to suppress that and take that source to make a weapon of war and destruction with it - but deprive mankind of the benefit of the energy, free energy that I offered them. Do you see how perverted they are?"

"I do, Lord, but it is a shame that innocent mankind must suffer."

"But mankind is not so innocent, from the highest to the lowliest. Pornography, slave labor, sex trade, stealing from the poor what little they have and the poor stealing from each other. The whole barrel is rotten from the bottom up. It is the selfish nature of man that must be regulated by God. Man cannot regulate man because he is so prone to corruption, so weak and easily persuaded to do what is wrong for his own gain.

"So, you see, it must come down to this. I must return and replenish the whole Earth, destroying the rot and corruption, pollution and degradation that man has created for himself. It won't be long now. Please hang in, there My little one, it won't be long."

I have to admit, I really, really yearned for His coming tonight and to be with Him, and I just sat and cried for a few minutes at my altar, my little prayer spot because I miss Him so much, and I want to be with Him so badly. And this world is SO messed up. So, it was a little word of encouragement when He said it won't be long.

"Oh Jesus, it seems like forever. And every day I grow older and more disillusioned by the burgeoning corruption found everywhere."

"I know. But I have given you stamina and you will hold up under these things as you have been. I will not let you fall or collapse - I hold you up, My Love."

"So, what do you want to talk about tonight?"

"The necessity of consequences.

"So many attribute to Me what should be attributed to man and Satan."

"It's not fair!"

"I know that, but for some reason they just can't bring themselves to see how responsible every human on Earth is for the approaching consequences. It is like a drunkard who continually blames his problems on others, when in fact his problems have been created by him and him alone. So, rather than point out the culprits, it's just easier to blame it on Me."

"Lord, they always cite the way you had the Israelites kill every man woman and child as they took over the Promised Land."

"Yes, because they were not present when the demons mated with the women, when the babies were offered up into the red hot, brass cauldrons for their God, Moloch - or Satan. They were not present when these little infants screamed the horrors of pain. They were not present when everything they owned was consecrated to Satan. They did not see that a cancerous, spiritual disease was implanted in every man, woman and child and animal. At least the innocent children are in Heaven with Me. Had they grown up, they surely would be in Hell with the rest of their family for torturing and brutally murdering innocent children. There is so much the world doesn't know, the world doesn't see.

"No, it's much easier to just blame 'God' and go on with a sinful lifestyle, having justified their choices because 'God' is not just or worth listening to or obeying.

"Not all have this mind set. Some are living a righteous life but still condemn me for religious wars and the like. They don't see the real set of fingers pulling the strings.

"But the ones who love Me? They do. They recognize the difference between good and evil. They know Me well enough to trust that if I lay the sword to a group of people, it is because those people are hell bent on living for Satan and propagating his way of life.

"And even at that, the Israelites still embraced pagan ways and even incorporated them into My Temple, and thus their downfall."

Just as an aside here, it's been discovered about Solomon's temple that there were several secret chambers. The prophets talk about it, where "detestable things go on." Where they worshipping detestable things in these chambers, in Solomon's Temple.

"You cannot mix good and evil - they cancel one another out. It was bound to happen that the Pharisees would be crooked, because for the sake of money and influence, Solomon and others allowed them to build secret chambers that honored their 'god.' It was bound for destruction with the first pagan woman Solomon took as wife.

"Let that be a lesson to you, how one bad apple can ruin the whole barrel. There is nothing quite like the beauty and comfort of a woman - it has shaped the course of history and been the downfall of many a civilization.

"So, when I am blamed for the evil in this world, it is out of ignorance and pride. Man does not know or understand what he has done to himself. And of course, he does not want to be frustrated or corrected, so he kicks against the goad. He blames Me, to justify his continuing sinful life. This, My Love, is why I must fulfill the prophecies in Revelation. Man must see what he has done to himself and where it has finally led him.

"Nothing I do is out of wrath, in the sense that man experiences wrath. For Man it is retaliation. For Me it is education, painful education - but the bed they made they must sleep in. Even at that there are so many things I have prevented that would have been horrendous, but for My mercy they were negated. So much will become clear to you in Heaven, you will come to understand so much.

"So, just be aware what is coming. It was not My choice, it was theirs. It was not My retaliation, it was their consequences. It was not done out of hatred for man, but out of love - to bring them to their senses. Everything I do has LOVE for its motive; not one thing is done for any other reason.

"Even conscripting souls to Hell; this is what they wanted, this was their choice to make. Who am I to override their free will? They wouldn't have been happy in Heaven anyway. I gave it to man so he could be free to choose. He could choose good or he could choose evil. What more could I do?"

"Nothing. Absolutely nothing. It's a pity people are so blind that they can't see You are not the author of their problems. They are - along with Satan's help."

"So now we have come to that decisive point in history where all things must be made right again. Pride and arrogance must be exposed, corruption must be purged, men must be given again a new chance to choose right from wrong.

"I am coming. It is time."

The Great Revival After the Rapture

April 6, 2015

The Lord bless you, Youtube family. I still haven't gotten my equipment up and running yet, so just keeping it simple here.

This evening as I was listening to the Lord, actually I was musing on some things – the revival that is supposed to take place before the Rapture. Which He has told me before is not going to happen. And I was thinking, 'What if I am wrong and am misleading my Youtube family – and that thought was weighing heavily on my heart.

The Lord began:

"I know you are frightened. I know how you feel."

"I'm so sorry Lord."

"For what? Questioning that perhaps it wasn't Me speaking to you about the revival? Let Me set your heart at ease. There will be no revival until you are taken in the Rapture. Yes, then revival as never before will break loose, and I will pour My Spirit out."

"But You just removed Your spirit when you took us?"

"How shall My people be converted without Him? Is it not written that He convicts of sin?"

John 16:8-11 And when He comes, He will convict the world concerning sin and righteousness and judgment: concerning sin, because they have not believed in Me; concerning judgment, because the world is about to be judged.

“Then why does Your Word say that ‘He is taken out of the way,’ which is the interpretation that most have about that line of Scripture?”

And it was interesting, because just then He quickened Psalm 85:1-7 to me:

You, Lord, showed favor to your land; you restored the fortunes of Jacob. You forgave the iniquity of your people and covered all their sins. You set aside all your wrath and turned from your fierce anger. Restore us again, God our Savior, and put away your displeasure toward us. Will you be angry with us forever? Will you prolong your anger through all generations? Will you not revive us again, that your people may rejoice in you? Show us your unfailing love, Lord, and grant us your salvation.

And that really stood out to me – their Salvation – which is the point that they will come to when they are convicted of their sin.

"So you see, He will be present and at work in The Great Revival.”

The Lord is calling this revival after the Rapture upon His people the Great Revival.

“You see, My Love, there is need for revival, but it will be shallow indeed until people are forced to see for themselves that their way has been death, especially My People and Your people for there is Jewish blood passed down through your mother's lineage. It was kept well hidden because of persecution. But nonetheless, you are a Jew."

“Really?”

"Yes, really.

"And I will say, many have Jewish blood and know it not. But I have told you that all men will see Me coming on the clouds of Heaven. All men means All men, it will NOT be hidden. No, I intend to see My people weep for having rejected Me. Does it not say 'All the tribes of earth shall mourn?'"

Then shall appear the sign of the Son of man in heaven: and then shall all the tribes of the earth mourn, and they shall see the Son of man coming in the clouds of heaven with power and great glory. Matt 24:30

"Lord, many say that is about Your Second Coming?"

"And yet it is true that the church is not mentioned after a certain point in Revelation, but in Revelation 1:6 John greets the seven churches"

Rev 1:6-8 He has made us to be a kingdom, priests to His God and Father-- to Him be the glory and the dominion forever and ever. Amen. BEHOLD, HE IS COMING WITH THE CLOUDS, and every eye will see Him, even those who pierced Him; and all the tribes of the earth will mourn over Him. So it is to be. Amen. "I am the Alpha and the Omega," says the Lord God, "who is and who was and who is to come, the Almighty."

"And this book was written in chronological order.

"It is my deliberate intention that My People know Who I AM. Without this knowledge they will not be able to repent. When they see Me they shall be struck to the very marrow of their bones in remorse for their sinful rejection of Me."

"Lord, You know the struggles I am having with the order of things in Matthew."

"I know that you are misunderstanding the order of things. The Temple will not be built until you are gone."

"So, does that mean You have spoken out of the order of events? It seems so clear that one thing builds upon another, but that comes before the Rapture. What am I missing?"

"Clare, I want you to rest in this, I will be seen during the Rapture. I will not set foot on the Earth - but I will be seen. My people will weep and mourn for having rejected Me. They will be left behind as the gentiles are taken to Heaven, then all Hell will break loose on the Earth; that will be the beginning of the Tribulation. I assure you, Satan will waste no time in implementing His evil schemes and bringing the anti-Christ to power.

"The Earth will reel like a drunkard. Not only will the accelerator upset the magnetic arrangement of the Earth's poles, it shall inevitably affect the planets along with the close approach of Nibiru and asteroids. Did I not say ALL Hell will break loose? It is intended that all of these things happen in close proximity, the judgment of this Earth will happen with great intensity.

"As much as I love them, the Jewish people are by no means innocent of greed and manipulation. The judgment for them will accomplish a two- fold purpose: their rejection of Me, and their manipulation in business dealings with careless abandon for the covenant I established with them, and that they should be responsible for the blood of the creatures of this world. They are culpable in this matter, extremely culpable. This is another of the reasons they are here for the judgment, they must sleep in the bed they have made. OK, are 'we' clear now?"

"Umm, I think so, but I'll have to reread all of this. You know how it is with me. I don't really get it right away."

"At least you do get it, My Love."

"Well, I owe that to You, Lord. It doesn't seem that there is any special sign for the Rapture except You have told me about Miami."

"Miami is no different than the WWII wars and rumors of wars. Because of the increase of knowledge the damage inflicted will be far beyond and more confusing, disorienting and devastating than ever before. FOR that reason, it will be an hour when I am least expected. You see with all the moons and feasts, I am expected. That should alert you right away that it can't be on a feast day, because you are expecting Me.

"Does it not say that when I am LEAST expected I will come? That was meant to be a hint."

"OK, well now that contradicts what people say about knowing the appointed times."

"Sorry."

"Oh Lord, you are indeed Sovereign."

"I will indeed do things at the appointed time, but I made it a point to exclude the Rapture, so why are you looking to appointed times?"

"Umm...I guess because it makes sense?"

"Exactly. And I already inferred that it would make no sense. So relax and stop trying to second-guess Me. I already gave you a very firm indicator, rest in this, Clare. Please do not sow confusion, hold to what I gave you years and years ago. Rest in this. Stop looking to guess what makes the most sense. You are all wearing yourselves out trying to resolve this issue using the stars and moon and the appointed times as your plumb line."

"Oh Lord...." I was just thinking at that point, 'Boy, I must really be a false prophet...' He answered without me saying anything:

"You are not a false prophet. I like what you call yourself - My Bride. And does not the Groom entrust His Lady with His secrets?

"Come here, My Love, I want to kiss you and hold you and rid you of your reluctance. Oh, when will My Love trust in Me 100% of the time?"

"Am I not getting there, Lord? As Lisa says, I am a work in progress. At least I'm not a work that's stalled."

"Well, I want you to reread this, absorb it deeply. There will be many who disagree with you about seeing Me in the Rapture. Don't allow that to intimidate you. Remember, you live to please Me, not what the more studied and intelligent think. Keep it simple, rely on Me, don't knock yourself out studying the Scriptures. I never created you to be a scholar. I have created you to be a Lover. That should have been clear a long time ago."

"Well, I love the idea of delving deeply into studies of the Bible, Lord. This is something I really look forward to in Heaven, where I'll have time - is to understand these things."

"Yes, in Heaven it will be safe. But on Earth, knowledge puffs up but charity edifies. In other words, you are safer little, unlearned and dependent on Me for understanding. I can impart to you in time so small it cannot be measured by human standards, the deepest understanding of the most complex truths. Whereas you could spend thirty years in studies of Hebrew and Aramaic and still fall short of understanding. So, trust in Me, lean not on your own understanding, and I shall direct your paths of understanding.

"My blessing is upon you and all My Brides who have chosen the simple and lowly way of Love."

And that's the end of the message. And I want to say, interestingly, the dream that the girl had when she was 13 years old that I posted just previously, He said that that was accurate. He said that that was exactly as the Rapture was going to happen. She saw Him, she saw the angels with the trumpet – and she was not a Christian at the time. So this argument that the people who are not Christians won't see, doesn't hold any water in the face of what she experienced in her vision. It certainly makes sense to me that the Lord would allow the Jesus people to see Him, in order to bring them to repentance. That totally makes sense, something I hadn't thought of before.

The Lord bless you, Youtube family. Thank you so much for posting messages and encouragements. God bless you.

Surviving the Coming Tribulation

November 7, 2015

The Lord bless you, precious Heartdwellers.

The Lord began tonight by saying, **"I want to talk to you about the coming Tribulation.**

"In all of history there will never again, nor has there been before, a time such as this. Men will be at their wit's end trying to figure out what to do next. Nothing will make sense to them and everything will be topsy-turvy. I am trying to prepare, now, those who will be left behind.

"There is no sense to accumulating wealth, position or power because everything will be scrambled and reorganized based on loyalty to the New World Order. Any Christian right now that is posturing for higher positions is going to hit a brick wall after the Rapture. There is no need to be alarmed, just informed. Those who are left behind will have to switch their priorities from making money - to surviving. And I don't mean surviving physically, alone. Yes, survival must also be spiritual, understanding and being sensitive to the movement of My Spirit.

"It is by My Spirit alone that protection will be rendered to those left behind. Nothing of man's design will bring peace for families, only My ability to save and protect will be found effective - witness Ruby Ridge. My dear ones left behind, you cannot count on guns to protect you. You must turn wholeheartedly to Me and ask for My protection. I will protect you supernaturally if I am your only recourse. Those who live by the sword will die by the sword."

Here I want to take a break and remind you of the movie "The Mission" for those of you who saw it – it's a wonderful movie for those of you who haven't. The final scene was when the mercenaries were coming in to kill all the natives, into the jungle. And there were two factions there – the group of natives that wanted to fight, led by one of the men, one of the Jesuit men, and the other faction was the one that wanted to pray. I won't tell you what happens at the end, but let's just say that it becomes obvious that the ones who prayed had a better ending than the ones that didn't and just came against them with guns and so on.

"But I have prepared an army of men and women to recover this country from the enemy. They will swing into action and have an active part in taking ground away from the Order. Never since the history of man has there been a time such as what is coming, and never since the history of man has My protection been as strong as it will be.

"But there are certain rules you must live by. Honesty is first and foremost. Vigilance over your own sins and bad example. The devils are clever and they know how to provoke a soul to cause a breach in their covering. Charity, humility and patience also score high on the list of things targeted and necessary to maintain My Protection.

"Come to Me immediately when you fall. Don't waste a moment. Make a sincere confession and renounce that sin. I will then restore your covering and add to it protection, and the grace to not repeat those sins. I have already taught you about judging others. The quickest way to lose your covering is to slander, calumniate, or gossip about another. Not only will the enemy use this to divide and conquer, he will use it to make you vulnerable to attack. The more key your position is, the more careful you will have to be about your heart attitude.

"Never disparage anyone who is sick or weak. Their prayers are essential and extremely important."

And we found that to be true in our mission, that the prayers of the elderly and infirm really bring about some amazing results.

"Your emotions will be your worst enemy. Sleep will be very important because of the stress you are under, it will quickly deplete your clarity of thinking and energy. This will be a time of survival techniques...especially spiritual survival techniques. Prayer and charity will increase your chances of survival and prayer will be your number one most powerful weapon.

"The enemy is very sly, and he will insinuate many things to turn you against each other. Sitting down and talking it out candidly, honestly, will completely foil his attempts to turn each of you against another."

I would like to add repentance to that. You know, once you figure out whose thinking was right or wrong, whoever has made a bad choice in their thinking or falsely accused, repentance is super important there and to ask the forgiveness of the other person.

"There will be much need for patience and deferring anger. There is always a reason behind a failure and it is always a test of virtue for you to bear it with charity and brotherly love. Remember: you will be judged as you judge one another. If you want mercy, you must first mete out mercy. You may see yourself as superior in the mix, but I guarantee - that will be your downfall.

"Somehow, Beloved, you must cultivate extreme respect for one another. It may look to you that another is inferior to you, but I look upon the heart. And he who loves more is superior, in My viewpoint. You may excel at many things, but if you have not charity, well... that will only buy you pride and vainglory. There are souls that are so interiorly kindly and well disposed that even the most brilliant and accomplished person is far inferior to them.

"This is no longer the world or worldly affairs you are dealing with. It is strictly spiritual and Our standards in Heaven are so far removed from yours - they are unrecognizable. Rick Joyner's books bring to the forefront the importance of charity and true spiritual vision. And remember, none of you have absolutely perfect spiritual or Scriptural understanding. Each person has a gift to add to the mix. Your task will be to find out and cultivate that gift and incorporate it. This will be a real trial of teamwork and deferential yielding to one another, and how well you take care of the weakest link will determine your success or failure.

"Whenever you feel threatened, your first recourse is PRAYER. This should be your very first response. There will be many misinformation campaigns, as there always are in war, to turn attention away from what is really important. If you rely on Me alone for your information, you will not fall for these side tracks.

"There will also be attempts to flush out believers. Be very careful of those who say that they're going to make an alliance with you, but underneath it all they really want to find out what your agendas are, so they can report you.

"Each person among you has a unique purpose. Try to discover that and nurture and honor it. Do not, under any circumstances, hinder a soul who is wanting to step forward and serve. Give them something to do, but do not deny them a job - that will seriously backfire on you. To feel needed, wanted and important is key to keeping the peace. When all work together synchronistically, all will feel satisfied. When things seem to be falling apart, pray against a spirit of Division.

"This will constantly be the enemy's course of action."

I want to say there, also, Lying spirits are responsible for division. Lying spirits, Beguiling spirits, spirits of Division, Miscommunication, Twisting Communication – all of that is involved in that dynamic of division.

"This will constantly be the enemy's course of action: divide and conquer, or set someone up for failure and conquer. Be ever so supportive when one of you fails. Come to their rescue with warmth, security and forgiveness. Reacting in anger will only empower the demons to cause dissent and dissatisfaction, which will gnaw away at the hearts of some until there is a strong current of mutiny and division.

"Never assume that something is good or a good opportunity. Always pray first and find out from Me if it is something you should do. Remember the story of the Trojan horse: everyone thought it was amazing booty from their enemy, but once they pulled it inside the citadel, its true intention became clear as armed soldiers piled out and took the city by surprise.

“All in all, success can be had through this most difficult of times. But understand, I do not measure success by survival or prowess. My standard is Love, and to die for Me is gain.”

"Do not fear those who kill the body but are unable to kill the soul; but rather fear Him who is able to destroy both soul and body in hell. "Are not two sparrows sold for a cent? And yet not one of them will fall to the ground apart from your Father. Matthew 10:28-29

Seek LIFE In Jesus

May 8, 2015 morning

"Would You speak to me this morning, my Jesus?"

"Yes, Love – I would.

"It is My pleasure to join you in this garden of your heart you have striven so hard to create for Me. I DO take great joy in walking there with you. My love, I tell you there is so much joy ahead of you and I. It truly WILL take your breath away! Come to Me frequently, now – I have much I wish to tell you for the sake of those who will find your journal. Now it is time to give them hope and prepare their hearts for the days that come on the Earth, for I will indeed be sure that just the right souls will find these words and it will be a source of balm, help and goodness for them.

"No, they will not know of the trials and sufferings that have brought them these words, but it is of no matter. I will repeat to them anything that was lost from your first journal, anything that is needful for them to know.

"I will share now that you have been a pure heart and a faithful soul to Me. The burning of the first journal was in obedience to Me. The losing of your second was the fault of the demons who hate your very soul. But this one, I will preserve from harm. I desire that you print it out each day now until I come for you. I wish to keep a record of our talks, our thoughts together, the rhemas that I give you for their sake."

I had been keeping a journal for two years before this point – and unbeknownst to me a Beguiling spirit had been interjecting messages into it, interspersed with the Lord's words. Once I found this out, and repented of the sin that allowed it – I burned the entire journal – 1,200 pages of it – to prevent ANYONE from reading those false words.

After this, I began a new journal – and whole chunks of it would just mysteriously disappear from my computer. It was only when I anointed my computer and prayed over the KEEPING of the journal intact that the Lord assured me that it would not happen again…

"Oh, My love – I love you with My Everlasting Love - yes, you smile now...because you have heard these words many times before from Me. They are Truth! They are My heart towards you.

"You have been a strong, obedient Child of Mine, and now you have become My most beautiful Bride. Soon, I come for you. Soon, the trumpet sounds and you will be lifted out of this poor body you dwell in. The pain will disappear with a shout – yet the work that has been done for Me through your suffering will stay on and on through many generations to come. This word that was spoken over you was Truth – do not take so lightly the words I give to you through the others at Inside/Out. (smile) This is a minor fault of yours, as you well know."

The other day, Jerri spoke these words over me in prophecy class: "I see a Rainbow of promises of God for you, vibrant colors not seen on Earth. Promises given to you that will last for everlasting, generation to generation will be blessed. There is a big, gold bucket at each end of the rainbow, you will have lots of "nuggets" to give out for others.

"I leave you now with these words: Have Courage. Have Faith. Be strong in My strength today. I am walking always just by your side. Do not fear what comes on the Earth today, or any day yet to come, as I know you do not. I write these things for the sake of the readers to come.

"This, My servant Carol, has fought the fight long, hard and with Victory in Me. She wishes with all her heart that you will do the same. Listen to the words I speak now for you each day until she has gone – they will be a source of strength, courage and wisdom for you. She is very little in her own mind...yet My power through her has the power to turn hearts to the Kingdom.

"Seek Me, you who read this journal. (These words have been lifted out of my private journal to be included in this book.) **SEEK ME, and I WILL be found by you. Read the words of the letters I have given to Clare that are with these words – they are Life, Instructions and the Path of Righteousness for you. Follow these words. Follow these commands I give you in order to LIVE!**

"For I call YOU now to My Kingdom, and through you I will call many, many others. You have been chosen by Me from the very beginning – to live at THIS time, to be found by Me at THIS time for the sake of many around you.

"Come, My friends – be faithful to Me and I will give to you the keys to the Kingdom."

The Alpha and Omega, the Beginning and the End.

Jesus – the King

It's Time to Let Go

May 8, 2015 evening

"Do You have a word for our Friends tonight, Lord?"

"Yes, Love, I do.

"Be patient with yourself, you spoke hastily and without thought just now – but you have caught it and I have already forgiven you. All is well between us, Dear One."

"Oh, how I love You, my Jesus. You are so kind to me....always so kind."

"Now, down to the business of the night. I wish to speak to 'our Friends,' as you so lovingly put it, about timing.

"In the days to come, timing will be of utmost importance to you: timing of when you eat, where you walk, how you live. Events will happen so quickly that there will often BE no time to be 'normal', and so many things will be left behind you in a swift move, many things that you will think are very important to you to have or keep.

"Now is the Time though, to let go – of everything. All things and possessions will mean little or nothing to you when the choice must be made between them and your lives or the lives of your families. So, I am warning you now: be prepared at any moment to move. Move from one house to another. From one place to another. From the city to the country, from one town to the next. For this reason, be astute in your thinking. Prepare for yourselves and those with you the essentials to life: a Bible, a few clothes, water, dried or canned food and a blanket or two. Keep these things handy in a backpack that you can grab to take with you at a moment's notice.

"Keep other, less important yet still-of-value things in a box nearby: these instructions, a computer if possible, flashlights, batteries, a few flash drives. It will be important for you to be free to travel lightly – yet these things will make your lives more bearable.

"The events that will soon come on the Earth are more horrific than any have even conceived. It will take great faith in Me to live through them, to avoid being captured and killed by the enemy.

"It is My wish that as many as will follow Me, listen to Me and obey Me - will live. For you will then walk into the Millennium and populate the Earth as I renew it and bring pristine cleanliness back to it. Yes, many will die in the next 7 years...but if you are faithful to Me and swiftly obedient – you will not be among them. I will protect and guide you where and when I wish. I WILL help you – but you MUST be willing to listen and obey Me at all times. I will be there always; My angels will be gathered around you, also. Call out to Me at any time, in any circumstance where you are in question, afraid, confused and I will answer.

"It will be important for you to be able to listen to My Holy Spirit with clear ears during this time. Ask Me, after you have called unto Me for Salvation, for the Gifts of My Spirit: the Baptism of Fire, tongues for strong spiritual prayer, healing, knowledge, and prophecy.

"Do not worry about the Internet at this point – I will preserve what I will preserve. Lacking this – I will Myself be there to teach you and impart these gifts to you.

"Take heart, Dear Ones! Have Faith! Soon the Father is plunging this world into untold chaos and judgment...but I have My perfect plans for you already laid in place.

"I leave you tonight with my Love and My blessings of Faith and Belief."

Your Jesus – the Christ.

Follow Jesus – Do NOT Take the Mark of the Beast!

May 9, 2015

"Oh, my sweet, dear Jesus – what have You to say to our Friends tonight?"

"I am here, Dear One. You have done well tonight – preparing with the Binding Prayer, trusting Me, preparing your heart to receive Me. Thank you, My Dear One. I have waited for you to come now.

"I enjoyed our time this afternoon together – thank you for taking that time away from the world and spending it dreaming with Me, as I asked you through Clare. This is what I desired – time, with no other thoughts than dreams of Me, our Home together, our time to come."

"I wish I could see You, Lord."

"I know – but you have given this gift over to Clare, to help her. Do you want to take it back?"

"No, Lord – You know I don't. It's just...sometimes...I wish..."

(He is lifting my chin up with His finger, even though I do not see it) **"I have shown you Myself at other times, Love. Rest in these. Soon, soon, soon, My Love – as you wished this afternoon – you WILL feel My arms holding you, REAL, solid-to-the-touch arms holding you as the One Who Loves you more than any other ever could. Be patient, My Bride. Be patient. I know you are doing your best with this– continue on just a little bit longer..."**

"I love You so, Lord – I feel light-headed and giddy at the thought that we are so very, very close now.... It's been a very long time of waiting, you know. My whole life! And yet when I look back over the years – they are as just a few short minutes..."

"This is the point, these are the thoughts I have placed in Your head tonight, Love. Life IS just a few short minutes – and eternity is very, very, very long. This is the idea that MUST be clear to those who are left behind you: Life is the ONLY time that you have to make this most important decision of all– the decision to follow ME, Jesus the Christ, in the days to come.

"There are only two choices, no matter what the government, your friends, bosses, families, or any other may try to convince you. Choose Me. Or Satan.

"With Me you will have Life Everlasting – from eternity to eternity in Glory and Life and Love more pure than you can ever try to imagine.

"With Satan...it will be nothing but pain, death, misery, endless torment and fire. The first death – of your body – will end with the second death: eternal separation from Me, the God Who formed you in your mother's womb, who breathed life into your very soul, who Loves you more than you can ever understand.

"So, tonight I appeal to you. Which do you want? The Enemy of your soul has filled this world with every device he could conceive of to lie, steal, kill and destroy you and all of mankind; to convince you that pleasure for the moment was worth trading away life Eternal.

"It is the same story as Jacob and Esau: blessings and riches traded in a moment of bodily pleasure, never to be exchanged again once the decision was made.

"I tell you tonight: BEWARE OF THE MARK.

"Man laughs at it, the government lies about it. But I tell you the truth: if you accept it, your very DNA will be changed into a son of Satan himself...and there IS no more redemption for you.

"Be wise, My children – be very wise now. Listen for Me. Listen for MY voice to help you through the days that come upon you, for they alone will give you life. They alone will guide you through the maze of death that Satan has designed for you. And even though the times will be torturous and hard – it is but for a short while. I will rescue you. I will be there, near to you. Call out to Me for Salvation first – and then for salvation of Life. (That you live and not be killed.)

I am near to you all. I am calling you to My side. Be wise, My Friends, My Children. Be Wise!

Your Loving Father, Abba (Jesus)

There is Very Little Time...Come to Me

May 11, 2015 morning

"Thank You for Your message to Clare last night, Lord. I heard well the part I was listening for – thank You. I have...more peace, now. Do You have more to tell our Friends this morning?

"Yes, My Love – write now.

"You did not flinch just now as I spoke to you in words of endearment long un-used. This is well! I wish to give you assurance that much and much of your past journals WERE from Me, and that especially the words of Love that I used for you were true and spoken from My heart to you.

"You truly ARE My Dove, My Beloved One, My sweet soul mate.

"Oh, Lord, thank You for telling me that. You gave me such beautiful things to think on – my Home in Heaven and what it looks like, mysteries about Nibiru and other things that could only have really come from Your mind. Thank You for the kindness of assuring me of these words of Love, these names that You gave me back then."

"Yes, My Love. My affection for you has never changed, but as you know, there was a great stain on your wedding gown that had to be removed. It is enough now – let us talk of other things."

~~~~~~~~~~~~

"I speak now to 'our Friends' as we shall call you. There is another issue that must be explained to you this morning.
~~~~~~~~~~~~

"Time. Yes, we spoke of this before a little while ago – but time is an issue that has many and many facets. This part of Time is concerning your souls.

"You must treat the Time that you have now as a fleeting, precious commodity, given directly to you by Me. Not to be used as you would, or to be given over to pleasure, gain or anticipation of spoils for many selling products, marketplace or business. These must become things of your past. I call all of you now to what I called My Brides to before I brought them Home: holiness. Increased sanctification. Yieldedness and obedience to Me and the Truths I have preserved for you in My Scriptures. I have brought a Great Revival upon the Earth one last time, and you have seen evidence of it. Do not reject the teachings that were spread abroad from it. Do not take lightly the words of Truth and Salvation that you have heard about. These Words and Truths are your very lifeline.

"The times you now live in will last a mere 7 years from beginning to end. Depending on the time you find yourself in when you have found these words is a mightily important thing to you. Perhaps you have been fortunate to be among the first to hear of Me, just after the Rapture. Perhaps you have been one of those who have received My Spirit during the sweep of Renewal that I brought upon the Earth in one, final move to gather in all souls who belong to Me. If this is you – then you have indeed been blessed.

"But I tell you the truth: if you are only finding these admonitions one, or two or even three years past that point – NOW is the time to accept these words that you have heard. NOW is the time that you MUST seek Me and be found by Me...for you are running out of time to make this decision.

"At the midpoint of the 7 years, there will again be a massive shaking, a major upheaval in not only the physical world but the unseen spiritual one. After this point – the forces of evil will be so strongly arrayed that it will be nigh unto impossible to live ANY sort of "normal" life in any way – if you have not yet bowed your knee to the ruler Obama and the evil ones that rule below him.

"Yes, I am pinpointing who the Anti- Christ is to you. Surely you know by now that he has become the very symbol of evil on the Earth to all who try to oppose him. Much death, much destruction, much disease, much harm has come to millions of souls who have tried to oppose him, and have died for their stand against him.

"You have found My words to My servants Carol & Clare, who were among many, many others scattered throughout the world spreading these messages to the world before I came and took them Home to be with Me in Heaven. You have yet a little time to make your final decision. You have been standing to the side, letting the enemy convince you that all is well, and 'they are better off rounded up and gotten out of the way of the REAL people'.

"I tell you now: these are but lies of the destroyer of your soul. You must heed them no more. Time for you is rapidly running out. I have preserved pockets of My people all around the globe – safe places where those who I have gathered in live and prosper in health and food and the supply of their needs. Take My hand now, and let Me lead you to them. Turn your heart fully to Me, and I will lead you there, where you may finish out this time in Peace, Truth and real Love – Love like you have never experienced, or have by now long forgotten.

"Time is your enemy now, My Child. You do not understand this fully now – but you will. Heed My words that are written here – you will not receive many more warnings with this much clarity. I work even now in your soul, your spirit to convince you that these words are True and Faithful, for they are spoken by the One Who is Faithful and True.

"Let Me in. Let Me find you, save you, and carry you into the wilderness of safety and salvation, for My heart longs for you to join with Me in My Kingdom.

"Come, My Dear Friend. Come! I wait for you. Come!"

Jesus – the Christ. The One Who died on the Cross for YOUR soul, and now waits with never-ending Love for you to come to Me.

How Great is My Love for You

May 12, 2015 morning

"What have You to speak about this morning as You call me to write, Lord? I am still reveling in Your love after hearing Your latest message to Clare..."

"Yes, Dearest One...it is Love that I wish to speak of this morning.

"My Love.

"Oh, Dear Friends of Ours, you have read this far in Carol's journal, and have surely seen the love she has for Me written everywhere in it. Have you thought this love peculiar? Do you catch even a glimmer of how deep is her love, how strong? Do you understand WHY this love is in her heart for a God she cannot see but dimly, in snatches, even at the advanced stage of her walk with Him?

"She has lived 61 years on this Earth, and 58 of them have been aware of Me and My Love for her. How is it, you wonder? How to love an unseen, and what you have thought, cold and far-off God?

"Oh, My dear, dear Friends. Know this: before you were ever born, before I created the world as you see it, you were a spark, a Creation in the very heart of God. The Father conceived of YOU – you, your mind, your heart, your soul...every part of your being, your body, your ways...and destined you to be born at such a time as this. It was no accident of mere human sex that brought you into being - no.

"The Father deigned that you would be born in the country you were, the family you were, the time you were. He ordered and ordained the school you would attend, the children you played with – and fought with. Every facet of your life, whether (from this time in history) you view that as well, or not.

"Sin brought trials, temptations and hard things into your life – many of them perhaps. You have been tempted by your enemy – Satan - to think badly of Me since the day you were born. But I have been there. My angels have watched over you since that very moment.

"During the times where you thought you were all alone, during the hardest parts of your life, during the times when you thought life could not go on, could not grow worse...I have been there – drawing you, willing you to look up and see Me there, pouring into your soul My love, My ways, My heart for you.

"Every time you saw a beautiful butterfly, or a sweet kitten and it touched a brief spark of joy in your life...it was I who sent it. Every time you heard a word of true love from a parent, a sibling, a teacher, a friend – I was calling out to you through them (whether they knew it or not) to take My hand and follow Me. You see? I have been with you through all things – good and bad.

"You may be thinking now, 'Well, if He loved me so much, why did such and such happen? Why did this and that occur? What does He mean *Love*, when... look at the world around us? Look at where I am right now???' These things are hard to comprehend, but set aside self for a moment, set aside anger and bitterness and reason with Me for just a while.

"Does an apple grow on a tree just like all the others around it? Are there not perfections and imperfections on each one? Do they not hang side by side next to each other - yet this one has a beautiful blush of color, that one stands duller and less appealing? Does not one get stung by an insect, and begin to spoil while it is even yet on the tree? Does one get picked and eaten and enjoyed – bringing joy to the one who has taken it - while another hangs there until the limb lets go, it falls to the ground and gets smashed underfoot?

"I tell you the Truth: these are still a part of My creation, still a part of the Glory and Majesty of Who I am, and what I have given to the Earth in My creative power. And I care for these thing as I care for ALL of My creation.

"Consider: a litter of puppies is born. One goes this way, with a family that will cherish and train and keep it in their home, giving it a life of joy and happiness. That one is given to a man with a dark and cruel heart, who beats it, abuses it and finally kills it. Do I not love both? Are they not both My Creation, cherished by Me? Will I not send My angels to gather it into their arms at last and bring it here to Joy in My world?

"Ah...you see, men do not believe Me in My Word when I tell them that My eye is even on the sparrow, and knows when every one falls. Nor does man understand how EACH THING in My creation is a part of My heart.

"You scoff at Me now, perhaps. Even Carol has gotten up to stop and think, and ask Me if this is truly ME giving her these ideas and words! But listen closely to what I am trying to make you understand here..."

"May I, Lord?"

"Yes – you may."

I didn't understand at all what He was trying to explain here with the apples – and I was beginning to wonder if it was really Jesus telling me these things. After I confirmed that it was – He opened my understanding a little more. I am an artist – and with each painting, each creation I make, a great deal of "me" goes into it. I feel almost motherly about the things I create, and secretly wish that all could feel as I do about them. So, I understood here, that ALL of what we see is His "masterpiece", and He, in this way, is a part of everything – literally EVERY THING that you see in the world. Even apples!

To further understand, look at a quote from what Jesus told Clare last night, as He was telling her about our Home in Heaven: **"You will see the transformations that Love permeating everything has made. The lion and the fawn will lie down next to one another and he will tenderly embrace the fawn as they nap. The otters will surface in the water with beautiful shells and drop them at your feet, begging to be petted. The bees will ascend in the shape of a heart and invite you to partake of their honey.**

"The sand beneath you will gently accommodate your shape wanting to make you comfortable. The canyon walls will have footholds and handles making climbing effortless, and on your way up there will be surprises like little caves lined with gem quality indigo azurite crystals. Eagles will invite you to sit on their nests and fondle their chicks. The leaves on the trees will rustle joyfully as you pass by and the grass will tinkle like chimes, greeting you in love with sparkling prisms of light glinting off of them and dancing off the canyon walls.

"Oh, the wonders of Heaven NEVER cease and all shall be yours because on Earth you lived for Me. So, now I will spend Our eternity delighting you with things you never thought of, but are extensions of what enthralled you on Earth."

Here He has told us that even the SAND, the TREES and the GRASS respond to His Love – as hard as that all is for us to comprehend and take in!!

"Thank you, My Love. You did well explaining that.

"My Friends. If I can consider an apple, a 'thing' that I conceived of, designed and by its very being declares My Glory – a thing most would not give a second thought to... Or care about a puppy that is a living thing in your eyes.... How much greater do you think I care about you? How much greater do you think my Love for you is?

"Ah, My Dear, Dear Friends! The love I hold in My heart for each one of you is far beyond measure, far beyond the understanding of man. You are My Creation, the highest order of My Creation. You were conceived in My Mind's Eye even before I formed Adam's body out of the earth of the ground, and then breathed into him My Life.

"Do you see? Do you understand even a little how I long for your soul to come to Me, to be brought into My Kingdom to live with Me for all eternity?

"I beseech you – think. Look around you at what is left of beauty in the world as it is right now. There is still a glimpse and a glimmer if you look for it. And think now, from this day on: every tiny bug, every tiny butterfly, every animal... yes even the plant Life that is still growing around you is given as a part of Who I am, of My Provision for what I have created.

"And I – the Creator of all of these things – Love YOU.

"Come to Me, My Friend! The world is ugly and harsh and dangerous for you right now, but do not run to the enemy's arms for your comfort, your solace, your provision. For I tell you the Truth: you will find there only death, disease, hate and destruction.

"Come to Me, My Friends. I offer you Life in all its glorious, original, pristine wonder.

"Come to Me, Friends. Come!"

The Source of All that has Ever Been,

Jesus.

Money, Self-Reliance...or ME. You Must Decide

May 11, 2015

"Do You have words for our Friends tonight, Lord?"

"Yes, I do. Begin to write.

"Our topic tonight is MONEY.

"Whether you have little or much, money will become a thing of the past swiftly in the days of Tribulation. You WILL be forced at some point to make the decision: will I take the Mark touted by the Anti-Christ – Obama and his new administration - in order to live/eat/survive?

"Or will I take the better way?

"Let's look at what each of these decisions will involve.

"It will seem logical. Cool. Intelligent. Prudent. 'No big deal' once all the various money systems, coins, currencies are in chaos around the world as the world economies collapse. The idea is already in the works: take a simple computer chip in the hand or forehead, and Viola! Open a door, turn on a device, pay for a purchase with the wave of your hand. Once the demons disguised as aliens show up, there will be an issue of allegiance, too. So, people will be brainwashed into believing that 'they' are right, but 'they' are wrong...and be driven to follow one course or the other.

"But the bottom line will be – follow Me... or follow Satan – no matter how convoluted the package appears.

"I have said before that taking the chip into your body will forever seal your fate. This is the reason: the chip will contain demon 'seed' that, once it is implanted into your body, will release another DNA into your bloodstream, and this will begin to permanently change and transform your DNA into what was once called a Nephilim. This process cannot be reversed, and will not be forgiven.

"This is why I cry out to you NOW to turn to Me, to give your life over to Me before it is too late. Better to be beheaded and join Me in Heaven and eternity, than to be able to purchase a few crumbs to keep you alive one more day. Rest assured, the powers in charge care not one whit whether you live or die, one way or the other.

"Their only goal, their only motivation in everything they are doing is to steal, rob, kill and destroy all of humanity, and convert them permanently into citizens of hell. Your life is worth nothing to them, no matter how strong you declare your allegiance to them might be.

"On the other hand, your life is worth everything to Me. I came to the Earth for your sake – I gave My life on the Cross so that you could make the simple step towards Me and be saved.

"Use Wisdom, My Friend. Be prudent. Think clearly about these things, and come shelter under My wings. Seek Me and I will be found. Knock and I shall open the door to Eternity to you. Ask, and you will find Salvation, Love, Joy, Peace and Eternal Happiness once your life is Mine.

“My love for you is never-ending. All powerful and persuasive. Given freely and without cost. Run now into My open arms. Do not be an Esau, exchanging your life for a bowl of pottage.

“Come, My Friends. Come.”

The King Who conquers. The Rescuer of souls.

Jesus.

CERN "I AM God and There Is None Other"

April 5, 2015

The Lord be with you, Youtube family.

I guess we're dealing with a rather serious message here. This message is about CERN.

All of my recording equipment is down. I can't tell you why, but I have two different units and microphones – professional recording equipment. And it's refusing to work - it won't even turn on. So, I think this message is probably NOT the enemy's favorite. I won't be able to edit this message, you'll hear a lot of "ahh's" and "hmmm's" but it's okay, it doesn't matter – the message is the important part.

"I want My Bride to approach Me with the confidence that she will be fully received. I am not some great and terrible king in whose presence you could be executed. No, to the meek, I am meek; to the fragile, every so gentle; to the fearful, embracing with open arms. But to those who are angry and cruel, I am fierce and protective; to those who deceive, I catch in their own rouses; to those who are wicked, I brandish the iron rod.

"In this way I protect My Bride and give to each one their just deserts. I have labored hard and long with this generation to bring them to repentance. Even in this hour I have presented to them the science of My Creation to bring them to their senses. And yet they persist in their obstinate unbelief to satisfy careers in the scientific community and avoid the inevitable ridicule that comes with proclaiming My Name.

"And so here we are at a critical juncture in history and I must contend with those who would pretend to be God. Even as Satan longed to ascend the throne, they have longed to outdo Me or at the very least set themselves on equal terms with Me.

"What shall I say to this wicked generation who toys with the very building blocks of creation? 'Carry on! Run your tests until you destroy all that I've created?' No, I shall let it backfire on them, for to them I say, 'I Am God and there is none other. Can I not withdraw the breath from your very bodies and to dust you will return?' But no, this does not occur to them, for they're blinded by their ambition to prove to the world they are gods.

"I will not tolerate this insidious behavior inspired by none other than Satan himself. I will punish and rebuke such as these lest they destroy the very ground they stand on. I am not a man that I should be mocked, nor am I deaf, blind and speechless like the idols they adore. No, I am their Creator, like it or not, accept it or not. What they are attempting to do will result in one of the greatest disasters the Earth has ever known. Each shall run to their own deep dwelling, but in vain. The waters will seek them out and they shall not escape.

"But you, My Bride, will be with Me in Heaven and we will dance and celebrate and explore the wonders I have created for you.

"Stand fast, My Bride. You shall see the glory and salvation of your God. Do not entertain fears, rather rest in My Provision for you, for I have gone to prepare a place for you that where I am. You, too, shall be in the house of the Lord, yet with your own lovely palaces where you may continue to grow in your love for Me in preparation for your reign on Earth.

"So rest and worry not, your salvation draws nigh."

What the Lord is referring to in this message is the CERN project. Which, I guess, they're trying to fire up the accelerator again this weekend. Maybe even at the time they think the Lord rose from the dead, who knows?

The Lord bless you.

Everything Seems Business As Usual

April 7, 2015

Good morning! I have an encouraging sort of message from the Lord. You know after all the drama of the weekend and thinking that the Rapture was going to happen, and then the Lord corrected us and gave is the idea that it wasn't going to be a time when we expect it.

I was thinking today, 'Gosh! It's just business as usual out there. Sunny day, trees are beginning to bud. Opportunities are coming up – life is going on, so to speak. And I thought, 'Lord, couldn't we have a more time? Or are we just a little crazy? Crazy Christians with Rapturitis, or whatever. could we have more time, Lord?'

Then I had a real burden for the souls who haven't really changed their lives, haven't really come to Him – even the Christian souls. We've had so many people on our channel who've had some beautiful experiences with the Lord, and are really getting deeper with the Lord. There's so much hope in that, for people who have felt alienated for so long. And I thought, 'If only we had more time!' Don't throw rotten tomatoes at me for saying that, because I know none of us wants more time – we all want to get out of here! In a way... But, I was thinking of that, thinking people are beginning to really, really show signs of life, and repent and wanting to be closer to the Lord.

So, that's kind of what this message is about. I began:

“Oh Lord, how I wish there were time. So many souls, so lost, so confused, I wish I could touch more. I wish WE could touch more.”

"I know."

“I wish we had more time.”

"I know. But we don't."

“But everything seems so normal, you know…”

"Buying and selling, marrying and giving in marriage?"

“Yes. The world seems to be so stable just like it will go on forever.”

"I know. But it won't. It's deceiving. So much is happening behind the scenes that very few care to know about as long as they can maintain the status quo."

“People are responding.”

"They are afraid. That’s why they are responding."

“Well, at least they are responding. Couldn't we have more time?”

"If you knew what I knew, you wouldn't ask that question."

“Well, every day I struggle with this, Lord. The world seems so stable, so normal - if it weren't for Revelation and for You, I'd think it would go on forever.”

"Aren't you glad you have Me?"

“Oh my goodness, life would not be life but a walking nightmare without You, Lord.”

"I know how you feel. I know how you feel because I weigh the pros and cons and I feel the same way. But we have knowledge of what's really going on, you don't. It is the status quo thing. ‘Don't upset my apple cart, let me get these apples to market, sell them, come home with a profit and go shopping. Just let me live my life.’

“This is where most are at. In the meantime, others are stealthily planning their assault. They rest in their plans because they know the masses are still filling their carts with apples and as long as that process can continue, they will be happy.

"Others, who value freedom of religion, freedom of speech, justice and security in those things - others are alarmed and filled with consternation, making plans to escape what they plainly see coming. Others yet are looking skyward, waiting for Me to rescue them.

"Clare, it's happening right before your very eyes, but life before you is lived in layers. To one layer it is the apple cart, to another it is dominance, to another it is freedom, to another yet, it is Heaven, but all the layers are before you. You each day must choose which layer you are going to live in. Which layer is your reality, who is your master, who you will serve. Until one of the layers explodes and takes away the rights of the other layers and the world is turned upside down and inside out and looking back, people will say, ‘How did this happen?’

"It happened because you chose to live in an isolated layer that appeared to provide all you needed. You didn't look beyond that layer because you were busy succeeding in this one. Then one day....well, it all ended, and left you standing in confusion. If you are one of the lucky ones who are still standing, that is.

"Nothing will be remembered of the fatness of the land when it collapses. Only bitter memories of what was lost. Then from the rubble they will seek Me. They will realize their love affair with the world left them naked and destitute. And when they find Me, I will embrace them, poor oil upon their wounds and raise them up in holiness.

"What I want to say is that you mustn't grieve over those who are left behind. No, this is their destiny because they chose to live in that layer of isolation where everything was provided by their own hand, where success was the entire focus of their lives. Yes, they chose this, and the world being such as it is, left them blind and naked before Me. And this I allowed to save their souls; for without it, well, Hell is filling up. They are not all bad people, just Godless, with no need for God. It is My act of mercy that their world comes crashing to an end. It is My love for them that allows such catastrophe. Only nakedness will bring them to Me, hungry for the comfort of truth.

"You see, once a man builds his house on the sand and the rains come and the floods wash it all away, well, then that man will consider the importance of building upon Rock, and I will be there to teach him. So, you see what is pending and inevitable is merely My provision to bring My children back to Me, in spirit and in Truth.

"Yes, it is harsh. Yes, it is brutal. Yes, it is seemingly unfair. But none of this occurs to man when he is busy exploiting the very poor of third world countries to buy his teenage son a car, or build a luxury home. All that matters to those of this mindset is the bottom line. And so they will experience the reality of the real bottom line of other nations, nations that looked to you for example in lifestyle and yet were hopelessly captive in a subservient culture and economy, while you continued to prosper.

"It is very, very sad, Clare. What you don't see is how these people are exploited and did I not create seed for the sower at a cost? But now greedy and wicked men scheme to find ways to force the poor to buy their seed. How much worse should I allow it to get? The cries of the poor reach My ears every day. They suffer the lack of even medical necessities, while in your country the medical establishment runs the lives of even the middle class and finds newer and better ways to get more control for more profit and flourish at the expense of the innocent.

"Oh it is so corrupt beyond all reason. Why should My Father allow it to go on for even one more minute? We have tried to turn the hearts of men, but their lust for primacy and luxury in the world has completely blinded them to their unjust lifestyles.

“Normally, I do not bring these things up to you, but I want you to understand - the facets of corruption I must look upon everyday are overwhelming and cry out for justice. And what is worse is the architects of these cultural crimes do not see they are destroying the very basis of their own lives by continuing to squeeze out every penny from the poor.

"Yes, this is only one facet, but it gives rise to unrest, hatred, despair. There is a reason Muslims rejoice in martyrdom: it's their one chance for happiness in a hopelessly corrupted and convoluted world. Living for a cause overshadows the pain of want and restores a man's sense of dignity when nothing is left to him but to die honorably. So, Satan has offered a chance for man to redeem himself and live in ‘heaven’ with all the things he could never have on Earth because of injustice. Should they not hate those bankers and world leaders that prey on the poor - many of them Jews?

“There is another sense of accomplishment: destroy the Whore. This, too, is honorable. So, you see? This problem is hopelessly complex. But when I come back to rule and reign, the iron rod will break the backs of those who would steal and denigrate even the lowliest human.

"Justice and honor shall be available to all who seek it. Opportunity to live honorably with a true vocation and necessary education will be available to all and yet no one will prosper without God. No one will, in the beginning, even conceive of life without God, without a serious devotion and desire to serve Me. Everyone will see the necessity of living in God, except those who are without a conscience.

"We must start over, Clare, from the bottom up. There is no other recourse. Do not lose hope. I am coming to set it straight. We will get it right, I promise you. In the meantime, try to look forward to a vacation in Heaven, even though I know part of you wants more time to help.

"I love you all with a love that only your God could have, a sacrificial love, a love that yearns to be spent to bring just one more soul in. I bless you and ask you to continue to refine your lives to make more and more room for Me. And one day, your suffering, prayers and hard work will be rewarded."

The Death of America

April 9, 2015

I came into prayer very late tonight because I was trying to answer some rather urgent messages from you, dear Family. Immediately, without having been more than 20 minutes with the Lord in worship, I saw us in black. I was wearing a black widow's garment and Jesus was wearing a black widower's garment.

He began, **"The death of America, spiritually and physically."**

"You know well what is being played on the surface: saber rattling, exercises near the North Pole, all of that is just for show.

"The man people call your president, the man of stealth and intrigue who gains office by deceit is merely playing to the masses, so that when destruction comes it will look authentic - when in reality it is no more than a superficial show to cover the destruction of all sovereignties, that only one may dominate the world. He has done a stellar job of destroying you, America. And this I have allowed, because you have played the harlot and slept with every passerby. While I, your Husband, stood by as each had their turn in our bed.

"And now what shall I say? ... *'the ten horns which you saw, and the beast, will hate the harlot and will make her desolate and naked, and will eat her flesh and will burn her up with fire. For I have put it in their hearts to execute My purpose by having a common purpose, and by giving their kingdom to the beast, until My words will be fulfilled....' Rev. 17:16*

"That indeed is what I say.

"Nonetheless, I am still with you, even as Hosea waited on Gomer to finish her whoring and grow weary of her paramours. (secret lovers) Yes, indeed, I am still here America, and when you seek Me with your whole heart you will indeed find Me, ready to reconcile you to Myself, says the Lord your God.

"So, in the heat of your injuries, turn to Me and I will give you comfort. I will wash and medicate your burns, I will dress them with clean linens. I will lead you by the right way and restore the ruined homesteads to you. Yes, you will recover, you will again be faithful to Me.

"I speak not to the detestable worshipers of Baal whom your capitol city was built for, no - I speak not to you, for you shall be utterly destroyed even in your underground country, you who feel so secure in your coffins. You I consider no more, for you shall be no more in My way.

"I speak to the hearts of America that continue to hold the vision I inspired. Those who refused to sleep with foreigners, those who could not overcome the greedy ones who held dominance and sway over a shallow and gullible people bent on living for their comforts. I am with you.

"Go forward with courage. I, Myself, will be with you and in the end, what has been planned for you will come to naught and again you will rise from the ashes to succor the world and be in accord with My Kingdom as it comes to free all men from the Oppressor.

"My peace be with you, sons and daughters of America, who hold to the vision of righteousness. Crippling blows shall you receive, but I will restore and find My pleasure in you once again as your country returns to Me. One Nation Under the God Who suffers with you, the God who loves you and bestowed great beauty on your land, and the God who surely will restore you.

“Hold fast to these words for they are faithful and true."

Provision and Instruction For Those Left Behind

April 22, 2015

The Lord bless you, Youtube family. I just wanted to thank everyone who has been so supportive and loving. Thank you so much, it really makes a difference. And it has helped to keep my heart in peace.

Tonight, the Lord changed the subject. Kinda funny, 'cause Carol said, "I've got a feeling the Lord's going to change the subject tonight." Well, He did. So I'll go ahead and share that with you.

He began: **"I want to talk to you tonight about spiritual growth. Much of what I've been doing with you all is about spiritual growth: growing taller, filled out, more stable, well-grounded ready for anything because your reality is in the spiritual dimension with Me, not the earthly dimension soon to be further emerged in chaos.**

"Not realizing what is coming, people are still planning as if this life will go on forever just the way it is now. That is why they will be blind-sided by what is about to take place. What I want for you, Clare, is to leave behind as much as you can to elevate people out of that dimension of chaos, which is something only I can do with souls.

"You see CERN, clones and the ruling elite will make many very serious mistakes that will impact their hiding places among the rocks of the Earth. Vaults of water and magma will open up on them with tragic consequences. They will cry out to those who engineered these spaces, 'I thought you said this could never happen!!!' But all in vain, only to be swallowed up into the abyss. This indeed will be their just desserts, and so I counsel all to have nothing to do with these underground bases, they are not safe.

"And yet I will provide safe havens in the deserted areas, places with abundant water, natural caverns and sufficient food. Just as the angels provided manna in the desert, so will I release to all sufficient sustenance."

I'll take a break here – that was a surprise to me! That the angels were helping to spread the manna in the desert. That was an interesting point.

"Many stores of food will never run out. Medical supplies and healing will also be sustained supernaturally by Me. Many will come into a full time healing ministry, tending to the sick and infirm, strengthening and giving comfort to those who have collapsed in fear, those on the edge of death, even some to be brought into the Kingdom in the last moments of their lives.

"I have some wonderful things planned for this horrendous time. Many a wall will come crashing down upon the enemy because of prayer. I will supernaturally and literally move Heaven and Earth to protect the holy ones. Some will be martyred, some will survive but all will be provided for. I will not abandon them to the will of their enemies. Yes, unsurpassed suffering will be witnessed but also unsurpassed glory and the triumph of faith. There will be many sent from Heaven as visitations to encourage and provide. My angels will be most solicitous for the welfare of the remnant I am shielding from the full force of My wrath.

"Listen carefully to the instructions I am imparting to you. Prayer will be your greatest weapon and I will teach you how to pray. It will flow from within you without any effort, so strong will My grace be among you. Prayer will well up from inside and overtake you in moments of fear and danger, and you will be kept safely hidden as well as have My Peace.

"Many will betray each other and only discernment by My Holy Spirit will alert you to who cannot be trusted. If you judge by outward standards: what is said, what they look like, how they act – if you judge by normal human standards you will be fooled. You must rely on Me to detect weak souls or souls sent to find you out.

"Again I want to say, this is for the left behind ones, this is not for those who will be raptured. It is important to have these things printed and easy to find."

"Lord, would you please fix my printer?"

"Tomorrow, it will begin working again. Begin printing tomorrow. OK?"

"Oh, thank you Lord." My printer has been out of commission for over a month – I just couldn't figure out what was the matter with it.

"Don't be afraid Clare, don't let the enemy do this to you. I know the temptation to be afraid is tremendous because you can see so clearly what is coming. But I have made ample provision for every moment of your life up until the Rapture. I want you, Beloved, to be an example of peace and security in Me, not a trembling little mouse in the corner."

I had to laugh when I heard that!

"And yet fear is no laughing matter. Rather, it chokes out faith and you mustn't let it gain ground on you. Recall My promises to you and how many times I have come through for you, Oh Israel? How many times did I provide hay for your horses, food for your table, gas for your vehicles, free places to live? Hmm? How many times... and still you doubt Me? Come now, what a disgrace you are, do you want to circle the mountain for 40 years?"

Deep sigh. "Forgive Me Lord. Jesus, I believe. Help my unbelief."

"You got your nose into some news of developing events and that scared you."

"That's true, Lord. I did."

"Well, it's better if you stay away from such things, they will most assuredly have a harmful effect on your state of mind."

“Lord, what about leaving supplies behind for our children? That continues to bug me – I wish we could leave something behind for them.”

"I have told you before, I have already provided for them. This would be an act of unbelief on your part. It would also be a powerful distraction. Can you trust Me with them? Do you think after all these years of serving Me, I will abandon your children? Is it not written that you will never see the children of the faithful begging for bread? I have powerful provisions for them, but because you can't see it, measure it, hold it, you don't believe. Your faith is flagging."

“Please Lord, help me. Truly I am a shameful servant.”

"Well, come here ‘shameful servant’, and let Me hold you and restore your faith."

So, at that moment I stopped typing and closed my eyes and thought for a moment. I could feel the Lord, and see His face, and He held my face closely with His two hands and said, looking deeply into my eyes only inches from His, **"Stop worrying about your children, I have ample provision for them It is all planned out and getting in the middle would only confuse things. Stop. Worrying.”**

“Okay,” I said, “Okay.”

"Trust Me. I want all your efforts on these souls I have sent you. Be a mother to them, feed them honey from the rock and wheat from the fields of Heaven. Oh, how jealous I am for these who are so in love with Me. Oh how I long to protect and nurture them! It is beyond your understanding to know how God adores a soul devoted to Him. How can you lead them in faith if you are weary and stumbling?

"Nevertheless, I will make up the difference, for My strength is perfected in your weakness. So carry on, lift the burdens from their hearts, adorn them with garlands of love from the gardens of Heaven. Nurture them, Clare, and BELIEVE that I AM has sent you to their side in these hours of mischief the Devil has devised."

I was starting to flag at that point and getting a little sleepy, and I figured maybe this was the end of the message.

"I'm not done yet, My Love.

"Just as in days gone by, when I supernaturally protected My people, so shall I protect those who must stay behind. There will be one among them who will be the designated the leader, and to him or her, I will give supernatural knowledge and wisdom. Protect this one who is critical to your mission. Let not the devils cause division, misunderstanding, murmuring and jealousy. Be on your guard against these poisons they will use to divide and scatter you all. Together you will survive. Separated, you will face many dangers without anyone to back you up. Do not let them divide and conquer. Be smarter than the enemy - walk in charity and humility and you will have no problems. Walk in self-will, selfishness, suspicion, and rancor - it will be your demise.

"There will be many testings among the groups, many testings. Painful decisions to make, life or death decisions to make. I will give you peace when the decisions are the hardest. Use lots to help you determine a plan of action."

Taking an aside here, Lots are what they used – drew straws or sticks or something. With Jonah, when he was in the ship to find out why God was against them in the storm, and of course picking the apostle to replace Judas they used Lots.

"I will be with you as I was with Israel in the desert. I will give you signs of My love, signs of danger, signs when you are going the wrong way, Signs when you are going the RIGHT way.. Be attentive, pay close attention to the signs I send you."

You know, when I think of signs, I think of heart-shaped rocks, the face of Jesus in the bark of the tree… I don't know – it'll be different things. But if everyone's on the watch for signs, then they're going to see them.

"If you suspect you have made a wrong decision, stop and pray it through. Better to wait on me than to move forward into a trap. There will be times to act and times to wait. It is in the times of waiting that trials will be the most difficult. Pray always, worship and thank Me for every safe moment of your journey, for every provision, for every time you evade the enemy. Use My Name as a weapon of war."

For you fight not against flesh and blood but principalities in high places and against evil rulers and authorities of the unseen world, against mighty powers in this dark world, and against evil spirits in the heavenly places. Ephesians 6:12

"Now, I want you all to remember how easy it is to fall into unbelief, to mistrust, to suspect, to be fearful. These are the weapons the enemy will use against you - forewarned is forearmed.

"Now, My Precious Ones, cling to My instructions, for in them lies life and death. Be not afraid of what man does to your body, only your eternal soul. Do not compromise for the sake of your body, your children, your wife, or for any reason at all. I will be with you to deliver you from evil. Pray often, 'Deliver us from evil.' Pray this frequently - it is a powerful prayer.

"That's all for now, My Love. Remember, I promised that your printer will work tomorrow."

"Thank you, Lord."

"I Bless you My Brides. Leave these instructions behind. Have courage and keep your eyes on Eternity." Amen

Put No Confidence In The Flesh

May 9, 2015

The Lord be with you, and bless you with His wisdom. The Lord came to me with a message for those basically who are left behind, and have work to do here. For some reason are not taken in the Rapture.

"Place no confidence in the flesh. Do not imagine for one moment that you can provide or take care of yourself without My intervention...or more properly without My complete control. When you place confidence in your own flesh: your ability to defend yourself, your ability to provide for yourself - you set yourself up for failure. There are those who are going to walk into the Tribulation with empty pockets and not a place to go, no food, no preparation at all. And yet they will be fully provided for every step of the way.

"When a soul puts all their confidence in Me, I am free to provide everything they need. Rather than providing and surviving, be about My business and all these things will be added unto you. Your insecurity and panic do nothing but give the devils permission to sift you, wear you out and cause you to move prematurely right into the enemies' waiting arms. But with your focus on bringing souls to Me, I am free to provide all you need. My faithfulness is your rear guard and covering.

"It is a lack of knowledge of Me that causes others to dive in and apply themselves to providing for their own needs. When you know Me, you know I have already provided a way out, complete with food, medicine and cover that will make you invisible to the enemy.

"This is for the benefit of those left behind, Clare. For the most part now, I am going to be preparing them through our times together"...my mind drifted onto the seismic charts for Yellowstone I saw today. Unbelievable – they were just these huge, solid bars of color rather than the usual squiggly lines that reflect and earthquake – really amazing. And I was thinking, 'Nibiru is bringing these Earth changes on and they knew all the time, they knew this was going to happen.'

"Yes, they knew all along. But rather than provide for the masses, they are counting on the catastrophic conditions to wipe out portions of humanity that do not fit into their genetic code.

"But let's get back to what is important here, My Love. The focus must be on charity and virtue, trust and faith in My ability to provide. Without these pivotal attitudes, they will not succeed. My protection can make you invisible. My protection can turn wild beasts away. My protection can save you from the ground giving way beneath you. My protection can provide water and food when there is none. I can do all things, and I will, for those whose agenda is to gather in souls to the Kingdom. Those who give and lead unselfishly, those who are honest and caring for others, these are the ones I will supernaturally protect and provide for.

"Many I will add to your numbers that need salvation. Their eternity is hanging in the balance and if you make their eternity your priority, I will cover you. Souls are going to be racked with confusion and fear, not knowing up from down, so severe will the trials be on the Earth. They will be so thoroughly disoriented that nothing can calm them down but a supernatural grace. A healing grace, laying hands on them and praying for My Peace to descend upon them.

"And for you who are called to heal, I live inside of you. Place your hand on the injured or suffering and imagine My hand moving from your heart out through your hand and onto the soul. I will do the rest. All you have to believe is that I AM and I LIVE IN YOU. This is all that is required for a complete healing of even the most dramatic sicknesses.

"Do be baptized in the Holy Spirit, do pray in tongues, do sing over people in tongues - you are speaking MY language and I am praying through you, the perfect prayer. Do not allow anyone to discourage you from speaking in tongues - the devils will use self- conscious, insecure and poorly informed souls to try and stop you from using this powerful gift. Don't let them. Now more than ever you need to pray in tongues. I will, for some of you, give the interpretation while you are praying which will inform you of what your true opposition is, be it man, beast or even your own self.

"There will be a great need for supernatural wisdom, so many different opponents will be coming against you. I will warn you of them if you make prayer your absolute priority. More than life itself, you need quality prayer time with Me. No one in your group can go without prayer. The ones who will not pray will be the weak links in your chain. They will betray you and make poor choices under pressure. Better that everyone stay in prayer and allow those who will not pray to go elsewhere - that is once you have done everything in your power to bring them to Me and still they will not acknowledge or choose to live by My standards. Let them go, they will only bring trouble upon the other members of your group.

"Towards the end, when things get the most chaotic, you will need to cleave to Me with all your heart and lean not on your own understanding or devices. I will inspire you with the proper steps to take, even in your dreams I will come to you and instruct you. Understand that the closer you draw to the end of events, the more chaotic it will become and the shorter the time before your deliverance. Pray for strength, courage, wisdom, compassion and peace. It is by your faith that you will be saved - the flesh avails nothing. Everything depends upon faith and trust in Me alone.

"You will witness people breaking down completely and unable to cope any longer. They will retire inside of themselves where they feel safe. All you can do for these is pray and be compassionate. My grace will carry them. They will be among you as the sick and disabled. Do all in your power to tend to them, do not grow impatient with them or cast them away - they may be your saving grace; because you took care of them, I will take care of you.

"However, if you must leave someone behind, give them a portion of food and water, pray for them that I will take over their care and commend them into My Merciful hands. Do not walk about in guilt - you did all you could and now it's My turn. You will be tried to your uttermost limits and when you reach those limits turn to Me and say, 'Lord, take over for me, I am at my end.' And I will give you the strength to carry on.

"Remember that My power is made perfect in your weakness. This is My chance to show you just how much you mean to Me and who I truly am in you.

"I bless you now with the peace that passes all understanding, courage and endurance. Run the race to the finish line. And remember that in all situations I am with you, and I will not desert you. Not matter what you face – I will be there with you."

The Hordes of Hell Have Been Released

June 20, 2015

The Lord bless you dear, sweet Youtube family. You are all so precious. I want to thank you for your prayers and for your support to of us. You've been doing a wonderful job, and we're having some breakthroughs over here.

I also want to thank you for your patience on behalf of the Lord, for putting up with sufferings and inconveniences for the suffering of the world. I know a lot of you are really, really suffering and you're taking it so well.

Tonight's message was pretty important, I think. I have two messages – well, I have a teaching and a message. The first message is "The Hordes of Hell Have Been Released."

The Lord and I were dancing. I was deeply, deeply drawn into worship tonight, and the sweetest most precious way. But I was interrupted a zillion times. That's what the next teaching is about…a new kind of "stupid" on my part.

(Maybe it's not so new, thinking of it…chuckle..)

We were dancing very tenderly, just quietly - He was embracing me and we were just dancing and all of a sudden I saw this black cloud coming towards us and going over our heads and passing over us. Something landed on the Lord's shoulder, on His neck. I looked at it – it was a vampire bat, it had canine teeth – wow! He picked it off His neck and He said to me:

"The hordes of Hell have been released.

“They have gone out into the world to stir up rebellion. Man against God, and yes, CERN does have something to do with it. These men are so blind, they have no idea what chaos it is going to mean for them and by the time they find out, it will be too late to stop it. It will already have a foothold and have destroyed half the Earth.”

Now, as an aside here, at the CERN facility they have a statue of Yeshiva that is lit up at night, right outside the building. Yeshiva is representative of the destruction aspect of life, and of chaos. So, the Lord is saying basically, these scientists are so blind that they don’t see the kind of chaos they’re going to create and what it is going to do to them.

“Lord, I thought CERN was affecting more outer space and these creatures were coming from some demonic planet or something.”

"Hell is in the bowels of the Earth and a particular dynamic of gravity has moved aside the protective shield I put in place to keep these demon-infested creatures from ruining the Earth."

As He was talking I kept seeing something like a huge, translucent, fish scale plate over an area of the Earth that had been moved by the doings of the accelerator.

"Clare, in fact it is very, very sad. I see these children messing with things they do not understand, thinking they will outsmart Me in some way, or be able to duplicate what I have created, thereby attaining equality with Me. Much of this is simply academic pride and a group of men and women climbing the professional ladder, wanting to perch on top and declare their brilliance to the world - that they are in fact equal to Me.

"There is one glaring fact they are still missing: and who created Me? You see, you can play with the building blocks I've given you, but they are still held together by My Love and My Power. Yes, they have rules that can be manipulated to produce various results, but they are all created by Me.

"Were I to remove the blocks, the universe would cease to exist and them in it. They would be nothing more than globs of energy floating around in a void. This, by the way, is Satan's goal: using their ambition to destroy them. Right now they can't see that. As I said, when they do it will be too late. But I will step in so the universe will not go belly up like a balloon who's naval has been untied.

"How I long to fellowship with some of these great minds that I created and breathed life into. But no, that would ruin their career. So, even though some of them know deep down that they are being called into the true realms of science, like Pontius Pilate they will not risk their careers by following that call. Pontius Pilate knew better than to crucify Me, but he did it out of fear that Caesar would ruin his career, because of the uprising if he didn't - and now look at his unenviable future in Hell. He was warned. They've been warned. But, lust for position and fame have overtaken them. Nothing short of a miracle can stop them.

"So, here we are on the brink of disaster. The hordes of hell have been released into the atmosphere of Earth and all they know is destruction and hatred for mankind and all I've created. So, they will manifest now in ways no one could imagine - to set to work, through mankind, the destruction of Earth. They will have their way, Clare. I have given it into their hands."

"But, Lord, what about the prayer 'world without end?''

"Oh, the Earth will be devastated, but it will not end. I will bring with Me a new Springtime. The beauty of a freshly created Earth - I will restore everything. The greater portion of those involved in the accelerator project are not evil, just very ambitious and without basic intelligence. They overlook the very foundations of life to pursue a way-out-there academic goal that will bring them fame and glory. That is why I say they are lacking in basic intelligence. A smart little toddler could easily prove to them that they are playing with a fire they cannot control.

"So, in essence, these hordes of Hell will begin to inspire men and women on every level to do things that will end in ultimate disaster. They will sit on the shoulders of people and suggest things that look innocent enough but will set a wave of destruction over the whole Earth, through the whole ecosystem, through the mass mind of man, controlling more and more the thought patterns and physics of psychology for their own irrelevant ends. Again, these are lacking in basic wisdom and intelligence.

"Not understanding God and morality, not being taught that as the basis for a healthy life, they have no fear of God, no understanding of how things are perpetuated. They have totally tossed out the idea of faith and religion and the significance of moral conduct and living Godly lives. Had they pursued the truth, and only the truth, they would have found how very foundational that is and would have had a holy fear of messing with things I created in a certain order.

"Well, I wanted you to understand, dear one. You are going to see an acceleration of evil from today onwards. Yes, evil is about to bite mankind, infect and destroy it. It will begin slowly but gain momentum over the days to come. Please, be steadfast in suffering, in putting up with the abundant annoyances that I allow in your life. Offer every one of them as wedding presents to Me.

"And for those of you who are carrying the heavy cross of sicknesses: you are holding back the wrath of God and helping Me to draw many into the Kingdom before it's too late for them."

“Lord, is there anything you can share with me about what's going to happen because of these hordes that have been released into our atmosphere?”

"No, not at this time My Love. But, you could share with them the embarrassing situation you found yourself in today and how it cost you dearly. Oh, I had some wonderful things planned for our time together and your focus on food robbed you of it."

“I'm so sorry, I could feel a special sweetness in prayer, I really wanted to be with You tonight, Lord. I’m sorry for not obeying…”

And if you want to know what THAT video is about, it’s called, “But, Lord!

CERN Wickedness Increases, Pride Protection

July 22, 2015

The Lord had a very interesting message for us tonight. A little background: when I came into prayer tonight, I was extremely distracted, because I've been getting things ready around here, cleaning things up and doing what had to be done to put things in order. And you know, once you get that thing going in your head, where you're nesting, and you're doing what you're doing...once you get going with it, you don't want to stop. It's hard to stop. And coming into prayer, I was a little bit disordered in my mind, I just wasn't as centered...Oh, I really want with all my heart to just get this stuff over quickly, so I can stay centered on the Lord.

The Lord was very merciful – He was extremely visible, 'cause I think He knew what I was fighting against – a lot of self-condemnation for having gotten into doing these things. But, in retrospect, they have to be done. So, He's on my side.

He began the message by saying:

"Just because you can't connect, doesn't mean I can't connect with you. Yes, it has to be mutual, but part of your problem is guilt, just like everyone else's. Let's put that all of that aside now. We have work to do."

What He was talking about was false guilt, not "guilt" guilt, but false guilt, and you know the devil's take advantage of that. Well, you know they give you these thoughts of false guilt, and they magnify them. And if you go with it, pretty soon you're running from the Lord instead of running TO the Lord. Or, you're afraid He's not going to speak to you or be with you in prayer time, because you did something bad. But, in all reality – you're being lied to. So, let's be careful with that, guys – the devil does that with EVERYONE.

"This thing with CERN is going to be a major hindrance to My Kingdom come, My will be done. However, I am going to use it to sharpen the warring skills of My Bride as she has never, ever been sharpened before. Every time Satan makes a move, I make a counter move. Every time he steps forward to hinder, I step forward to arm. Like I said, the world has never seen the likes of what My Warring Bride is going to do with the anointing I am sending.

"All I want from her is seriousness of intention. Not heavy fasts, but moderate intake of calories and moderate self-denial and pressing into prayer."

"Jesus, am I hindered by my medications?"

"A little. But I need you to be stable and functional."

"But You could do that without these pills."

"I have My reasons, Clare. There is a certain shame associated with being dependent on medication. It most certainly lowers the image of self-sufficiency that promotes pride and comparisons with others."

And I have to admit, that's true. When I was young and strong and didn't have any physical problems at all...oohh, that pride was just running strong and really high. And He's definitely whittled me down by allowing this – the negative part of me, that is. I was feeling an emotional pain inside while we were talking, and I said, "Lord, what's going on in my heart right now?"

"You are grieving for what is yet to come. It is the innocent who suffer the most, and that pleases wickedness more than anyone can understand. Nonetheless, I will have My Triumphs. My daughter, you are so concerned with your selfishness, and yet you don't see what I see. You are devoted to Me with all your heart. I know your weaknesses and I don't count them against you because, truly, you love much. That you cannot feel that love is to your benefit - that you not get puffed up.

"But by your actions you have proven - more than proven - to Me that you care, even deeply, for Me and all that matters to Me. With many of My Servants I have to keep things hidden from them. Feelings, devotion, manifestations of their love, fruits of their service to Me. I hide these things deliberately because they are weak in humility and I must protect them.

"It is when a soul begins to see what 'they' have done that trouble starts. As long as they stay ignorant and forgetful, they are safe. When they begin to take the credit and see themselves as somebody or someone, well, if things don't turn around quickly, that's the beginning of the end. Sooner or later, Satan will engineer a fall for them, and because they aren't listening very carefully, they are taken down.

"That's why I want to say to all My Brides: I am going to release gifts to you to overcome what Satan has planned. Be very, very cautious not to attribute those to yourself - you will be infected very slowly with a demon of pride. Pay very close attention to your thoughts and feelings that you do not start to feel good about who you think you are becoming or what you think you've done. This requires a closely studied caution and an absolute obedience to Me. I will correct your course at times. I will take detours or stop things mid-stream so you won't skip right over the workings of the enemy and allow it to take root in your souls.

"This is what I have done and will always do with Clare, as long as she is willing. She has shared with you transparently, which has helped you to see how I work in a vessel's life. If only you would follow the way I have led her and stay transparent to yourselves and others, I could prosper you and those around you that you might grow in My anointing and gifts without them being stolen from you by the enemy.

"Humility, charity and transparency are your greatest weapons against the enemy's moves on you. So often, it is the gate of charity and the covering of humility that is weak and easily invaded. If you know these things and put them to practice, happy will you be. There is no temptation that has overtaken you that you cannot see that I've provided a way out.

"That is - unless you are operating in Pride. Pride works in degrees. There is ALWAYS pride, ALWAYS. The only way to overcome it is in stages. I release grace, I watch for your response, I watch the enemy's moves, and wait to see your response. If you come to me contrite and broken, we can continue on to the next level. You may not have sinned through pride, but you feel yourself going that way. That's when I need you to nip it in the bud and come to Me deeply contrite, before that infection grows and spreads through your whole life. A little leaven raises the whole batch. As it takes root, it multiplies and spreads like wildfire not only in you, but in those around you who are not paying close attention."

I just want to clarify something here, where He said, **"If you come to me contrite and broken... I watch the enemy's moves, and wait to see your response."**

You know, when pride starts to invade your space and your thinking.

"If you come to me contrite and broken, we can continue on to the next level." Then He said, **"You may not have sinned through pride, but you feel yourself going that way. That's when I need you to nip it in the bud... before that infection grows and spreads through your whole life."**

So, in other words, you may not have acted on pride, or sinned through pride, but can feel yourself moving in that direction – kind of an undercurrent of feeling good about yourself. THAT'S when He wants you to nip it in the bud, and come to Him contrite, that it's even gotten THAT far in your nature.

"This is why I deal so painfully with Clare when this sin tries to take over. There will always be a little, but by degrees we will snuff it out. Constant vigilance is required that it not begin to spread again. As you overcome the temptation to pride I can continue to anoint, bless and increase all you put your hand to."

You know, when He said that, about how it will spread again, I thought of cancer. They operate on you and take out the cancer, but they are constantly vigilant to make sure that it doesn't pop up in another place. Well, pride is certainly spiritual cancer of the worst kind.

"My children, this is the way I work through My chosen vessels, whom I love so very much. Those that are wicked take off with pride and go their own way. Eventually it is to their ruin. They would not pay heed to attitudes in their deepest being. They allowed the world to seep in like leavening in a bowl of flour.

"So, here I have laid out My plan for you. Satan is about to make his moves through CERN. Wickedness will increase, along with it your anointing to defeat every tactic of the enemy, AS LONG AS YOU ARE VIGILANT NOT TO GIVE IN TO PRIDE.

"If you begin to get lax, I will withhold from you My anointing. You will then seek Me with your whole heart and discover how the enemy has entered in. If you deal with it appropriately, I will return the active anointing to you and we will continue to grow together. You, from virtue to virtue, and anointing to anointing. It is because I love dearly that I tend to you this way...I would rather see you without any anointing than lose your soul to the devils.

"How do you know the difference between the enemy's opposition and Me withdrawing the anointing? Have I not given you tools? Do you not have what you need now to discover what's going on with you? Use the tools you have been given. I want to see breakthroughs. I want to see you with your second and third witness."

And I want to say here, guys, that when you use the Bible or the Bible Promises, and the Lord confirms something to you – you have something to stand on. You can stand on that word, and you can get through any opposition, because it's the Word of God that you're standing on.

"I tell you the truth, if you do not use what you've been given to the greatest extent you may very well not fulfill your calling on this Earth. There are many forces against you, lying spirits abound, and it is My desire to see you so close and tight with Me and knowing My thoughts about your situation that you not fall into any of these traps.

"Some of you will be equipped to move into new territory because of these second and third witnesses. Others will be lazy and because they do not have the assurance that they are in My Will, positively, they will draw back and lose what could have been their missions.

"You will find increasing opportunities to move forward in your anointing, but you Must Stand on the Words I Give you to Hold on to Your new Ground.

"I am with you in this. Do not grow discouraged. But cleave to My Words."

Do You Feel Condemned?

September 25, 2015

Forgive me for not being with you yesterday, but I was exhausted and having problems with that dental work that was done, and NOT able to function normally. But I'm back tonight and sincerely thank you for all your prayers, they definitely have helped.

Tonight the Lord brought up forgiveness – forgiving ourselves.

Isaiah 1:18 "Come now, and let us reason together," says the LORD, "Though your sins are as scarlet, They will be as white as snow; Though they are red like crimson, They will be like wool."

"In these days, My people are stressing way too much about their sins. Their sins have become like mountains of condemnation and few among you believe that I've truly forgiven you."

You know, I've noticed that on our channel, guys. There's been quite a few people who've said, "I think I'm condemned, I'm going to hell, the Lord's not going to take me in the Rapture." And you're not living in sin – you just have this vague sense of being condemned. Well, I think tonight, the Lord's going to clear up where that's coming from. This is super basic to our walk, that the Lord died for us on the Cross, and He paid the price. And if you're contrite, if you're sorry for your sins and you turn and repent, you don't have to worry about being left behind OR condemned. Let's go on with what He had to say:

“Why is it, My people, that you cannot accept My forgiveness? Why is it that you believe condemning lies from the lying mouths of your enemies? How many times must I plead with you to BELIEVE, just believe and you shall receive? How many times must I die on the cross again to convince you that your sins have been washed away?

“Many of you are lying in beds of condemnation, from the time you awake and become conscious to the very moment you drop off to sleep. Your sins weight you down. You've asked for forgiveness but you do not believe you have received it. Rather, you believe the lies of the evil ones who continually bombard you with falsehood.

“Take every thought captive, My Dearly Loved Ones. Every thought. Don't let it pass on into your heart or your inner places, do not feed on these deprecating lies. I will tell you how you must act. Consider the little toddler. He waits until his mother is out of the kitchen, then slides a chair over to the counter, leans way into the counter and takes the top off the cookie jar...all the time keeping an eye on the door.

"He knows he isn't supposed to be taking cookies...somehow he has that much sense. So, he waits until she isn't watching before he attempts to raid the cookie jar. Carefully he sets a handful of cookies in his pocket, puts the lid back on the cookie jar, climbs off the chair and moves it back to the table, and quickly runs outside with the cookies before she catches him. Then as he eats them, one by one, he begins to consider that he just did something wrong. They taste good, but he feels badly. I am working in the conscience of that child, until he is ready to repent. I'll make it easy for him. He left crumbs on the counter, his mother sees the crumbs and finds the little guy in the corner of the yard facing the other way putting something in his mouth. She walks over to him and says, 'Child, did you take some cookies?' He wipes the melted chocolate off his little hands, looks up at her with mixed emotions, guilt from stealing cookies and satisfaction from having finished them. Caught in the act he has no other response, 'Mmm hmm, I sorry Mamma, I sorry.' Then in that moment of confession, true contrition rises from within him and tears well up in his little eyes. He really is sorry. He did what was wrong, he knows it, he repents and asks forgiveness.

"What kind of God am I, My children? Shall I grab you by the arm jerk you up, drag you into the house and beat you black and blue? Or shall I sit you in time out so you can think about it for a few moments and have another discussion with you, 'Do you know what you did?' It was wrong, Momma. 'What do you say?' I'm sorry. (a little tear drips from his eye.) What shall I say at this point? 'I forgive you. Go and sin no more.'

“Later on you're playing and you start to feel badly. If you could see, a demon is on your shoulder, telling you, ‘You're bad - you took those cookies.’ You lay down for a nap, more demonic voices, ‘You're a nasty little boy. You stole from your mother.’ Later, when everyone's coming to the dinner table, ‘You should be in time out, you don't deserve to sit at the table.’ This repeats itself day in and day out and before long you feel so badly about yourself there is no hope left, why even try to be good, you're doomed.

“This is how the enemy demoralizes you. Some of you have lived through this kind of childhood where your parents were the voice of the demons. They continually beat you down and told you how bad you were. They never let you forget one thing you did wrong. Every time they got upset, they brought up the past and beat you with it.

“Do you think I am like them? Well, I am not. When I see the contrition in your heart, I wipe away your sin and whisper, ‘Let's try again. We'll do better next time.’ I wait patiently for you to realize what you have done, what the consequences are, then I embrace you, working with you until you can overcome that temptation.

"On the other hand, the demons beat you day and night mercilessly. My Children, when will you learn the difference between My voice and the Lying demons? When will you take Me at My word, 'I forgive you.' When will you take my hand and try again rather than running the other way? Don't you know that condemnation begets condemnation? The demons rail on you because they want you to rail on each other. They want you to become so discouraged you will never come forth with your gifts, you will never believe I can use you, you will never believe you are of any consequence in My Kingdom. Or that you're saved and you're going to Heaven.

"But you are! Each and every one of you are equipped with precious gifts I need in operation to fight against the enemy at this time. Each one of you is endowed with power when you pray. But you will not ever come into the Throne Room boldly, if you feel badly about yourself. You will never venture forth to touch another soul if you feel unclean and guilty. And if you dare, to the enemy will say, 'Look at your sins you have no business helping them, God can't use you.'

"Guilt and condemnation are the number one tools used by the enemy to disable a Christian. This is what the demons are taught, 'If you want to bring a Christian down and make them stop, bring up their sins.' And sadly, it works! But forewarned is forearmed. If you know this is the area of attack, you can come before Me repentant and go into battle fully equipped. What better way to demoralize a man that to make him feel badly about himself? Do you see? You are victims of psychological warfare if you give into the lie that your sins are not forgiven.

"My people, it is time to grow up. You have got to go into battle confident of My Love and forgiveness. There is no more time for wishy-washy faith. You have communed with Me. You know My nature is love and forgiveness, along with a helping hand up. You have been with Me, and to be with Me you know Me and you should now have the confidence to act on My word, to fight the good fight and take every thought captive.

"That is another reason intimacy with Me is so opposed by the devils. They know that if you draw nigh unto Me in tenderness and love, you will be washed clean in My forgiveness. You will walk away encouraged, strengthened and ready to love even as I have loved you.

"But if you never attain to that intimacy with Me, you are still prone to think of Me as harsh and condemnatory, calling on the experiences from childhood and school when unjust punishments were leveled against you. You are judged guilty and imprisoned mentally when the demons rail on you day after day and you've not had any authentic and intimate time with Me, where I hold you, forgive you and equip you to try again. You carry over your head a permanent cloud that says, 'Guilty.'

"And finally, you must BELIEVE in My forgiveness. BELIEVE I suffered and died for you on the cross. BELIEVE that though your sins are blood red, I will wash them white as snow. Did I not forgive David, a murderer and adulterer? Did I not forgive the Pharisees and Roman soldiers…'Father, forgive them, they know not what they do.'

"So if I have forgiven them, how is it you cannot accept My forgiveness for your sins?

"Very simply, you are listening to demons who are disabling you through condemnation. It should be clear to you by now: condemnation belongs to demons, conviction belongs to My Spirit. When I convict you, there is a sweet, sweet sense of being sorry for having offended Me, and with it comes a real desire not to repeat the act, and I am with you in that moment, encouraging you to call on Me for strength in the future.

"When the enemy condemns you, it is to convince you how bad and worthless you are, that you are doomed and can never be used by God, you are utterly lost and useless. Along with that comes overwhelming shame and a desire to run from Me instead of to Me. Once you are convinced to run from Me the spiral goes down swiftly into hopelessness.

"Mark My words, when you feel that you are feeling what is being put upon you by Satan's servants.

"So, now I have given you a lesson in how to recognize My gentle convicting thoughts and thus escape the trap Satan has set up to bring you down into disgrace permanently disabled as a Christian. Take it to heart, My Dear Ones, take it to heart and refuse the guilt that belongs to Satan and his servants.

"I bless you now with a sweet sense of My never-ending love and compassion for you. Walk in My forgiveness. Though your sins be as scarlet, we have reasoned together, now they are white as snow."

SECTION FOUR
Messages to Help You Know How to Hear From the Lord

Prayer That Prepares Us For Intimacy with Jesus: Dwelling Prayer

June 19, 2015

We call our form of prayer Dwelling Prayer, because we are dwelling with the Lord according to His promise that if we love Him, we will obey Him and He will dwell with us. (John 14:21) We have a playlist that explains the Scriptural basis for dwelling prayer: I'm Calling You

Before you begin, use the binding prayer. It begins with repentance for our sins and shortcomings. When you come to the prayer part, be sure to proclaim it with authority, taking authority through Jesus' name over the people, spirits and manifestations in the list.

We enter into the Lord's presence with praise and thanksgiving, worshipping Him in spirit and in truth. You may do this with or without music. We prefer to be drawn to Him through the lyrics of a worshipful song sung directly to Him, but you may feel more led to pray and worship - even in tongues - without music, just going directly to Him in your heart.

As we worship, images may come to mind, like Jesus standing nearby. These are not usually just imaginations you make up, they are sanctified images that God puts before you in your imagination. Don't brush them off, rather take them for the real thing.

Continue to worship, but pay attention to what you see in the 'spirit' or your sanctified imagination. The Lord may invite you to dance, may walk with you on a beach or sit with you in a garden. Be sensitive to the imagery around you in the spirit, then go with Him. Stay focused on adoring the Lord, and His love will draw you into Himself - you will feel His affection for you, you will sense that He is happy to see you. Stay with it. 99.9% of the obstacle in seeing and hearing the Lord is our own unbelief or false guilt. Don't take your time with Him lightly or brush away images - that's how unbelief manifests.

He may begin 'talking' with you by putting thoughts in your inner mind...like a spiritual voice. He will always be kindly, gentle, and affectionate with you – never, ever harsh or condemnatory. He may even ask you to write down or journal your conversation with Him. This is a good thing to do, then you can go back and read from your journal to see what He is saying and gain confidence in listening to Him again. You can also answer Him and this will become a time of dialogue between the two of you.

Jesus will always be very pure in your presence. There will NEVER be a hint of impropriety or sexual advance. He might hold you tenderly or kiss your forehead but there is never any hint of sexuality. He is God. He is Pure. He is a Virgin. His affection is strictly for the purpose of revealing to you that you are His precious soul Whom He loves infinitely, in a personal way.

During this time, you can pour out your heartfelt prayers for others to Him. As you become more accustomed and comfortable listening to Him, you will find that you slip into His presence with more ease every time you are together. He is always present to you, whether you hear or see Him or not. He is always there, usually at your right hand.

If you have fallen and done something you feel conviction about, DON'T RUN FROM HIM...run TO Him. Don't be afraid to confess and apologize to Him - that brings Him great joy and He is quick to forgive you and give you the grace to stay stronger next time in temptation.

People ask us, "How do you know for sure it's the Lord and not a demon or familiar spirit?" Our answer is that you will know by the fruit. There is a God-shaped place inside of you that no demon can fill. As you become better at prayer, you will begin to sense that place, when it is full and when it is empty. You will above all feel a deep, lingering peace and feel the strength that you need, because God is indeed with you.

You will not feel shame, confusion, condemnation, although you may feel conviction and apologize, asking for forgiveness. The fruit of that apology will be Peace and His love for you as well.

Some people use a verbal formula, asking the person appearing as Jesus in your vision "Do you confess that Jesus Christ has come in the flesh? I wouldn't trust just 'yes' as an answer. The right answer would be to hear a repeat of what you just asked: "I confess that Jesus Christ has come in the flesh." Based on John 1:4.

I have seen similar Scriptures asked of demons during a trance meeting and they replied in the affirmative but we knew they were lying. So, we really don't trust that way of verification.

If in your time with Him you start to feel anger, hatred, condemnation, hopelessness, jealousy, frustration, or sexual stirrings - that is not the Lord. Pray the Binding Prayer again. Go into worship again, maybe spending more time in worship and using music this time. We have a playlist of songs that always work to bring us into His presence.

Always remember that at all times, the Lord's presence is loving and gentle. Anything other than that you should be highly suspicious of. Pray the Binding Prayer again.

If you have come from a background of witchcraft or been dedicated as a baby to Satan, or have any history with Ouija Boards and the occult, you may need deliverance before you can be sure it is Jesus you are speaking to.

If you have any history of mental illness in your family, or instability, be very careful to enter the Lord's presence through worship and do not follow any extremes of thinking or emotions. You are now dealing with the spiritual world and just like going to a shopping mall to get something you really need, there are predators that hang out at those malls, too, wanting to make a connection with you for evil purposes.

Wherever the Spirit of the Lord is Strong, there are strong cross currents in the demonic realm as well. Why? Because anyone who is close to Jesus in spirit and in truth is a threat to the kingdom of darkness, so the demons are present to do everything they can to discourage you from this kind of relationship.

But the Lord protects us and leads us. If you encounter turbulence, don't be frightened; seek out an answer with us or another qualified group.

Remember at the mention of the Name of Jesus, every knee must bow, every tongue confess that Jesus Christ is Lord.

Use that name, "In the name of Jesus, I command you to leave and never return." Or the Binding Prayer, that is still the most effective prayer we have found and we keep it updated, so the most recent date is the best version.

You are the beloved of the Lord, it is absolutely true that He desires your company more than you desire His.

Getting A Word From the Lord

June 26, 2015

Your word is a lamp to my feet And a light to my path. Psalm 119:105

This channel is not just about intimacy, it's also about learning to hear from God on your own. Just about every other e-mail or private message that comes to us from our different sites is requesting a word from the Lord. But, He has asked us to keep our focus on teaching you to get your own words. Nothing mysterious about it, "Seek and ye shall find, ask and it shall be given to you."

When I first became a Christian, the church I was attending did a Bible study by Evelyn Christenson, called *Lord Change Me*. It was then that I learned to listen to the message within a message. In this very simple book, you are taught to read a section of Scripture and listen for the Lord's voice in a personal way, guiding you in your everyday circumstance. That is called a Rhema.

There are different levels of training, and as you mature, the Lord will take you into deeper waters with this practice. But for now, let's keep it simple and start with the concepts.

There are two Greek words that describe Scripture which are translated "word" in the New Testament. The first, logos, refers to the inspired Word of God and to Jesus, Who is the living Logos.

In the beginning was the Word [logos], and the Word [logos] was with God, and the Word [logos] was God. John 1:1

For the word [logos] of God is quick, and powerful. Hebrews 4:12

The second Greek word that describes Scripture is rhema, which refers to a word that is spoken and means "an utterance." A rhema is a verse or portion of Scripture that Holy Spirit brings to our attention to address a need for wisdom and for direction. So, when we are reading our Bible, all of a sudden something on the page catches our attention and is quickened by Holy Spirit for a current life situation. If we are listening very carefully, we hear the Lord's wisdom for us, right at that moment. It does take a little practice.

Man shall not live by bread alone, but by every word [rhema] that proceeds out of the mouth of God. (Matthew 4:4).

Jesus said, "The words [rhema] that I speak unto you, they are spirit, and they are life" (John 6:63).

When God gives a rhema for us to act upon, He often confirms it by a second rhema, that "in the mouth of two or three witnesses shall every word [rhema] be established" (II Corinthians 13:1).

"So, then faith cometh by hearing, and hearing by the word [rhema] of God" (Romans 10:17).

When the angel told Mary that she would have a child: "Mary said, Behold the handmaid of the Lord; be it unto me according to your word [rhema]"(Luke 1:38).

Jesus told Peter he would deny Him. *"Peter remembered the word [rhema] of Jesus, which said unto him, Before the cock crows, you will deny me three times" (Matthew 26:75).*

This is how we get our confirmations from the Lord. Our opinions about things don't matter, it's God's opinion that matters and when we want an "outside of ourselves" confirmation, we pray and open the Bible and begin to read. But, rather than using the entire Bible, we use a Bible Promise Book by Barbour Publishers. It's a book that has Scriptures sorted by different topics, so when you open it you're immediately in the midst of Scriptures about a topic like Brotherly Love, Help In Troubles, Marriage, Parent's Duties, etc. etc. As we begin to read, some of the lines will begin to really resonate deeply in our spirits. At that point, we stop and linger, soaking in the anointed words and allowing them to minister to us.

So, the way we receive guidance from the Lord is to simply pray for guidance.

As it is written: *If any of you lacks wisdom, let him ask of God, who gives to all liberally and without reproach, and it will be given to him. But let him ask in faith not doubting. James 1:5-6*

My sheep hear My voice, and I know them, and they follow Me. John 10:27

That Voice has a resonance in our hearts that no other voice can duplicate.

We approach this like an innocent little child.

Truly I tell you, unless you change and become like little children, you will never enter the Kingdom of Heaven. Matt 18:2-4

Very simply, we earnestly pray for an answer and open the Bible or the Bible Promises and start reading. As we read, one of the Scriptures written there will come forth and stand out. That's Holy Spirit making that word come alive in our hearts and minds, or a Rhema - a present-time utterance of Holy Spirit directing us according to our needs.

We prefer to get three Rhemas in a row in order to clarify and establish the Lord's train of thought. We also prefer to pray over the Bible Promise book before we open to receive a word from Holy Spirit. We have found that the enemy can also, somehow, manipulate the pages to bring up a reading counter to what God has for us. So we simply say, "In the Name of Jesus, we bind a lying spirit off this book." Believe it or not, we have many times caught the enemy infiltrating our readings! So now, for safety's sake, we always pray that prayer along with, "Holy Spirit, please guide me through this book."

Some would accuse us of fortune telling, but they aren't familiar with drawing lots, as it is used by the prophets of old, as well as the Apostles, who drew lots to choose the replacement for Judas in the first chapter of the book of Acts: "Lord, you know everyone's heart. Show us which of these two you have chosen to take over this apostolic ministry", then they cast lots, and the lot fell to Matthias; so he was added to the eleven apostles.

So, when we use the Bible Promises, we are asking the Lord (who knows everyone's heart) to reveal what is necessary for us to make the right decisions.

Trust in the LORD with all your heart and do not lean on your own understanding. In all your ways acknowledge Him, and He will make your paths straight. ...Proverbs 3:5

It is SO much easier to do it right the first time, than to plunge headlong into our own wisdom and make a choice not pleasing to God - and in the end, costing all a great deal. I would much sooner act like a five year old child throwing myself on the mercy and wisdom of God than to receive a precise report prepared by a human - who at best has limited knowledge.

Coming to God seeking wisdom was called an oracle in the Old Testament. Bible scholars call oracles 'Communications from God'. The term refers both to divine responses to a question asked of God and to pronouncements made by God without His being asked. In one sense, oracles were prophecies since they often referred to the future; but oracles sometimes dealt with decisions to be made in the present. In the Bible, the communication was from Yahweh, the God of Israel.

In times of idol worship, however, Israelites did seek a word or pronouncement from false gods (Hosea 4:12).

Many of Israel's neighbors sought oracles from their gods. THIS you could call fortune telling.

Why were oracles given? To help God's people make the right choices. There were "decision oracles" and "pronouncement oracles." Decision oracles came when people asked God a question or sought His counsel. For example, David needed to know the right time to attack the Philistines. So he asked God. The answers he received were oracles (2 Samuel 5:19, 2 Samuel 5:23-24).

Saul, the first king of Israel, was chosen through an oracle (1 Samuel 10:20-24). In that case, the communication from God was through the casting of lots. The falling of the lots was considered an oracle from God. So, this is a well-established practice from the holy prophets and patriarchs in Scriptures, not some "new age" or fortune-telling thing, not at all. This is serious business with God.

When we come to the Lord prayerfully to be instructed through His Word, we must remember that He is God and not a slot machine. He may choose to bring up something totally different than what you asked Him. There may be things in your life that He has been wanting to address for a long time and when you ask about one thing... you may very well get an answer drawing your attention to another thing.

There is a learning curve in hearing the Lord's voice through Scripture. We have to slow down our thoughts and restfully read the Scriptures. At first, you might say, "What in the world does that have to do with my question?" Well, I don't know. That's for YOU to meditate on until Holy Spirit illuminates it for you. There are no shortcuts. We all have to suffer through the toddler stage. It is painful – but SO worthwhile!

For instance, if I get really, seriously ill with something unusual, and it hasn't yielded to anointed prayer, I may ask the Lord, "Why am I feeling so badly?" Did I do something wrong, was His protection lifted because I strayed out of the corral? If He gives me the chapter on 'Salvation' or on 'Parent's Duties', it is safe to assume that, right in this hour, someone's salvation is hanging in the balance and my fast offering is going to tilt the scales. In which case, I will be happy and receive it like Simon 's cross.

However, if He gives me readings under the 'Guilt' chapter, or 'The World' - I'll know immediately the devils have been allowed to sift me for an indiscretion.

Let's say I'm invited to a conference with a speaker I really respect. I come to the Lord and ask Him if I should go and He gives me the chapter on 'Joy' and 'Loving God'. I'll take that as a confirmation that He will bless me if I go. However, if I get 'Lust' or 'The World' or 'Lying', then I will not go.

Let's say I was nosey on the internet and found something that caused me to fear. It was something that could possibly hurt us, and I gave in to fear. If I prayerfully ask Holy Spirit to tell me if this is something I should be concerned about, I might get the 'Help in Troubles' chapter, or 'Guidance'. Then I would say it is something we should be prepared to deal with.

However, if I got the chapter on 'Lying,' or 'Fear,' or 'God's Faithfulness,' I could relax and not worry about it.

As I said, it takes time to interpret what the Scriptures mean. Not everything comes easily, in fact there are many times when we just don't know what to think and we have to put it on the shelf and pray for better discernment. This is a learning process and Holy Spirit is your teacher. Each day you will learn more and more and more about how God thinks in different situations because you are constantly going to Him for advice.

There are some people who are too 'grown up' for this kind of discernment...they must find their own way. But we've been using it for 35 years and we can testify - it works.

One thing to be aware of, in all discernment situations - if you are attached to a certain outcome, or you want things to go your way, you'll have a real hard time understanding your answers. You have to be willing to completely yield to God's wisdom in everything. Ouch! There are times when you might as well not ask, because you're not going to obey Him, anyway.

Let's be real honest here: when we want our own way we're not willing to yield to God's way, and rather than pretend that your readings were confusing and you weren't sure what He was saying...well, better to not ask, because you're so attached to the outcome and not willing to hear anything else. In that case, you must be willing to pray, "Lord, I am willing to be MADE willing for YOUR answer."

Jesus Teaches on Discernment

December 12, 2014

Here's the message that I just promised you in the previous video, and, to fill you in on what was going on when I received this message, the last few days I've been assaulted with accusations that I'm not hearing from the Lord but from a demon. It hasn't been a clear-cut accusation; just a subtle hint…an undercurrent…a quiet questioning.

The Lord began, **"I want you to be totally at rest, like a child on her mother's lap."**

"Is this really you, Lord?"

I've been plagued with this fear all of my Christian life, and one reason I have is because I came from the New Age. I had to make the change from The New Age to becoming a Christian. Believe me, the last thing in the world that I wanted was to be able to speak to the Lord, in the sense that I was so afraid that I'd be deceived. That's a little background on why I'm so cautious.

As I came to sit down to praise and worship, I immediately saw my handsome Jesus, dancing with me, with a twinkle in His eyes. My Spirit just leapt inside of me! I just knew it was the Lord! He smiled and said,

"You can't deny it's Me now, can you?"

And, no, I couldn't. I knew, indeed, that it was Him! We danced for a very long time. But I grew weary of the music. It became noisy and 'in the way,' so I turned it off and sat, quietly, and I pulled a card from my daily rhema Box. It said, "Oh, how wonderful! Oh, how marvelous, is my Savior's love for me."

By the way, I encourage all of you to make your own daily rhema Box – it's like a Daily Bread box, an index card box, and in it on index cards, you can write down the Scriptures that the Lord's given you, the Prophecies, the Promises, and all kinds of things. Just put all of the cards in that little box, and when you're high and dry, and you just can't connect with the Lord, and you can't hear Him, and you feel like saying, "Where are you, God?" Go and get three cards from your rhema Box. Pray to the Holy Spirit first, and bind any Lying Spirits from the cards in the Name of Jesus, and then pull three cards from your rhema Box. That will give you a really good reading on where you are, and it will really help you to 'pull out of the ditch,' and to trust the Lord.

Truly, He was there, before me, smiling, and He said, **"All I want from you, Clare, is to receive My love."**

He began crying. **"It has taken Me so long to get you to accept my love. Please, please, don't turn Me away. And, by the way, every one of those messages was from Me. Every single one."**

"Lord, I still have doubts about Iran. Why would you give me that message?"

"Didn't I show you Obama, long before he was even visible or elected?"

"Yes, that's true."

I'd had a dream and a vision, before he was elected, and when he was giving his acceptance speech, I immediately recognized him as the man in my dream that the Lord had shown me, something like seven years before.

Anyway…just then, one of my cats came in and meowed at me, wanting to be picked up, so I lifted her up onto my lap and arranged her so that she'd be comfortable. She didn't budge; she just settled in while I petted her.

"You see? I want you to be just like her. When I come to hold you, melt in My arms, and fall into the deep place of trust. Rest, and receive the love I long to shower on you; the love that transforms all of your wounds into beacons of light, that can touch others with My healing power. I long so much to be totally received by you, and all My creatures. But they're so fearful; so scrupulous; so afraid of going astray, and hearing from a dark spirit, rather than their God. How I wish they would trust Me more."

"But Lord, you do allow deception."

"Every time I have allowed it, I have also delivered you from it and clarified why I allowed it and restored you, haven't I?"

"Yes, Lord, you have, but that's why I'm so cautious. I suspect much greater pride lurks within me than you've allowed me to see. And so, I'm afraid of being deceived."

"I have no argument for that, My love."

"Only…even if He slays me, still will I love Him. Oh boy!"

"You must be willing to be wounded for your own good. You must trust that I will not let you go far, before I correct you. And you do have a Covering."

That would be my husband. I'm very careful with my Covering, to make sure that anything that I get is from the Lord, because the last thing that I want to do is be deceived or to deceive others. That's the last thing I want.

"So, you can trust me, Clare, to provide you with accurate information, as long as your charity and humility are intact and growing. You mustn't ever let yourself grow lax in charity, or get 'too big for your britches.'"

And I'd add here that not relying upon the discernment of your Covering, in some ways, puts you in that position of being 'too big for your britches.' I think that I've mentioned before – if you've seen my other videos – that if you don't have a Covering, you can use a Rhema Box; you can use a little book called The Bible Promises Book, and pray to the Holy Spirit, and ask, "Is this the Lord I'm talking to?"

I'll tell you guys, I do this every day. You can laugh, and you can accuse me of 'Bible Roulette;' I don't care. It works! The Lying Spirits get shown up for what they are when I use The Bible Promise Book. There are times the Lord allows me to be tested one step further, and I have to bind Lying spirits off The Bible Promises, but He does reveal the truth. He uses the Rhema Box, and He uses The Bible Promises, and readings from Scripture.

"You mustn't get lax in charity or 'too big for your britches.' I try to pull you down and back in line gently. I can't help it if your pride causes you to overreact to My corrections. Sooner or later you will come to the point where you can tolerate it without becoming despondent, or rebellious, as you always do. Besides, what about that little flutter in your conscience that tells you something is not right? Are you listening to that? Yes, you have been listening, but be a little quicker to obey, when you hear that flutter. Keep your conscience clean. Always keep your conscience clean, and you will have very little to worry about in the realm of discernment. It is only when you stubbornly grab the bit in your teeth, and take off in your own direction, despite your husband's warning. But I must let you learn the harder lessons."

"This is an ongoing lesson, My Beloved. This is the fine art of discernment, and the more you abandon the purse of your own opinion, and renounce your own self-will, the easier it will become for you. But, for now, I am indeed holding you, and how wonderful it is, to have you in my arms; to see your tears of love; to hear your heart so eager for My words and so willing to obey. All of this is stunningly beautiful to Me and the very joy of My heart. Please, oh please, never give this up! You are so dear to Me! I am so comforted by you, and I derive great consolation from your love for Me, Clare. Great Consolation! And as you can see, there is so much suffering I must endure from My creatures.

"My heart needs the tender love of all My Brides."

Jesus Answers His Bride on How to See Him

March 28, 2015

The Lord had a wonderful message tonight; there were many, many answers. I've been getting so many questions about how to become more intimate with the Lord, how to have a deeper relationship with Him, how to see Him, how to hear Him. And He's been listening in on this, and tonight He weighed in on it and explained what He is needing from us, what we need to do in order to clear the way to have this intimacy with Him.

Before I go into that, I'm going to read how He began with me tonight, and to share a little bit about the Rapture and so on. We've been kind of looking at that and feeling the time getting shorter at least as this Passover Season comes around.

Tonight when I was with Him, and He was holding me so tenderly and showing me the many faces that I've adored Him in – probably three different faces that I really feel capture His personality and His moods, and just His gentleness. And when He began to appear to me more as in the Shroud of Turin – the pictures by Ray Downing, I was a little uncomfortable with it because I hadn't seen Him that way before. Tonight, as He held me, it's like His faced morphed into all these different images that I'm so fond of portraying Him, as well as the Ray Downing one, the one from the Shroud of Turing.

Thank you Lord for holding me so tenderly and showing me the many faces I have adored You in...and melding them into one.

"My Bride, I didn't want you to feel alienated from Me, I truly am all those things to you. Yes, indeed the pictures you have used capture unique facets of My person and I have no objection to you using them.

"I only want for you to be acquainted with My actual face so that you will in no way be shocked when you finally see Me."

"Oh, Sweet Lord, how kind you are to me."

"Oh Sweet Bride, how I love you."

"You certainly show it in so many ways, I am totally overwhelmed over Your gifts to us." (and then He goes on, my husband Ezekiel – he's been carrying a cross, he's been carrying something. So I said to the Lord, 'Please comfort him, Lord - please pull Him out of the place that he's in.')

"My Love, he is carrying a very heavy cross for Me right now. Shall I remove it from him?"

"Well, no. Perhaps if I explain that, he will carry it with more confidence." (And he is carrying it very peacefully, but I know it hurts.)

"Perhaps. But he has offered himself to Me as a total sacrifice so many times, and I rejoice to share with him what I must endure on behalf of souls."

"But Lord, I thought you endured all that on the cross?"

"Sins, yes - but the dynamics of brewing situations, no.

"There is much tension in Heaven right now as well. We are all on the edge of our seats, so to speak."

And I wanted to say that a dear friend of mine had a vision of the Lord on the edge of the seat of His throne. Angels had trumpets in their hands, at their sides – and they were all watching the Lord on His throne. And He was sitting on the edge of His seat, I think, looking at the Father. He was waiting, waiting...

"But Lord, I thought you said last night, 'a date has been set'?"

"I did indeed, and that is what we are waiting on. You know how it feels to wait. However you have not, nor will you ever know, what waiting for this moment is like. It is like none other in history. It is horrendous. Waiting, waiting, waiting."

"Can You tell me more?"

"No, My Love, except that you are very close."

"Close in time or close in thinking?"

"Both.

"Listen to Me, Dear One, hold up under the pressures of this life only just a little more. Don't grow weary in well doing as you began to feel today. I would say to you, you will receive your reward - but I know better. It is not for reward that you do this. You truly have been made a shepherdess, laying your life down day after day for the sheep. This is what I have always wanted for you."

"Thank You, Lord. You've done this beautiful work in me."

"There are many who wish to have this relationship with Me. I exclude no one, let that be made clear. My arms are wide open to all who seek Me...until they find Me. I am not an easy catch. I need to know how much I am wanted, I need to see a relentless Bride searching high and low for Me. Then, I shall surprise her with My presence. Most people give up way too easily - this is the majority of the problem.

"Most people give in to the lies of the enemy, 'You're not worthy.' Nothing could be further from the truth. Unless you want to say, 'Unless you are willing to seek Me until you find Me, you are not worthy.' Now that would be correct.

"The other issue of purity is also major. Two facets: one is that the more stimulus you glean from the world, the less sensitive you are to My presence, My still small voice, My gentle breeze and embrace.

"The other facet is uncleanliness. Feeding on the filth of this world makes a heart very soiled and unfit as a habitation. The house must be clean or at least committed to cleanliness."

"Wow, Lord. We needed to hear this!"

"I know. Oh, how I love each and every one that is seeking Me. That is why I am here to explain the direction they need to take. You know the things that offend Me. Sin offends Me very much. Sin in clothing, or lack of it, sin in violence, crime, hatred, gossip, backbiting, jealousy, adulteries. Soap operas are the epitome of sin and extremely noxious to Me. Like your-nose-in-fresh-dog-excrement noxious. I mean very, very bad. These things not only offend Me but also the Heavenly court, the angels and the saints. Yet in your world they are matter of fact, part everyday life.

"If My Bride wants to find Me, she must lay aside these things and purify her heart and mind from all forms of entertainment that portray sin. This means music, clothing, behavior, speech, murder mysteries, wars, things that portray sin in any form. I don't have a problem with biographies that show the progress of a soul coming to Me, that doesn't make entertainment out of their sin, but simply portray where they were and where they are coming to. It is the scintillating entertainments that spoil the perception of the delicate and clean things, dulling the senses and offending Me greatly.

"Understand that I, too, must endure what you are watching and thinking about. I, too, am in that bedroom watching unspeakable filth. I, too, am at that murder scene with all its suffering. I, too am present at that intrigue that will steal and ruin the lives of hundreds caused by greedy men. These things HURT Me.

"Please My Brides, do not watch these things in movies or TV they are SO hurtful to Me. Do not listen to music or look at magazines, billboards, pictures that depict suffering and sin."

"Lord, I remember how you recoiled at some of the images I was going to use for the nuclear war video."

Yeah, I was working on it, and I really sensed that the Lord didn't want these images in the video.

"Oh Yes, horror of horrors, I created that soul! To see his very body on fire disturbs Me deeply. Remember, I was there when that soul set fire to his body. I, too, felt the suffering. I had to work with his soul, determining his destination. No, No! Do not trouble Me with what you look at, listen to, think about. No. No. Do not put Me through that.

"How can I embrace a Bride, when her mind is full of filth such as this? These things have half-lives, they linger and linger and linger. Over and over again I must see these things as they are recalled to your memory.

"Do you understand, 'Blessed are the pure for they shall see God.' Do you now understand why so many cannot find Me in their prayers? Yes, seek Me until you find Me, but first, clean your house. Come to Me clean, create a throne room in your heart that is undefiled with the filth of this world. And I must say it is not only filth, but worldliness that is offensive to Me.

"Carnal preoccupations with cooking, sewing, decorating, buying, selling, having this and having that. Shopping. Wanting this and wanting that. Oh, those idols are detestable to Me and when I find that kind of clutter in a heart, I want to run the other way. And when I see that a soul prefers that to My company, well... My heart collapses in sadness. Oh, how could you prefer these worthless idols to Me. How could you?"

As a break here guys, I have to say, I am guilty! Guilty, guilty as charged – I have done that. I have gotten distracted on the Internet, I've gone shopping – sometimes when you're upset, you go run to the store and go shopping, and walk around – that kind of thing.

"I'm not talking about when you fall into a mood, or are deeply hurt and disappointed and you head for the Hagen-daas and a movie. Although keep the movie pure. I'm talking about making a conscious decision to forego time with Me in order to do useless things. That's why I get so disappointed with you when you follow rabbit trails on the Internet. What a waste of time. And you are getting much better My Love, not following news stories that bait your curiosity. Much better.

"These are willful sins you do not recognize. Pray: 'Oh Lord cleanse me from my unknown sins.' When you get done surfing, you feel conviction, 'You know, I shouldn't have wasted all that time.' Your heart sinks a little, knowing you've disappointed Me. Not only have you wasted time, you've also filled your mind with unnecessary cares. Then you speak them out to others and pass them around, so you not only affect yourself but others as well, giving them a bad example.

"Do you see what I see, now?"

"Yes, Lord, even for the first time, I am understanding some things and why I feel a certain way after doing something that wasn't your perfect will."

"Well, My Brides, I am not saying this to condemn you, do you understand that? I am answering your prayers. This is what I require of you, this is why you have such a hard time seeing and hearing Me. Work on this and I will bless you with visitations and consolations. I promise you.

"Well, that's enough to chew on for tonight My dove. Thank you for responding to Me so readily. All the dear ones on your channel have been on My heart, and now we can all work together to fulfill your dreams and desires to be with Me.

"I love you all dearly and tenderly. I am coming for you. Prepare yourselves."

Well after that word, you're probably thinking, what's left to me to watch? You know, sometimes we feel like we need a distraction, something to change the subject. Well, we watch children's movies (that aren't atheistic, we're careful about that) and nature movies. Documentaries as long as there is no obnoxious content and simple cartoons like Simon's Cat or Animal Babies. You know, something like that is humorous and cheers you and changes the subject, especially when you're dealing with counseling souls – it gets kinda heavy after a while.

We are pretty simple in that way, you could get much more heady with intellectual programs and interviews and biographies. Just don't walk away from these things all cluttered in your mind, and be sure that there's really nothing impure in that, that they're rated for children and the general public. NOT R-rated – oh please don't watch anything R-rated. Even PG-13 is questionable.

Thank you all for listening to our channel. My heart has been burdened for you as well, in helping you to be able to get in touch with the Lord in this way. He's not excluding anyone. I do want to draw your attention to some of my earlier videos – I did quite a long series on Intimacy with the Lord. Everything I gave you in that was given to me by the Lord. It's just that since they are earlier videos, people aren't going back to them.

But I really encourage you to check out the playlist, and in the playlists you'll see the ones on Intimacy, those playlists. I think they would be very, very helpful to you.

Also, I hope you're listening to the music I put together on a playlist, which you can find on my main channel page.

The Lord bless you with a sweet, sweet experience with Him. Please don't be discouraged or think that you have so far to go. One step forward in the journey, He'll match it with a hundred steps and it won't be long before you are right where you need to be. He will bless you with your efforts. You don't have to be perfect – just desire to be there and He'll do all the work.

SECTION FIVE

Messages to Show You the Attitudes He is Looking for In You

Come to Me, My Lost and Lonely Ones

July 15, 2015

"No good thing will I withhold from those who love Me, according to My purpose for their lives. I have not forsaken anyone. People forsake Me. They don't trust Me when their prayers aren't answered according to their advantage, as they see it. This causes so many to fall away from Me. They have no concept of how I love them or how infinite My wisdom is. Rather, they blame Me for the things that go wrong in their lives, even though it is Satan who is the culprit. They come to Me and pray that things would be different, but I cannot answer them with what they want, because I see the path ahead and I know the road they must travel.

"From time to time, you get atheists who have been jaded by phony Christians, or Christians less than perfect...yet when atheists act badly it goes by unnoticed. I wish they would apply the same standards to their atheist brothers and sisters that they apply to My children. I wish I could tell them, 'My Children aren't perfect any more than you are... but they ARE forgiven. And many, many are trying to change with My help.' You don't always see what's behind that Christian's life. You don't see what they were like before I got ahold of them."

“I'm thinking of myself now, Lord. Whew! not good, not good at all. Selfish, proud, deeply entangled in materialism and impressing people. Not able to form deep friendships, give or receive love. But, something in me changed, when the Lord got hold of me. It took years for Him to change me. But it did change. I’m not perfect, I still have problems with all those things, but not anything like I was living before.”

"Love came into your life. The kind of love you had always dreamed of: a holy, loving companion. I came and revealed to you Who I was, indeed. And who you were, to Me. So special, so very special. You had never had anyone treat you like that, you had never ever been understood by others. You never felt secure in your life until I entered into your heart. You knew beyond a shadow of a doubt that I Am God and yet 'have nothing better' to do than hang around with you: guiding you, protecting you and teaching you about My Kingdom.

“Your church experience was not any better than any of your other experiences - you weren't accepted there any more than you were accepted in the non-Christian community. But, one thing you did have: a personal relationship with Me. You touched the hem of My garment, day after day, and through that you survived the bad things that happened to you even at church.

"You see, religion and God bear no resemblance to one another. Religion is a system fostered by men to get closer to God. Whereas, I embrace you without the rules and regulations, even without the knowledge of My Name. There are those who know Me in their hearts and spirits and follow all I ask them to do. Then, someday when the time is ripe, I reveal Myself to them.

"Yet, there are others who have been handled so roughly in their lives, they have no hope of love or of being accepted. I must surprise them with My Love. I must take them in a moment they are least expecting and shower them with My profound, unconditional love.

"There are many who blame Me for every bad thing that has happened in their lives, because they don't want to give up their sin. Somewhere, inside their hearts, they hear My voice - but the world and its allurements overpower them and they ignore it until it's too late.

"I am always calling, always waiting, always with them, wanting to bring healing into their lives. But, they must at least be willing to give up sin and receive My Love. The pleasures of the flesh call much more loudly than I, so I must wait until the flesh is old and weak. But, even then there is no guarantee that the bitterness they are holding onto will allow them to hear Me. So, I allow them to languish in nursing homes until I can reach them and bring them Home.

"Oh, how sad it is when a soul has closed the door on My Love and has nothing in this world to turn to. Alone, abandoned many times through their own fault, they are so convinced of their own personal righteousness that there is no room for repentance. All is the fault of others - they were the innocent victims. God is to blame for all.

"Clare, I want you to love the unlovable. Go out of your way for those who have rejected Me. Be My hands, My feet, My mouth and My ears. At least in that final moment, I can reason with them. I can remind them of your kindness, even when they didn't deserve it. This, many times, is the very last straw on their resistance and they break...a flood of tears, a deep knowledge of their sins and an even greater knowledge of how enormously special they are to Me...so special, that I endured torture to bring them to Heaven with Me forever. I treasure them, I love them and I embrace them, never to part.

"These are the days when many souls will be rescued in this way. That is why I am constantly admonishing you to love the unlovable. They are the most destitute of all, even and especially those who have known wealth."

"Lord, You are blamed for all the terrible things the Israelites were commanded to do. Few seem to care to find out why You did what You did, when you ordered the armies to murder men, women and children and just totally wipe out a town. People don't understand that, and that's why they see You as being too harsh, a terrible God."

"They did not hear the terrifying, heart-rending screams of infants, when they were laid in red-hot, metal bowls and sacrificed to Moloch. They did not see the perversion the people had with the animals - not even the animals could escape their wickedness. They did not see the mating rituals with demons, who impregnated them with evil and demonic powers. Little has been understood down through the ages as to why My people had to destroy every living thing. Yet, My Word is not lacking in explanations. I make it clear that the wickedness was beyond repair.

"And now, you are approaching the Days of Noah, as it was in the Days of Noah. Yes, every perversion and wickedness will be allowed by law. Fondling young children, sex with animals, men with men and women with women - all of it is coming, just as surely as I Am. It is here, but still shunned. Not for long. The laws that have been signed and are in the works will make every detestable practice more legal than pornography. Now there will be no age limits - all may come and see and try it for themselves. After all, it brings pleasure, and pleasure is your right and your freedom.

"I am calling to you, My Children, My wayward ones. Forsake your loneliness. Forsake the lies, the darkness, the confusion. Come. Come to Me, all who are weary and heavy laden. You will find rest for your soul and unconditional love for your heart. I will never turn you away. I will never forsake you – rather, your life shall grow brighter and brighter, going from glory to glory. I am not a man, that I should lie. I have good in store for you, not evil. I have gifts and talents for you, things you've longed to do. Who do you suppose put that longing in you? Now I want to bring fulfillment and happiness to your life. Your sins have only brought you grief and disappointment. It's time to make a change, time to release all the old baggage and start anew: fresh, born again.

"I am calling to you, My lost ones. Come to Me. I will embrace you and ring you round with songs of gladness and thanksgiving for returning to the very womb that bore you. Yes, I will dress you in fine linen and place a ring upon your finger, sandals upon your feet and we shall walk together as one. Just tell Me you are tired of being hurt. Tired of hurting others. That you are sorry for the sinful things you have done. Ask My forgiveness - then hand over your life to Me. I will cherish you. I will lead and guide you. I will never forsake you. I will lead you by the hand into Eternal Joy in My Father's Kingdom in Heaven, forever."

'Jesus, forgive me, I give you my life. Teach me, lead me, never ever depart from me.'

Turn to The Lord (song)

Turn to the Lord
He's longing to see you
His arms will enfold you
In love forever more
Turn to the Lord

Return to the Lord
You're called and chosen
And now that you're broken
He's calling you back home
Return to the Lord

Turn Back to Me
Your worth is not in silver
Nor days filled with pleasure
Nor things you can measure
They're lost forever more
Turn back to Me

Come, come to Me
My love's without measure
And you are My Treasure
My joy forever more
Come here to Me
Come, O come, here to Me.

I Want Your Whole Heart, Jesus Said

February 17, 2015

God bless you Youtube family. This is an entry from our book *Chronicles of the Bride*, October 27, 2007.

What's very interesting about it is it really correlates with the last two things that I had posted about intimacy and communicating with the Lord. This is another confirmation to that Valentine's Day video that I just put out. I came upon it totally by surprise. Again, it was the Holy Spirit's reading.

We picked up the *Chronicles of the Bride* today to get a reading and it opened to this page. We trust the Holy Spirit to pick out readings for us. He did it and brought up something else that would be very helpful to us in our desire to hear the Lord clearly.

By the way I had two people report back to me that the binding prayer has worked for them immediately. One of those people has had a tremendous battle hearing and seeing the Lord but he had a break through immediately. If this is given by the Holy Spirit then He knows what He's doing. He knows what the devils are up to.

When I came into worship today I saw a devil in the corner and he was fuming mad. It was a large devil and nasty looking. Like a miniature Satan with a large head. He was so angry with me. I had barely got the name of Jesus out of my mouth and he was gone. So somebody is upset about that and that's good.

I'll begin this message then:

Jesus said, **"Trust Me child I want to speak familiarly with you. It is a good and wise thing to test the sprits, however within so much time in a known relationship it is important to move forward and be natural; that you may enjoy the consolation of friendship in a comfortable way. This is the way I want to be with you. This is the way I want to be with all of My children.**

"Yet so many are busy with other things, the cares of this world and their allurements soon build a wall of interference by which I can only communicate myself to them in circumstances, in distant ways. Many say I speak to them in and through My written Word. Just as with so many other things, I brought the Scriptures forth for their edification and good, but also for their hardness of hearts. I knew that men were weak and easily pulled away by their wandering minds and flesh. I could speak familiarly with my servant Moses, as one man speaks to another. But the rest had to hear Me from the spoken Word in My inspired writings."

I believe what He is saying here, is that the Scriptures are necessary for teachings and edification and He is present to us through His Holy Word. But in the beginning, when God walked with Adam in paradise, written words were not necessary since they conversed with one another on a daily basis. In Heaven, too, we will always honor and treasure the Scriptures as God's Word, but we will again have Him to speak to us familiarly on a daily basis because our hearts will be renewed with tenderness, holiness, and with nothing of the world to distract or pull us away from our full intentions on Him.

Jesus continues, **"And so, which would you prefer? To have a guest you spoke to only as through a curtain - or to have a guest you could see and hear and converse easily with?**

"I have placed no barrier between Me and My disciples but they regularly keep a wall between us. I love and cherish them with all of my heart and I would that all would come to know me intimately.

"Pray for this grace, but know that it comes at a cost. Are you truly willing to change your lifestyles to accommodate that kind of closeness with Me? It will surely mean a serious change for most. Are you willing to put away all of the distractions in your life and make room for Me exclusively? Can you make the sacrifice of many things; friends, books, entertainment, and so on?"

I want to say that that has been a struggle for me. I think one of the things that brought me to my senses was the understanding about the Rapture. Before I really knew that the Rapture was the real deal, I think I was a little sloppy.

When I found out the Rapture was real, I looked very seriously at what I was spending my time on. I came under heavy conviction when I went off to go shopping for entertainment, so to speak. Like when I would go to look at something just to get my mind off problems. I put that stuff away totally. Instead of doing it maybe once a year I just put it totally away. I don't do it at all. There is a cost and it is challenging but it is so rewarding.

"I'm here for every soul I create. I never change, nor do I sleep or rest. I am constantly looking at you, waiting for you, yearning and longing to spend time with you, and speak to you My heart. You have only to gird up your courage and try. I will most assuredly meet your efforts if they are fully from the heart with no preconceived opinions of your own. Give to Me your whole will and intellect. Ask to made again as a little child. Peacefully wait for Me and be patient and I will visit with you in ways before you never imagined.

"Only make room for Me. I want your whole heart. Your strong and earnest desire and pursuit of Me and Me alone. I will give you the abundant grace but you will you avail yourself to it?"

That's the end of the message.

So with that in mind I pray for you, myself, and all of us that we can continue to put the world outside and leave it outside. That we may continue to expand in that intimate space for the Lord; in time of silence and precious space for us to commune with Him.

The Lord bless you, Youtube family and thank you for tuning into our channel.

SECTION SIX

Messages to Show You How Deceiving Spirits Work

How Deceiving Spirits Work

December 6, 2014

Ezekiel: Welcome to Heaven Talk. Dream, visions, comment and discussion on all things Heaven. I'm Ezekiel.

Clare: And I'm Clare.

Ezekiel: Here in the foothills of Taos, New Mexico, the Sangre de Cristo Mountains. Good Evening!

Clare: Well, YouTube family, we've really had a heart for people who've been sorely disappointed because the Rapture didn't happen around Thanksgiving as we had mentioned before. And in fact, I have a letter from one lady; I'll read you a segment from it.

She said, "Part of the reason we were both so fooled by these 'end dates' for the Rapture (as we thought of them,) was it gave so much hope that the abuse and hardness of this world would finally be ending. The Lord told us a few days ago that He allowed us to hear these dates because we wanted to hear them so much (we were too attached to the answer, so the demons were able to step in.) That He's been here with us all along and He loves us. So, we're praying that our words are clean and that our discernment is good, but I don't feel like I have any discernment at all.

Clare: I think a lot of us felt that way in this last week or two weeks.

Ezekiel: Yeah, it's been kind of foggy, off and on.

Clare: Yes, like some kind of static storm, or something like that, very static-y and stormy.

Ezekiel: Yeah, some definite oppression interference.

Clare: It's so subtle, you know. This oppression is so subtle that we don't really realize that it's an oppression. And I think that there's an art form to that that the demons use. They make it subtle, so that you don't notice it, it just kinda of creeps in on you.

Ezekiel: Yeah, yeah. Well you wake up some days and you feel like "Where am I? What? Lord you just spoke to me, or I thought you did?" Or you flip back to your journal and see what the word was He gave you or what your Scriptures were, but you don't feel it. And I think sometimes there's a – we can't really trust our feelings can we?

Clare: No, and the demons definitely toy with our feelings. And I have already put out just a Youtube with a very simple message from the Lord. But I think it would be good to read it again tonight just for you, just to kind of spark our conversation here. I have it on my computer, so forgive me for looking to the side.

The Lord began:

"My heart is deeply grieved by the many deceptions My Bride has fallen into during these last days. Did I not warn you that many would come in My Name?

"Nonetheless it is not your fault, as much as it is the fault of the shepherds. So let Me begin by saying, 'No one knows the day nor the hour.' Not even I. You do know the season, and yes, this is the season."

Clare: We all know that! Real strong feeling of that!

Ezekiel: Close. Right at hand!

"My Bride you must be more clever than the demons assigned to you. These vile creatures know you better than you know yourself. And that's why knowing yourself has become so important."

Clare: And He gave a list of the things, the way that the different doors open so easily. And I'll go through that real quickly.

"Pride, Flattery, Self-seeking, is the number one open door for their entrance...they tell you, you are so special, and so different than the others, you are specially chosen to receive secret knowledge."

Clare: So they play on your pride and your vanity.

"And may I say, all of you, each and every one, all of you are unique and special in your own way. Period. So don't let them tempt you by putting you on some kind of pedestal. And as far as secret knowledge goes, now you are taking on the New Age mentality that capitalizes on the esoteric."

Clare: You definitely don't want to go there. And you know that I wanted to make a point about that. Any time in the Christian community that there's a sense that someone has 'secret knowledge,' that they have a special relationship with God that is so special and that he confides all of his secrets – I mean, the Scriptures do talk about confiding things to your prophets – but when it becomes a thing, when it becomes like a movement, when people get drawn into the idea of the mysterious, and the esoteric, and the 'highly advanced' and so on and so forth – this is NOT the Lord. That is definitely the devil's trap.

Be careful about saying that it's a move of God because it's producing some exclusivity and bitterness and that's taking the Lord's name - Yeshua, Yahweh, and using Father God, and using the name Jesus, and some people are highly offended that you use the name Jesus and I want to tell you, the demons know what the name Jesus means. We've been in deliverance situations where we use the name of Jesus and it works perfectly. There's not one issue with that name. The issue is I think more with people who kind of get puffed up and proud and say "Well, this is the right name and this is the way you should say it." And it causes scandal and division in the body.

Ezekiel: Confusion.

Clare: Yeah, confusion. It's like, people are used to calling the Lord, you know, especially older people, by the name of Jesus and the Father and so on. And we . . .

Ezekiel: Cuts a whole heck of a lot of nice praise songs, doesn't it.

Clare: Oh yeah, there's all kinds of praise songs we can't sing (if this were true), and because some people are so adamant about this, it's really pride that causes them to rise up and condemn other people who don't use the "proper name" for the Lord. And I don't think this is a good thing. I think we need to be really careful. I think it's beautiful that people use the Hebrew names and feel comfortable with it.

But for the ones that don't feel comfortable with it, we need to cut them some slack.

Ezekiel: Yeah I mean we're swallowing camels, right, and straining out gnats. You know, we're warned not to take part in foolish arguments, aren't we.

Clare: Exactly and that's another good point. I mean, I don't want to argue over these things. It's ridiculous.

Ezekiel: Divide and conquer. Divide and conquer.

Clare: And I think that we are probably in the not too distant future going to do a segment on the suffering of the Lord, and maybe we can bring some of that up tonight. The visions that you've had of the Lord's suffering because people are ripping and tearing at the body. Could you share that?

Ezekiel: We're just crucifying Him all over again. In fact, the meeting I mentioned earlier - I got to a point that I went to the hardware store and I bought three railroad spikes and before this man passed away (the way he did, it was unfortunate and tragic) - at the next meeting I was going to come and just lay those spikes on the table and walk away. You know? Try to kind of let him get the message. How many nails are you going to continue to drive into the body? How do we assassinate? We've got to remember, that lady at the church we just talked about, or that sister or brother, the preacher or pastor, that's Jesus that we're taking a bite of!

Ezekiel: We can't do that – that's like a cancer eating the body. You know, eating itself.

Clare: Right – right. And like you've said so many times before, is that if you have a child who's challenged or disabled or someone does, you don't point at the child and say "Look they can't even walk!" or whatever. You don't say that to the parents.

Ezekiel: That would be very hurtful.

Clare: You're very compassionate, and you pray for them. You pray for the healing of that child. I hate that bumper sticker "Christians Kill Their Wounded" – but you know what? There's substance to that. And a lot of us, (and I notice even on Youtube,) we get some rather harsh remarks. (laughs)

And you know, God love 'em, I think some people think they are doing the Lord a favor by bludgeoning other Christians into knowledge. "You WILL know the truth! I am going to tell you the truth now!"

And it's just sad, even amongst the denominations, I mean we've experienced the Lord in the Orthodox Church, you know the one with all the ceremonies. We've experienced the Lord in the Evangelical Church, in the Pentecostal Church, in the Methodist Church. We've experienced Him in the Catholic Church. It grieves my heart when people speak against a denomination and speak against things and oftentimes there's no substance to what they're saying. They don't know.

Ezekiel: Parroting. Just parroting what someone said, and someone said, and someone said. I have a friend who was in Northern Africa for some time. He told me, "Even though I'm an Evangelical Christian, I hadn't seen a Christian forever. I was in these Muslim nations and states and provinces. And I was like a hungry, tired, thirsty man looking for water. I came upon a group of monks in a Coptic (which is Egyptian) Christian church. And the priests and the monks came out - I didn't care who they were, what they were, what their name was. I saw that Cross. I knew that they were Christian. I saw the Scriptures, I didn't care – I was so glad to see another Christian! It had been a year!

Clare: Yeah, and you can really feel the presence of the Lord in another Christian.

Ezekiel: You may need to know each other by the Spirit.

Clare: Absolutely. I mean, these are the same people right now who are being beheaded for their faith. You know, while we are at our shopping malls and our daily jobs.

Ezekiel: Even their children. Even their children!

Clare: Children are dying for their witness to the Lord. And they're in these Coptic churches.

Ezekiel: Not just Coptic, you know - Palestinian Christians, others – the Christians of the East or Middle East, or whatever.

Clare: Right, right. Not just evangelicals, but these are people who are in the churches that have liturgies, and they are dying for the witness. They won't renounce the name of Jesus, and that's why they're beheading them.

Ezekiel: Yeah, so you know, I'm not here to argue somebody's rite or ritual or history or as many would say, man's precepts or such. I don't care – we all have the traditions we have in our families. In our cultures. I don't care. When they love Jesus and they're willing to lay their life down on the line? Man, it put me to shame.

Clare: Yeah, well we all have traditions. And some of the traditions are Holy Spirit inspired, and some of them aren't. I think the ones that aren't - we need to get rid of.

Ezekiel: You know the argument these days is "Oh, we don't have religion. We don't have religion, we just have faith." What IS that good religion – you use the word religion? To feed the widow and the orphan. You know, give it a break guys. We are just, we get on these little – we're fundamentalists as well, aren't we, over here in this country. Fundamentalism, whether Shiite or Christian, is dangerous. Let's be careful that we're not putting Him back on the Cross and bludgeoning Him with the whips and driving the nails.

Clare: Well, you know, moving back to this whole thing on discernment, and you know, even though that is a little bit off the topic of discernment, it's a very good point, because when we criticize other people, we open ourselves up to demonic manifestation.

Ezekiel: Deception, deception big time.

Clare: Oh my gosh. In our marriage, I mean, we found out early in our marriage that if we come out of a place – let's say we're wounded, you know how it is when you're wounded in a church. If you come out of that church wounded, and you go home and you talk about it and you start to cop an attitude about the people and what they said and what they did. And then I noticed we'd start fighting between ourselves. And we noticed this pattern for a few years before we finally 'got it', DUH!

Ezekiel: We started to say, "What opened the door?"

Clare: We got it. What opened the door? We opened the door by criticizing other people.

Ezekiel: I think that's the quickest way the Lord will bring any of us down, is the minute we open our mouth -- our heart. We might not even say it, but a heart judgment. He's going deep to the things that matter. The judgments of our heart and our mind. We're all wounded and we all need healing. He has been so firm with us, I mean to the point of breaking us into fine powder over the years, to stamp out any judgment – we just can't have it.

Clare: Yeah. And it will affect your discernment, and the Lord will allow you to fall. And of course, as we judge others, we'll be judged. That's another facet of that the Lord warns us about.

So, I think I mentioned **the first one was Pride**: flattery, self-seeking was the number one open door.

And then **number two, Loneliness** is the second open door. We're talking here about how mistakes in discernment happen, how we allow the enemy in. So, Loneliness is the second open door. Failed marriages, feeling of being isolated, bitter failures in business or in church, rejection and wounds from others in the Christian body -- these are all things that can leave us -- what's the word -- wounded and debilitated and open to an attack from the enemy. Because he looks for you when you're weak. He wants to hurt you when you're down and you're weak.

Ezekiel: Wounded fish syndrome.

Clare: Yeah. He sends – he waits, he watches, he sets up situations so that you'll get injured. Then he comes in on the heels of that and starts pounding you. And then you start pounding the other people and then that opens the door wider and it just gets worse. So, Loneliness and failed marriages and isolation, that also is an open door.

The **third one is Attachment** to anything you want. Along with it goes self-well, disobedience, thinking you know better. Oh boy, have I been guilty of that.

Ezekiel: How many times have you gone to the Lord and it's like: "Oh, please say yes, oh please say yes." Or "Oh please say no, Oh please say no! I don't want to have to go over there, tell me this in this order . . . " You know. And He's given you Scriptures on brotherly love and everything, but we're actually trying to get some Scripture to justify us not going to see the sick sister or brother because we're lazy and we don't want to go! You know - attachments like that – attachment to the outcome of whatever it is you are trying to discern. "Oh I need this to be the Lord, I want this to be the Lord, because I want this vision so much" or this 'whatever' so much.

Clare: Remember, just not so long ago, I had an opportunity to buy a label maker and a CD burner, and I thought "we really need this" and the Lord put His foot down. And I was just, oh, I was just so upset about that.

Ezekiel: You were crestfallen.

Clare: Oh, I was terribly crestfallen. Here I loved to work with graphics and Photoshop and we need labels on our DVDs ... and He said "no". And I had to go with that, you know, but not without a little bit of an interior fight. That's for sure. (laughter)

Ezekiel: Poor Jesus! (laughter)

Clare: That's right!

Ezekiel: She told me one day, "You better pray for me, the Lord and I are having a fight." I said, "I am going to pray for Him!" (laughter) Just kidding!

Clare: Oh Lord…. OK. So that's the open door – Attachment. If you really want something the demons will oblige you. And they'll say you can have it, just to get you off track.

And then **Self-hatred came up as a fourth**. The survival instinct kicks in to counteract the terrible self-image we have of ourselves, whether real or imagined, to keep yourself from giving up on life. We tend to construct a fantasyland of being special, to protect the projected ugliness that we're so afraid to see. So, we create this fantasy world and the demons are only too happy to oblige us in that.

Ezekiel: Oh, you have all kinds of neat visions and dreams and words and everything. But you know, are we willing, as you said, to be made willing to just be honest and look at the truth of who we really are and who we're really not? The Lord's trying to get the false stuff out of the way so He CAN give us the good stuff!

He's not trying to hurt us or take away our life…

Clare: And we're not half as bad as we think we are on one level.

Ezekiel: No, no.

Clare: But the other thing that the Lord was very careful to speak to me, and I am going to share that to you – He said:

"Now I am going to advocate two way communication with the use of Rhemas."

Clare: That's an illuminated word from the Lord, which you can get from a Bible, or a book or a bumper sticker or a billboard.

Ezekiel: When something just stands out to you on a page.

Clare: Yeah, yeah, and there's a flutter in your soul, in your heart. You can feel the Holy Spirit has arranged that --whatever you saw. We have a special way that we do that and I'll be showing that to you in just a second. So, you may be familiar with the little daily bread boxes that people put on their tables. Well, it's a system very much like that except it's using a book. And the book that we use is called The Bible Promises (which I have a different cover on it now).

Ezekiel: People will give it to you for Christmas gifts – Precious Bible Promises, or whatever.

Clare: Things like "Repentance", and different readings will come up.

Ezekiel: Don't just stop at the title, like "Oh I got Repentance", or "Oh I got God's Love, so I can do this." Actually read the Scriptures and see what He's trying to say. In fact, what He's had me doing lately, when a Scripture stands out to me in a little book like this or a devotional -- go look up the Scripture so that I can read into the chapter and see what He might be trying to say and more narrow it down or flesh it out more fully. Right?

Clare: Right. Well, the reason I'm bringing this up is because this has saved us from many false words. We'll open this little book and it will open up to "Lying", and "Lust in the Flesh", and "Jealousy", and "Lying" and we'll know that we've got a Lying spirit.

Ezekiel: Yeah, and this is not "Dip for Script" or some kind of Ouija or crystal ball or that.

Clare: So the Lord, He's actually verifying that He wants us to use this. Because you know, if the people who thought that the Rapture was going to be before Thanksgiving had done that, they would have gotten "Lying" and they would have realized they had a Lying Spirit telling them all sorts of things that weren't true.

Now, this is what He said. He said:

"I don't care what the devil has planted in other people's minds about this being divination or childish. They are wrong. And unless the motives turn to divination, there's nothing wrong with it."

"I will explain: If you are seeking Me for the sake of obedience, and you pray to the Holy Spirit and ask for what He wants, the Lord will protect you. But, if you are seeking answers out of insecurity, or wanting to foretell the future, have secret knowledge, or impressing others, you are bordering on divination"

Clare: Watch out! Then you are into borderline divination, and the devil has a counterfeit for everything. So it's legitimate to have a Rhema or a word from the Lord, and of course the devil copycats that with something evil or he puts in people's minds that it's wrong.

Ezekiel: Well, I'd like to also say that many of us, when we first came to the Lord, we didn't know how to do a Bible study, or do this or do that. We just, by the Holy Spirit, began to read the Scriptures at some point. And it was amazing how He would lead a lot of us as new believers exactly to what He wanted.

Some of us just closed our eyes and stuck our finger on a page. (You gotta be careful doing that, you might get something like "God has utterly rejected you.") Ahhhh!! (laughter). But what we do when we get Rhemas, whether from our Scriptures or the little Bible Promise or devotional book, something – we make a card, a file card, like a little recipe card. And we keep them. Man, we've got boxes of cards from years back. And every now and then, when I need a confirmation outside of myself, I'll ask my wife or someone else to pray and see if they can get a word from the Lord. I probably won't even tell 'em what it's about. But I'll go to one of those little daily bread boxes – homemade daily bread boxes . . .

Clare: Yeah, that we put together, with index cards.

Ezekiel: And I don't like to go to hers, because they've got some tough, disciplinary, fasting hard words! But when I really need to know, I go to the hard boxes! (laughter). And sure enough, He'll give me something real loving and tender and good. But, a tripod stands on three legs, right, and testimony is verified on two or three witnesses. So we really believe in a second and third witness from the Scriptures.

Clare: Navigation. You know, like you're out in the ocean and you get one reading but you need another one to intersect that so that you know exactly where you are. Well, I never did quite finish reading what the Lord had given me after He said that that's borderline divination, when you're trying to foretell the future. You know, that's not what this is about.

He said: "Your motives have to be pure and detached from your own personal agenda. My priests and prophets used this form of acquiring discernment with Me far before your culture made it popular. So, I endorse the use of the Bible Promises or the Scriptures to receive understanding from Me when other means aren't working. Ideally, you should feel the truth deep within your soul, a place no demon can enter or imitate."

"Remember, the devils look for your weak point, they know your history, they capitalize on that. It's easy to tailor the deception or should I say the bait, to hook you. So if you know yourself and understand My ways, you will be less likely to grab the bait and run with it.

"Doing anything to impress, influence, or please others makes you vulnerable and easily manipulated. Any kind of selfish ambition, what so ever, makes you an attractive target for the demons.

"Even your desire to be used to help others, if it's not moderated and strictly mandated by Me, can also make you a target. In short, any impurity in your motives can make you vulnerable; wanting a title, to do or be someone different or important, to control, influence, manipulate others, it opens the door wide to demonic manifestation.

"So your safest posture is pure love and devotion to Me and Me alone, and to love your brother as you love yourself."

Clare: And these are just guidelines that He's given me because there are so much pain right now. Discernment is so difficult. There's such a proliferation of evil and demons are constantly finding new ways to deceive us.

And if there's sin in your life, if there's unconfessed sin, He will let you fall. Whether you use a Bible or you don't use a Bible to verify it, He will let you fall if there's sin.

So your motives not only have to be pure but your life has to be pure. So many times, we don't know that we're sinning against the Lord. Like He's brought up pride to me in an area that I never even imaged I was prideful.

Ezekiel: We've come so far in this protective shell within the church and the killing of the wounded, that we certainly don't let anyone know about anything. We're not vulnerable and we're not going to confess our sins one to another, so even good friends won't share their weaknesses. Why? Because all of a sudden that friend gets on the Internet and types a bashing letter about whatever. It might not even hit you, but they're talking about your situation. And if you're not comfortable with that and they didn't ask your permission, it makes you feel terrible. We have got to be able to be transparent and real with each other without the fear of "they're going to use it against me" – you know? Backlash. And we think, people are terrible for confessing their sins to a priest or something. Wow. You know, same kind of fear. If we can't share our burdens . . . safely – we've got to be safe.

Clare: Yeah. Well, I think that pretty well wraps it up. We wanted to share the Lord's heart with you on discernment, and encourage you. And give you some guidelines that He's used with us for many, many years to verify when He is indeed speaking with us or when we've let a familiar spirit in.

Ezekiel: And don't be afraid to ask for help with discernment. I mean, no person is an island. Notice I was inclusive – male or female (laughter). Ask others to pray for you and for situations – and you don't have to give them all the details. It's even better if you don't sometimes.

Clare: So I thought it might be a good idea just to take a moment and show you some of the different things that we use for discernment.

First of all, first and foremost, the Scriptures. Any really good Bible will work. But something that speaks to you for sure, something that has a real meaning to you that you can understand easily.

Sometimes I'll take a reading from The Ways of the Desert Fathers, which is some ancient wisdom, ancient Christian wisdom. Praying with the early Christians.

Another person I like to use just for encouragement is Laurie Beth Jones. She has a number of books that are Christian motivational. She takes examples from the life of Jesus and applies them to worldly situations that we might find ourselves in.

I also like Rick Joyner and I'll get a Rhema from one of his books sometimes. It's nice to have a little bit to choose from sometimes and to have a little color in your reading sometimes. You don't always want it to be just black and white Scripture. Sometimes you can use someone else's viewpoint. It's very useful to help you see something in a new light.

And then, here's The Bible Promise Book that I was talking about. It's just straight Scripture and it's organized by topics like: Fruitfulness, God's Love, Brotherly Love, Lying, Jealousy, Lust, Eternal Life. It's really, really useful because it is pure Scripture and it is broken down into different subjects and topics.

Here's one of our card files. (shows box with index cards in it.) It's a big'un! It's a double sized one. But we'll make a card and sometimes we'll color it and do different things with it, depending . . . it's just Scripture written down, or a word that we received in prayer, or prophecy that someone gave us. We'll write it down on a card and we'll keep it in here. And then on those gray, gloomy, foggy, misty days when you just don't feel like you can quite connect with the Lord and you don't know the reason why, I'll go to this little box and I'll pick three cards out to get my bearings. And it's just amazing how the Holy Spirit is reading your mail. I mean, He's right there with you.

You're trying to please the Lord. You're trying to be obedient. You're trying to love Him and give Him your life more fully. He's not going to give you a snake when you ask for a fish.

The problem with a lot of these people who claim they've heard from the Lord is that they don't have any external backing. They don't have verification. There's a few that do and they talk about their back-up and their pastor and so on. And of course, my husband and the words that we use here.

But if you don't have a husband and if you can't really trust people at church, use the Scriptures and The Bible Promises or homemade Bible promises like your own little book. These are my own little homemade books that I've done and they have different little readings in here. Just a little reading like that, it says: *I will cut a road through all my mountains and make my highways level (Isaiah 49:11).*

You know, something like that at a time when you're facing monumental challenges can really, really, really encourage you and give you hope. It confirms that you're on the right path; that you're going in the right direction.

I think that a lot of people, if they had recourse to this method of discernment, they wouldn't get off into trouble as much. The Lord would be able to rein them back a little more easily by giving them a word that they could meditate on and that would apply to their situation. And that's what's so wonderful about using confirmations is that they are so on target, that there's times when you say "Wow, I don't think I could have said it any better myself! Thank you, Lord!" And "From all those pages in the book, You gave me this reading. It's just what I needed to hear."

So, I want to encourage you all to press in and do hear from the Lord and do persist with that. Because it's a skill, just like typing is a skill, driving is a skill. It takes time to learn it. Don't give up because you failed – that's the worst thing you can do and that's what the devil wants. He doesn't want people discerning God's clear voice in their lives at all. He wants to sow confusion, so don't give up.

God Bless You!

Tag Along Monsters, When You Fall...

December 12, 2014

Tonight I want to share with you a message that I wrote. There'll be a message from the Lord in the next message after this. This is basically something I wrote based on my experience. I call it "Tag Along Monsters".

The devils are opportunists and tag-along monsters. God has given us a tender place in our souls, a place where He speaks without words. A gut-level place where He guides.

It is written, *"You will hear a voice, 'This is the way, walk in it. Whenever you turn to the right or the left" Isaiah 30:21.*

But, our insidious enemy, the vicious ones, the accusers of the brethren are constantly using this against us in our walk. We know when we offend God with some thought, action or thought action. This is His gift to us, to keep us spiritually healthy. But what do we do once we've recognized our fault? Well, I can tell you for years, I would go run and hide. I've been walking with the Lord 25-30 years and I can't tell you how I spent many, many years running and hiding after I blew it.

But generally speaking, we tend to cower and avoid Him, just as Adam and Eve did in the garden. The evil ones are standing there encouraging us to do what we somehow suspect or know is wrong. They're saying, "Oh, it's okay, really. You can do this. God won't be offended. Or, "He'll forgive you, really. It's just a little thing."

And once we've committed the fault, the devils come back and say, "See? You're good for nothing, you can't be faithful for one hour. Now God is angry with you – He won't hear YOUR prayers! You aren't worthy of Him. And forget ministering to others!"

At this point, we run for cover instead of running into His waiting arms. All the while, HE'S looking on with mercy and compassion. This fall, which He most likely allowed to humble us, is our opportunity to grow in humility and faith. He's waiting with open arms and kisses, to receive us back into fellowship, wanting to strengthen us and assure us of His love, which is impossible to earn. He loves us because He is God. And Love is His nature –He can't help Himself. He IS Love! He created us for fellowship with Him, He enjoys our company. He's not like an earthly father, waiting for us to prove how good we are before He showers His love and approval on us.

So, what are we do to? The sooner we forget ourselves and turn to Him, knowing that He will forgive and restore our peace, the sooner we'll be happy again.

These little tag-along uglies know this – so they work energetically to cause toxic guilt that paralyzes our relationship with God. We have to learn to outsmart the little monsters, and go directly to the Lord when we've fallen short. Confess our weakness, our sin, and ask forgiveness in all humility. This needs to be done without delay. The longer we delay, the more monsters accumulate on our backs, shouting how worthless and bad we are.

They take a certain delight in seeing a Christian cowering in guilt, while they invisibly go on beating us with self-hatred and condemnation. Oh Boy, can I relate to that – this stuff is NASTY! And it sticks, unless we deal a decisive blow to these crippling lies.

Don't let these tag-along monsters paralyze your relationship with the Lord. Turn directly to Him with all confidence, knowing that He will forgive you immediately and paralyze your unwanted company. They'll have to look elsewhere for a new victim.

Sometimes, consequences of our sin linger on as we repair the damage we've caused. In all humility, receive this from our Good Shepherd's hands with a docile heart. He will turn what was meant for evil into good.

Be teachable, be meek and confident in His loving arms and you will TERRIBLY upset and even depress the little monsters who have worked so hard to separate you from God.

Who shall separate us from the love of Christ? shall tribulation, or anguish, or persecution, or famine, or nakedness, or peril, or sword? Romans 8:35

So, in conclusion, I just want to say that the most threatening thing in the world to the devils, the demons, to the kingdom of darkness is a discerning Christian in intimate communion with the Lord. That is a VERY, VERY threatening person. So, they do everything they can to keep you from becoming intimate with the Lord and learning how to discern the truth from falsehood.

Be encouraged, press in and know that the Lord is mercifully waiting to pick you up every time you fall. Boy, it that weren't true, I would NOT be here right now!

The Lord bless you and increase your wisdom and discernment.

Secret Rapture, Three Days of Darkness, Our Discernment Process: True or False?

December 14, 2014

I've been asked several times what I thought about the prophecies where the chosen-out ones were waiting for the 3 days of darkness that is to happen before the Rapture. As the prophecy goes, during these 3 days the chosen ones will be raptured ahead of the Bride, trained for 3 days, and return to the Earth in glorified bodies. I was asked to join them by one of the women. I honestly sought the Lord about this without wanting an immediate answer, because I didn't want to influence my answer by my own desires.

Sometimes our desires are so strong that they eclipse the Lord speaking to us, because He is very delicate and gentle. It sounds absolutely fabulous to me, I have to admit. I was torn between fulfilling my mission and not enough time because of the impending Rapture. Somehow being allowed to return to the Earth during the tribulation to help with the harvest would be an absolute dream come true. Let me say right now this idea was really awesome and the answer to all my conflicting feelings about being taken before my time, so to speak.

Well, the Lord knows how I am and as He was advising me about another situation with one of the women involved, He mentioned this to me. Before I tell you what He said, I would like to take you through my steps in discernment and share them with you. When I first heard of the secret rapture I felt an immediate check in my spirit. Deep down in my gut, something didn't feel right - but I put my feelings on hold and patiently listened to the explanation being given. Then a more firm check in my spirit caused me to stop right there. I took it to my covering, my husband. His immediate reaction was the very same as mine. Something didn't feel right. I have to admit I was a little disappointed, because it would have solved all my problems with not finishing my mission here on Earth.

The next step is Ezekiel went to The Bible Promises three times for a confirmation from the Holy Spirit. He bound the lying spirit before He opened the book.

The first reading the Holy Spirit led him to was under the heading of Lying. *"A false witness shall not be unpunished and he that speaks lies shall perish" (Proverbs 19:9).*

Let me stop right here and tell you I am not accusing anyone of lying - but I don't care how solid your prophetic gift has been: God alone is without error and perfect. We all make mistakes. Sometimes a lying spirit will tag along and that is to say you could be having a perfectly good and valid conversation with the Lord and there may be a pause and He may, for His own reasons, allow that demon to interject something untrue. I will not even venture to say why He does, because there are many different reasons. All of them are very good for our souls. At that point, it's not God's messenger that is lying, it's a lying spirit saying something untrue. So, please don't jump to conclusions and please don't accuse someone of being a false prophet, or that they're lying.

The next confirmation was under the heading Jealousy.

The Scripture that registered with him was in *James 3:16, "For where you have envy and selfish ambition there you find disorder and every evil practice."*

I want to take a moment and say something about this. I think it's really important that we never, ever judge a person's motive when given a prophecy. Only God knows the motives of that person. That's His job. To take on His authority and take that upon ourselves is not right. That's what I believe. Who knows where the selfish ambition is if it's quickened by the Holy Spirit and that's the aspect that He's communicating with us. It could very well be with the intention of the demons, for sure. If it's a misled prophecy, the ones who gave it have selfish ambitions and they have motives. The motives are to confuse us and to cause division. Not every single thing that is given to us in Scripture will necessarily apply to the situation. The Lord may just be calling your attention to ambition. It's something we need to just sit with and discern and not get all worked up over it. Look at the aspects of it that you know apply and let the other things go. Don't fall under condemnation, accuse, and don't be harsh. Look for the dynamic that is quickened to you. In any case if it's selfish ambition or jealous that particular reading is not a good indication that this whole concept is true. It's another red flag.

The reason I mention The Bible Promises so many times is very simple; each one of the chapters is divided according to content so it's a lot easier to discern what the Holy Spirit is saying to you in The Bible Promises than it is if you were to open the Scriptures of the Bible. There's a great deal of conflicting information on both pages depending on which copy you have and size of print. The nice thing about this book is that it's divided into topics and segments. When you prayerfully ask the Holy Spirit to lead you through the Scriptures using The Bible Promises, you're able to find more continuity in your answer than if you were to find something on the two pages of your opened Bible that give you different situations of what's happened. It makes it easier to discern. That's why we're so fond of using it. We've been using it for 30 years. It's done a pretty good job of leading us, as far as I'm concerned. We feel like our lives are in the place that He wants them. Yes, we have a lot to learn, that's for sure, but we feel like we are in the right place in the right time. Boy, that's invaluable to have that kind of peace.

We also go to the Scriptures. Many times we use that as a jump off point. We'll get a Scripture from James, for instance, and we'll read it in context and get an understanding of the situation and how it was meant. Sometimes the Holy Spirit brings up more about the situation just by mediating about that simple word. This is what we use to discern because this is an outside witness. It's a second and third witness. When you don't have two or three reliable people that you can go to, to confirm, you're pretty much on your own. Being on your own is dangerous. We need to know one another by the spirit and learn the ways of the spirit and the move of the spirit in order to navigate through our lives, especially as things become more treacherous with betrayals and people being handed over to death and so on. We need to be able to tell by the spirit who is authentic and who isn't.

The third and final reading was under Humility.

"A man's pride shall bring him low but honor shall uphold the humble and in spirit" (Proverbs 29:23).

This one was inconclusive. There are two different ways to look at this. One is to say that, "Well, maybe I'm too proud to accept something different like this and different from the ordinary. Maybe I'm just too proud." Some people would say, "If the Lord didn't say it to me, then it's not true." This kind of reading could be pointing right to us. On the other hand, it could have to do with pride involved on the other end. We don't know and we certainly don't want to assign motives to anyone anymore than we like having motives assigned to us. The combination of those three reasons was not a sign at all that this prophecy is true. It pretty much shot it down.

So in conclusion, the Spirit of the Lord in Ezekiel put up a caution sign and then He confirmed it with three readings.

After that, my sweet and loving Jesus came to instruct me about a situation for a woman who dearly loves the Lord with all her heart, but had been drawn into a deception. The Lord said something very gentle, **"They are misguided. There will only be one Rapture."**

After that, I went to The Bible Promises to make sure it was from the Lord and He gave me three confirmations and it was Him speaking to me. Plus, He told me something about the lady I was praying with and it turned out what He told me was true. So, everything in that conversation with Him proved out.

I want to emphasize that the demons have access to any knowledge in the world that is existing. This is a little a side note for you - I think this is worth mentioning. Don't let it confuse you about this topic, but just something to remember. So - they can see the situation that the lady was in. They could have told me that and it wouldn't have been supernatural knowledge but rather inside information by seeing the situation. Just because you hear, "So and so is going to be at your door in 30 minutes" doesn't mean that is from God. The demons can see very well who is on the way to your house.

True prophetic knowledge is knowing what's going to happen before it happens without surmising it based on evidence, based on observation. Such as when Paul told the ship's captain not one man would be lost after the ship wreck (Acts 27). The probability of someone being lost was very high, so when he said not one man would be lost he was speaking from supernatural knowledge.

Now, I want to look at the prophecy itself. Examine each thing on its own merit. First of all, let's look at the three days of darkness. My experience with this prophecy is that there is some substance to it. It came from a good Catholic source. I based it on the person who operates in the gifts of knowledge, healing, miracles, and lived an inapproachable life. There were others as well who prophesized the three days of darkness going back over 100 years and they were reported to have lived holy lives. That's real important that the source was holy. Their version about the 3 days is that there would be a time near the end of the Great Tribulation where the demons of hell would be released on the Earth and that anyone who was outside and not protected by the Lord's angels would die instantly. The instructions were to seal up your house and not go out for anyone or anything. Another part was that you would hear relatives' voices being imitated by demons crying to open the door and let them in. In the end the Lord and His angels would bind and destroy every last human and this would constitute a purification of the Earth from evil. True or false? I'm not convinced one way or another in my spirit. I don't have a strong leaning, so honestly I'm not sure. Since the sources are good it might possibly happen that way.

My conclusion is that if I need to know about this, the Lord will remind me of it and fill me in on the details if this is something necessary to me. If it's not necessary to us, then we're really wasting our time running after it to find out whether it's true or not.

In examining the dynamics of the prophecy: "Is there any room for vanity and pride?" Since this specifically talks about the special "called out ones" - then yes. I believe there is plenty of room for vanity and pride. The next question I would ask is, "What is the motive and the fruit from the event?" I believe there is a possibility of very good fruit since it talks about working for the Lord to bring in the harvest before the Rapture. That seems good and noble to me. "Can it be found in the Scriptures?" There are parallels in Exodus and in other places. "Does it agree with Scripture?" This is the final and most important aspect to look at. This is where it falls short. No, it does not agree with any references to the Rapture, at least to my knowledge.

So, my conclusion about this prophecy is that it is false. With that said, please - let's remember no one is perfect. I'm not perfect. We're all opened to deception and if you think you aren't open to deception well... moving right along.

Dear family, let's stay little, tucked away in the Lord's heart where it is safe. Let's not find fault with anyone or accuse. Let's not assume we know more than others. Let's just keep our eyes and ears on Jesus and cry out to Him for answers. There's nothing wrong with examining something and testing the spirits to see if they be of God. There's nothing wrong with examining a prophecy or a doctrine. That's not being critical of others. That's just being sensible and wise. We have to do that from time to time. We don't have to lay condemnation on them if they've made a mistake. That's totally unnecessary and what it does is, it injures the Lord. Not only does it injure that person but it injures the Lord.

This is His body and we need to treat it with kid gloves like you would an infant. You don't want to discourage or wound anyone. If we trust that the Lord will make the way straight for us and not allow us to be deceived, that's important too. Many demons have gone out into the world and they are very clever trying to deceive even the elect.

If we stay little and teachable not trusting in our own understanding, I believe the Lord will not suffer us to be misled for very long. If we have a sincere heart and we are seeking the truth and only the truth, eventually we'll get to the truth. If we're trying to defend something like a favorite idea and we fight off all other forms of logic concerning it… then we're in trouble, because then we've got an attachment to something. Our attachment is stronger than knowing the truth and that's not good.

In conclusion I want to quote this Scripture, because I feel that it applies here. "Trust in the Lord with all your heart and do not lean on your own understanding. In all your ways acknowledge Him and He will make straight your paths. Be not wise in your own eyes. Fear the Lord and turn away from evil. Do not despise the Lord's discipline or be weary of His reproof for the Lord reproofs Him whom He loves as a father his son in whom he delights" (Proverbs 3:6).

The Lord delights in all of us, especially those who are really committed to serving Him. You look at prophecy in light of that. Wherever the prophecy came, from the intentions were good and obviously they love the Lord enough to serve Him with their whole heart and their whole lives. We need to encourage one another when it comes up that maybe we've made a mistake. We need to say, "It's okay, I've made mistakes everyday."

The bottom line is, if we don't have that attitude, then we're in pride and if we get into pride He's going to arrange a nice fall for us. He's going to remove His covering and allow the demons to trip us up. It's super important that we receive the truth from Him and that we're willing to be corrected. When we are corrected or when someone else is corrected, we are to be very gentle, loving, kind, and understanding. If we were in that person's place we would have done the same thing.

God bless you family.

Discerning Between The Three Voices You Hear in Prayer

December 20, 2014

I'd like to share with you three things that I have learned over the years about listening to the Lord, and knowing for sure that it's Him you're listening to. The title of this is "The Three Voices of the Spirit". Life would be so much simpler for souls that really want to hear and obey God and please Him, if they could only hear His voice clearly and know for sure, it's Jesus.

I've consistently, all my Christian life, heard three different voices that come from three different sources in the spirit during prayer: the voice of my mind, which sounds like what we would call "talking to ourselves". On a day-to-day basis, it's a running dialogue of opinions and chatter. However, when we're seriously listening for the Lord, it tends to tell us what WE want to hear.

The second is the demon's voice, which sounds affectionate, reasonable, persuasive, and very compatible with our own thoughts and desires. It tells us what we want to hear or what makes sense. At other times it accuses us or other people, drawing us into judgment, which the devils know is a way to open the door for them to come in and sift us. If they can't get away with lying to us about good things to set us off course, it will switch to the discouragement mode.

And third, the Lord's voice, which also sounds affectionate, reasonable, and at many times much like what we sometimes perceive to be our own, because He is always renewing our minds with His thoughts. His instruction is gentle and does not provoke us to judge others. Rather, He encourages us to be long-suffering with them, as He is with us.

So those are a kind of light overview of the three different characters of the voices that we hear when we're praying and we're in the spirit.

Now how it all started for me, I began hearing from the Lord by writing in my journal. I would journal my heart, and my feelings, my desires and then wait and listen for the Lord to respond. At first this seemed to work beautifully – but then I began to notice contradictions and things that were predicted that didn't come to pass. Red Flag!!!

This is why I can't just indiscriminately write down what I hear. I have to go deeper. The Scriptures say in *1 John 4:1 Test the spirits and see if they be of God.*

Okay, so how are we going to test them? Well, a lot has to do with listening very carefully to the attitude and the demeanor of what you're hearing. As I said, one sounds like we're talking to ourselves and sounding more regal and authoritative - like God. The second sounds very affectionate and reasonable and persuasive - that's the demon. The Lord's also sounds affectionate and reasonable, but He's gentle and doesn't provoke us to judge others. And let me tell you, the demons are really smart. They'll do that – they'll sound like the Lord and they won't provoke you to judge others. They'll make it a little harder for you to know. But there's that sweet space in your spirit, down in your gut, where you know that you know that you know it's the Lord.

I just find it very hard sometimes to be confident that it's the Lord when I'm communicating with Him about something I'm attached to. People say, "Well, but I hear the Lord in my heart." But here's what the Scriptures say in *Jeremiah 17:9: The heart is deceitful above all things and beyond. The heart is perverse and unsearchable. Who can know it?* So that's tricky, too! What's in our hearts isn't always what's Holy and right and Godly.

So, I was very young in the Lord and insecure and these contradictions would throw me into a panic, especially because I'd been a New Age practitioner for 12 years before the Lord rescued me. I wanted to base everything in my life on what the Lord told me to do, because I'd made such a mess of my life for the first 33 years. I was so sick of "following my star." Let me tell you, I was ready to obey and to follow the Lord.

When I was first saved, my very first experience of hearing the Lord speak to me was through the Scriptures. I opened my "new to me" big family Bible three times prayerfully. I've never forgotten those readings. Little did I know they would define my mission in life. I never expected anything like these readings so I was detached from them. They were Moses and the burning bush: Out of the burning bush I've made you to hear My voice. The second was the story of Esther, fasting in prayer. And the third was the call of Jeremiah to speak out about the things that the Lord showed me that needed correction, and to encourage.

So truly, the Lord does direct our lives individually in the Bible and there is merit in seeking a word from Him directly through the Scriptures. And to this day, those words still define my mission. I think it's just a matter of trusting that God will open that Bible to the right page. It's a childlike trust. It doesn't come easily for us because we're so mental and so controlling. The whole idea of letting go of control and allowing something to open to the right thing is just real scary and alien to us.

But it's a matter of letting go and taking Daddy's hand, like a little child, like a 3-year-old or a toddler would take the Lord's hand and just walk with Him. He wouldn't ask, "Well, where are we going? What are we going to do? And when are we coming home?" He wouldn't go into all these mental gymnastics to secure his future. He just takes the Lord's hand! That's what going to the Scriptures for a confirmation is like.

Okay, so I want to give you an example of three clear messages about the same topic as you'd hear them in your prayer time and write them down, believing it was Jesus speaking to you.

The first one. When I began singing, I wanted to have a powerful voice, and in prayer when I was seeking the Lord, I heard "Work your voice and it will be powerful."

Okay, the next voice: "Your voice will be much more powerful than that singer you so admire. She's very good, but your voice is outstanding. Work it day and night and you'll get there." Okay, that's the second voice.

The third voice: "Your voice is unique to you, just as other singers have their own beauty. Don't copy other vocalists. Work consistently and you will in time blossom into your own."

Okay, so, a little question here – which one do you think is the Lord?

1) "Work your voice and it will be powerful."

2) "Your voice is outstanding. Work it day and night and you'll get there."

3) "Your voice is unique and blossom into your own uniqueness."

Well, in the first one, I was attached to having a powerful voice. That's a caution, a red flag. Anything you're attached, you're likely to tell yourself. Also, I felt a check in my spirit when I heard this.

OK, the second - it plays on my vanity. It judges and criticizes another singer and it directs me to over-do my practice, which might even lead to vocal damage.

And the third voice – it contradicts my desire, but it encourages me to become who I am.

So, after time had expired, I began to see that that's not my style, to be powerful. That's not what comes naturally to me as a form of expression in song. And not only that, but the songs the Holy Spirit gives me are not suited to power, but to gentleness and softness. Later I figured out I was telling myself "You will have a powerful voice" because that's what I wanted to hear. I was attached.

So, I learned after many years of failures you cannot just trust a word that plays up to your attachments. Or should I say you can't just trust ANY word you hear. You have to discriminate, as the Scriptures instruct us to.

When we have been in worship and the time comes for us to sit quietly before the Lord and to listen, there's a potential for three different voices to be heard. But only ONE is the voice of God. If you just indiscriminately write down what you're hearing, you run the risk of being directed into a path that is not yours by your very own flesh, or by demons who will guide you into judgment, which will bring repercussions. Basically, they're setting you up for a fall, because they know that when you judge, you go out from under God's covering, and then they can step in and sift you.

But when you clearly discern Jesus speaking to you - you've gone over the three options and you've decided "This is the Lord. I can feel it in my spirit and there's nothing to indicate that it's from the enemy." When you clearly discern that Jesus is speaking to you, the whole world can come against you. I could lose my voice for a month to laryngitis, or not have any opportunities to sing and it wouldn't matter. Because the Lord gave me His word about my voice, and all I have to do is have faith in what He told me.

So, it's really, really important guys. Don't just write down anything you hear. Please! Please! Discriminate, as the Scriptures teach us to do. Test the spirits. You don't want to end up at a dead end later on because you just took anybody's word for it.

Well, the Lord bless you and help us all to have better discernment.

Demonic Obstacles against Hearing and Seeing Jesus

February 15, 2015

I received a beautiful message from the Lord that I think will really be edifying to my sister Brides, as well.

I've been having monumental problems seeing and hearing the Lord clearly, lately – to the point where I've just collapsed in tears. You know, I love to post things that He says to me, but I can't post them unless He speaks to me, so that's part of the tension of it. The other part of it is, I love to be with Him and it's so comforting to be with Him and that's where all my strength comes from. So, I reached that point again today and I said, "Lord, I can't live without You anymore. I just can't. You've gotta do something."

And when Ezekiel and I sat down to do our devotions and readings together, Ezekiel opened our book *Chronicles of the Bride* to the entry that was from Valentine's Day, 2007 – wow!

And this is what it said. It addresses this very problem. Here we are on Valentine's Day.

~~~~~~~~~~~~~~~~
~~~~~~~~~~~~~~~~

My Unbelief And Fear of Deception

February 14th, 2007

The Lord Jesus is very present before Me.

"Why do you avoid Me?" He said.

I had been busying myself with many things and finding excuses not to get into prayer. I believe this was a result of false guilt. Many times I have felt guilt for doing things that were God's will but I was unsure of that at the time, so I just did the best I could to discern what would please Him the most. But the enemy sends in lying spirits that accuse when we are innocent, so that we will avoid the presence of God.

Okay now, that was from the journal of 2007. Interestingly enough, that is the EXACT problem I was having today. I thought that I had done something to offend the Lord, or that I hadn't repented sufficiently, or that I hadn't recognized my sins and He was waiting on me. Wow, the exact problem, 8 years ago.

Before I had a chance to answer in reply to His question, "Why do you avoid Me?"

He said, **"Fear. You are afraid. You have gotten into this habit through disobedience because you were afraid of what I would say. But now that you are making every effort to be obedient, there is no reason to fear. I want to speak to you face to face, this way, everyday."**

Now, this isn't just for me, guys. This is for you, too. The Lord loves to hear, love to be with His Bride and loves to communicate with you.

I had begun to fear deception. He responded to my unspoken thought as He always does, **"I know you fear deception but as long as you remain humble you need not fear that I will allow you to be misled."**

(I can only pray that His grace will warn me when I am not humble and am entering into the sin of Pride, the most difficult sin to recognize in ourselves.)

I was listening but not writing because I wasn't sure that it was Jesus yet.

He said, **"I want you to be writing this conversation down. About this fear of reprimand; I am not a man who says unjust things and puts unjust judgments on you. I am God...remember? You are My Bride."**

I felt so unworthy, so ashamed I could not even look at Him even though He was holding my face in His hands and I sensed, tenderly looking into my eyes.

"You still don't know how I feel about you...what you mean to Me...do you? You still don't know, do you? We are One flesh, My Beloved, I want you walking with Me everyday, talking and walking together hand in hand. We are One."

Now, I'd like to take an aside here, when He's says we're One flesh, He's talking about through communion. And I receive communion every day.

I had been asking Him earlier, "Since we have to be on this Earth, couldn't You talk to me all the time?" And I realized as I began to pray tonight, that I have been nervous around Him in these experiences, even though I have had solid confirmations and the discernment of my husband that this was indeed the Lord and not a familiar spirit.

Despite the beautiful wedding we had, this awesome palace, and swimming together, I still feel so formal with Him. When He said this, I realized that false guilt was underlying our encounters.

Gee, I wonder who could have sent that in?? That false guilt…hmmm.

Yet, when He looked at me, I felt like a vapor that merged into His being. Nonetheless, I have continued to feel inhibited in His presence.

Jesus said, **"I want to begin with a new level of trust. One that will allow us to communicate clearly. There is much I have to tell you and I heard your musings tonight about 'Who will be my instructor in Heaven if we are constantly increasing in understanding?' Well, the answer is, I will - not only in Heaven but here as well. We are One, and it is My desire and intention that we speak familiarly, not through a glass darkly. Not through a veil nor a tunnel, nor in any way impeded. That's My desire."**

I began to cry because that is the most wonderful thing I have to look forward to in Heaven: no more confusion.

He replied, **"My Beloved, My Precious, no more confusion, here and now."**

I thought about it for a moment.

"Your agreement?" He asked.

"Lord, I agree, please help my faith."

Jesus replied, **"Do you expect Me to let you fend for yourself? Do you think your unbelief comes as a surprise or catches Me off guard, as if I didn't anticipate it and already have a provision for it? I've already conquered all your enemies, remember?"** He looked at me tenderly, and a little hurt.

"You still have so much to learn about Me, and how I love, honor, and cherish you. How deeply I desire to be with you - fully present, familiarly. Just like we are right now in this moment.

"Happy Valentine's Day, from Me and all of Heaven. You will be lonely no more. Since I am coming to take you away with Me soon, we are preparing you to be accustomed to us. (The Body of Christ in Heaven, the Great Cloud of Witnesses) Your transition will be as simple as walking through a door way."

And, you know – when He said that "everyday He wanted to be present" to me, He is expressing His heart's desire as it was in the Garden of Eden before Adam and Eve sinned. You know, He came everyday to be with them, in the cool of the Garden.

~~~~~~~~~~~~~~~~

Well, after I read this entry during our devotions from Valentine's Day, 2007, I just sat there and broke down in tears. I couldn't do anything else.
~~~~~~~~~~~~~~~~

"Lord, You've answered my prayers I've felt so condemned and I didn't know why."

"I love you," He said, and began to sing a song He gave me in 2013, which I'm working on right now, BTW. I'll probably be done in a week or so. It's actually a song where He sang the melody in the first line. The title of the song is, "I Love You" and it's Him singing that to His Bride.

The Lord continued, **"I want the joy of your countenance to shine on Me, your God. I want to see Me reflected in that sweet face. Don't let unbelief saddle and bridle you anymore, Clare. No more. Please, no more."**

I thought about the analogy He gave: To saddle and bridle is to give the one riding me total control over everything I say and do.

He went on to say, **"So much of what I have said, you have heard and dismissed as familiar spirits and your own mind. I want you to pray for the Grace to increasingly know the difference. You need to know the difference more clearly. So much of what I have said, you have heard."**

And I kind of sensed a little frustration in His voice when He said, **"So, now here we are again at this place where I must convince you it is Me, and no other."**

So, I asked Holy Spirit to give me a reading to confirm through Bible Promises that this is Jesus speaking to me: And I opened to Hospitality. *I Peter 4:9-11* is what caught my eye, and I felt it had the anointing.

Be hospitable to one another without complaint. As each one has received a special gift, employ it in serving one another as good stewards of the manifold grace of God. Whoever speaks, is to do so as one who is speaking the utterances of God; whoever serves is to do so as one who is serving by the strength which God supplies; so that in all things God may be glorified through Jesus Christ, to whom belongs the glory and dominion forever and ever. Amen.

And I thought about it for a minute, and said, "Lord, I don't get this. Hospitality. Are you trying to point to something I haven't done? I'm not taking good enough care of our homeless guest in the front house, and so You're withholding Your presence from me…is that what it is?"

So, I opened to Bible Promises again, and I opened to probably the most beautiful reading in that whole book: *As a young man marries a virgin, so your Maker will marry you. Isaiah 62:5*

So, obviously, no. It was not that I was guilty of neglect. No. Hospitality has to do with my gifts.

Well, at that point, He said, **"It's your gift, Clare. It's your calling to be a light in the wilderness of this world. Use your gift. Your gift is hearing and recognizing Me, too. That's why you got Hospitality."**

Okay – taking a moment here. We're a Light to the world – and you can't put a light under a bushel basket – you need to put it on a hill. And many of you who are listening to this, know that you are called to be a light to the world – and that's a gift. A gift to share. So, it's imperative for you, too, to be able to recognize the Lord's voice, and discern when it's NOT His voice, so that you don't mislead other people, as well.

I mean, we can never mislead people by quoting Scripture or by properly, in context, talking about Scripture. But, people HUNGER for the Word of Knowledge, a Word of Wisdom – they hunger for something special, a word in season. And, as Lights in the world, the Lord has given us light in our hearts and our minds, and speaks to us Rhemas – illuminated words from God that we can speak over other people.

So, it's so important to be secure when you open your mouth and know that it's God speaking through you. As a light, it's our duty to make sure it's God, and not someone or someone else speaking through us. As you know, that's a big topic of mine, and I've got a lot of videos about discerning the Lord. And here we are, adding another one. But, He gave me some techniques here that are pretty neat, and I'm going to go on to share with you.

So I asked Him, "But why is it so hard? What is standing in the way? Truly, tell me, Lord, Please."

He began, **"You have many enemies trying to confuse you and steal your gift. Trying to erode your confidence with false guilt. They don't want you to have this gift, and you'll have to fight for it, and fight to keep it as well. That is the naked truth."**

"Wow! So if I bind those enemies, I will recognize you more clearly?"

"Eventually, yes. But you need to work at it and be diligent in targeting the monsters."

'Monsters?' And I thought about my video "Tagalong Monsters" which is a technique the devils' use. They tag-a-long on a word that the Lord is giving you.

"Monsters," He repeated. **"Thieves. Liars. Devils. This is where your problem lies. Fix this and we will be much clearer."**

"But can't You clear the air for me? I've asked You to do that, and I've prayed over our time together."

And He said, **"I would rather see you take authority and teach others to as well, than to do it for you. You understand that?"**

"Yes, I suppose I do.

"Well please, Lord – give me some names. Like the handles of the demons with which I can grab hold of them, which I can use to clear the air. "

I was taught early in my Christian walk that it was important to have the name of the demon that was oppressing you. And so I asked Him to give me some handles.

I heard **"Lying spirits, Beguiling spirits. These are your major enemies. Fog, Brain Fog. Curtains. Voices. Vehicles of Disturbance. Hindering, Obstacles and all Vehicles of Demonic Oppression."**

"Ohhh...That's a list."

Now I'm feeling the need to renounce and repent as well, after He said that.

"I renounce, Confusion, Self-doubt, False Guilt and spirits of Propaganda that lie about the faithful character of God. I renounce any Pride within me. I repent of all prideful thoughts. Lord, I present my contrite spirit to You and call upon Your Faithfulness and Mercy to forgive my sins. Restore and protect that which You wish to do with and through me for others. For it is written, *"The Lord has heard the desire of the poor. Your ear has heard the preparation of their heart. Blessed are the pure in Heart, for they shall see God."*

I shortened this, I condensed this, so I'll read the condensed version: *"For thus says the high and exalted One who lives forever, Whose name is Holy. I dwell with the contrite and lowly of spirit in order to revive the hearts of the contrite." (That was taken from Isaiah 57:15 and Matt. 5:8 You hear the desire of the poor - Psalm 10:17)*

Then the Lord continued, *"There now. You have a prayer and a technique for clearing the air and moving the heart of your God to respond to your entreaties. This truly is a tool for you and for others to clear the way for our trysting time."*

By the way, I looked up "Tryst" in Webster's and it says "Private, romantic rendezvous between lovers."

He continued, **"Oh, Clare. I do so want you to put an end to the interference. It is very important to me and to those who are serving. Please see to it that it works and share it with the world. I will honor these prayers, both for the weak of heart and mind, and for the strong who've been under great oppression."**

When I received communion, I saw myself as a Bride – but I was in a casket with my hands crossed over my bosom, and a pink tea rose crown. I was alive – but I was sleeping. I prayed, and Jesus bent over the casket and took her by the hand and raised her up.

"My Bride," He said. **"No longer sleeps the sleep of those who are deaf and dumb. Now she hears My voice in newness of life, filled with Joy and Life Eternal."**

And as I rose up, it was Springtime and everything was new and green and jubilant. Including me!

And the Lord began, **"This is what I have for you on Valentine's Day. Don't ever let them separate us again, Clare."**

And when He said, **"Don't ever let them separate us again",** what He was talking about was, NO ONE can separate us from God – no one. But they can interfere in the communications, which make us feel separated. That's an illusion. We're never separated from God. But there are times when we feel distant from Him, which I've gone into in other videos. But in this case, when He says **"Don't ever let them separate us again"** He's talking about in communication. Take authority over those things that are trying to block your communication with the Lord, or trying to effect it in any way.

"Don't ever let them separate us again, Clare. Use these weapons of war that I have personally armed you with, and do battle bravely, My Bride. Continually protecting our relationship and teaching others to do likewise.

You are My Beloved. I love you."

The end of His message

So, what is exactly the point of this message and His teaching?

Well, first of all, the Lord has given us some new weapons to use against the enemy who is trying to intercept communications back and forth between the Lord and you, and the Lord and I. These are new weapons and I would really appreciate some feedback from those of you who are having the same struggle, if you see a difference. And that will be important, because then we can refer these things to other people and they'll see what this has done for you in your life, and have confidence to do the same with their own messages from the Lord and their own quiet time.

Some of you who've been struggling are not going to struggle anymore, it's going to be really beautiful.

And the second point of this, which is kinda funny, but nonetheless is pretty important – you'll notice that Valentine Day's message was eight years ago to the DAY. Eight is the number of new beginnings. Seven is completion, 8 is new beginnings.

You'll notice at the end, that I had the vision right after I received communion, of rising up out of the casket.

Well, I've gotta say, guys – if there's hope for ME, there's hope for you! Eight years it took me, eight years...and I've still been flailing around with the same problem. If you think YOU'RE thick headed, or obtuse, or think you're a slow learner...or think you're unworthy. I mean, anything that you're thinking negatively for yourself – I've already manifested that in my life. I've already done all those things and I AM all those things.

And look what the Lord has done with ME. If He can do it with me, He can do it with you. There couldn't be a worse case of flightiness and forgetfulness, I don't believe, there could be a worse case than what I am. And I'm not saying that pridefully, 'cause there's not any pride to be had in that - it's rather shameful. Understand if He can do these things with me, and He can pull me out of these things and teach me how to hear Him clearly – He can do it with you. I promise, He can do it with you

This message is especially to increase your faith, your hope and trust in the Lord. I hope it really helps you and please, do us a favor, and give us some feedback on this technique. Let us know how you are coming along. Thank you so much.

The Lord bless you, Youtube family and I hope this Valentine's Day message touches your heart and makes it easier for you, too - to communicate with the Lord. And I'd love your feedback. I've been using these prayers today and so far so good. We'll see as time goes on just how well it's working. The Lord bless you.

You Must Have TRUE Discernment

May 25, 2015

My Dear Family, I have another message for you tonight. Something that I think is really, really important to our spiritual health and survival.

Guys, we've got to go deeper with our discernment. This is EXTREMELY important for our survival. There is a place within a place, so deep and personal that NO ONE can transgress it. It is your God Space, your conscience. And not anything the enemy can penetrate. It's protected by the Lord.

This is a Holy place. I need you all to cultivate your ability to hear from this place. There are many who have gone out with clever arguments against some of the most profound relationships we can have with God. I want to say that a clever person can use the Scriptures to prove or disprove the same thing at any given time. They can pull up all the Scriptures to defend their viewpoint, and another person with the opposing viewpoint can do the EXACTLY same thing. We have to be wise as serpents and gentle as doves, or we're going to lose the relationship we have with our Lord.

When you listen to a prophet and your heart begins to throb with fire and love for God – do you suppose that prophet is speaking under the anointing of the Holy Spirit or in their own flesh? Can a person speaking from their flesh inspire the fire of God in your hearts?

"My sheep know My voice, and another they will not follow." John 10:27

But then along comes a clever intellect to sow doubt in your mind, about the authenticity of what you heard. And you, My dear ones, must have rock-solid discernment so that you can NOT be swayed by clever arguments. These are tortuous times, and even the Elect can be deceived. It's you responsibility to develop your perception from deep inside your God space, or you will be led astray by powerful people and lying signs.

Because the Lord does not always send clever arguments. In fact, more often than not, it's His power working in us that bears witness that this is from God.

Did Paul not say, *"I was with you in weakness and in fear and in much trembling, and my message and my preaching were not in persuasive words of wisdom but in demonstration of the spirit and of power, so that your faith would not rest on the wisdom of men, but on the power of God." I Cor. 2:3*

And the fire that burns in your heart, when you listen to someone speaking - that's the power of God. The fire of the Holy Spirit driving you on into the depths of a relationship with the Lord. So, there's great need for discernment here. Either you hear the voice of Jesus or you don't. And some are being tempted by clever arguments to deny what they feel and know in their heart is real.

"My sheep know my voice and another they will not follow."

This is true discernment. To know what is true in the depths of your being and not let anyone steal it from you. There's no replacement for this kind of discernment. You can't reason it out in a discussion with human thinking.

People twist Scriptures to fit their argument and will twist your thinking right out of reality and cause you to lose your blessing. This discernment has to be cultivated by intimacy with the Lord. It's something much deeper than the intellect and you've got to have it if you're going to survive.

So please, my dear Brides. Avail yourselves of true discernment. Do not allow men to steal these things from you, but hide them deep in your heart. Do not give ear to the enemy cleverly seduces with words of wisdom. You KNOW in your heart what the voice of God sounds like. Cleave to Him and do not give the enemy the opportunity to steal from you.

"My sheep know my voice and another they will not follow."

SECTION SEVEN

Messages to Give You Hope: Heaven and What is Waiting For You

Your True Home

(Taken from Chronicles of the Bride)

September 21st, 2007

"How I long to gather you to Myself. Press on toward the goal to win the prize for which God has called You Heavenward in Me. For I will bring you to the joy and peace of your eternal home.

"When you arrive, you will see souls going to and fro, all very natural, all very orderly according to My Purpose. You will see, that just as upon the Earth, My People will be serving, praying, praising, and working along with the Salvific Plan for all souls, even until the end of the world.

"Though glorified and perfect, you will yet resemble the human state that you previously lived in, only purified, reflecting Me, and My Own Image authentically and genuinely. You will all be perfectly humble, with perfect divine charity, wisdom, and grace. You will love Me and one another with absolute sweetness. Holiness will abound, and permeate everyone and everything, as with the words to the precious nativity song, 'All is calm, all is bright.'

“I will reach you there, instantly, without the slightest delay when you call. I will spread My cloak over you, and draw you again and again to My Heart, that you may drink fully of the consolations of your God.

“Blessed be the days to come, when I ring you round with songs of joy, with festive tunes and celebrations. How wondrous a thing it will be, when I your Lord, gird myself about with a fine linen sash, and begin to wait upon you at My Father's Banquet. Although you measure your days at present with hours and minutes, it will not be so there. In Heaven there is no sense of time, for it does not exist. All things are eternal, and each occurrence, circumstance, activity simply flows into and out of another.

“We will work on earth. We will live for souls, and for the salvation of every one of them. As many as will be saved, we will accompany as a Great Cloud of Witness. We will pray, interceding, and ministering to the Heart of Our God on their behalf, and assisting them with many graces, intervening in their lives.”

Heaven and the Millennium After the Rapture

April 1, 2015

The Lord started talking about Heaven and the 1,000 year reign. So this is going to be a fun subject to share with you – it will definitely be a welcome break from all the heavy stuff.

"You will be everything you ever wanted to be in Heaven. All the vices and sins you've struggled with on Earth, in Heaven will be gone. Let's just say it will be a wedding present. You will immediately be transformed and all sickness of spirit will be washed away. It will just peel off and wash away to reveal My glory dwelling within you. A total transformation."

"Will there be classes for learning?"

"No, I Myself will teach you. You will feel the desire to know something and I will reveal it to you. You will feel the desire to play something and it will roll off your fingertips; to sing and perfect pitch effortlessly sustained will escape your lips. Everything will seem magical to you at first, until you become accustomed to knowing and doing everything effortlessly."

"Lord, this is hard for me to accept? Won't we all be working together as teams?"

"Yes, teams you will have, learning experiences you will share, more like what you would call a lab. You will do things together with others and cooperation will be so joyous. Harmony will be something you have always longed for, but rarely had. It is intoxicating to work together as one where all of the many come together to bring about good. You will love it. Your deep desire to work with groups will be fully satisfied in the best possible ways.

"You will seek to see something, and I will escort you. Nothing will be impossible to you, except evil. This is yet another gift, because in Heaven the door has been closed to evil; it will not enter, it will not entice. My daughter, you will not feel anything evil, this too is a gift, a grace I will impart to you.

"Everything in Heaven is effortless."

"Can I have an evil thought?"

"No my love, you will never have an evil thought again. Not only because the devils cannot buffet you there, but also because by Divine Grace all wickedness will be washed out of your system. You will be sparkling clean and glorified. You will be content beyond anything you could ever imagine. You will see into the future and know whatever is necessary to you. You will never guess at anything again. You will never fail to understand Me again, or anyone else for that matter. You will have perfect vision into hearts, that you may help them escape death and decay.

"You will have perfect discretion, timely and sensitive. You will understand the ways of men without effort and easily be able to guide them back to center. You will appear glorious, because you will be like Me. Like Me in so many ways. You are going to love how I transform you. You are going to be unspeakably happy and satisfied.

"I wanted to share with you some of the joys of Heaven because you've had a couple of very rough days, and I can see it has weakened you and stolen your joy."

“Oh Jesus, it hurts me so the lies and calumny spoken by uninformed souls. Oh it truly hurts me so deeply, and I know it is an obtuse spirit, a brick wall I can never penetrate in my own timing.”

"That's right. It is not yet time, but My promise to you, Clare, is that you will be working with me to open their eyes in cooperation with My Spirit. When we return, so many things will be changed. First of all, there will be signs and wonders in the sky that will cut many to the quick and instantly turn their hearts. Then you will be working with soft clay and I will give you wisdom as you have never had.

"Oh My Love, how you will rejoice at the elegance of My plan, its depth and breadth, height, and length. Oh, how magnificent it is! And your wisdom will be as the waters in the ocean, you will understand so much. And it will make you so humble that none will be able to resist your sweetness."

“Will I be with You always, Jesus?”

“You will know Me even as I know you and nothing shall ever separate us, nothing.”

“I don't understand, I thought there would be times apart?”

"Not apart as you understand it in your world. We will be in complete union and you will never miss Me, because I will be dwelling inside you. Nothing will interrupt our sweet communion together, because in Heaven there is no sin, no pride. This has its advantages and disadvantages, because we will share sorrows together as well as joys."

“But I thought I wouldn't know about Earth doings.”

"Not until the end of the Tribulation. Yet you know how you grieve when I am rejected. Well yes, that will still be there, you will feel that. When we return to Earth and as you work with souls, you will be acutely aware of my feelings for their deeds and you will have instant knowledge of how each situation is to be handled, even punishments and corrections."

“Will there be many punishments when we return? Will people still be hard headed and rebellious?”

"You will at first see vast improvements in the attitudes of men and women, but corruption goes deep and some will manifest quickly. Others, it will emerge slowly even over generations. You will be able to see clearly the consequences of sin carried down through families. You will work to change that but some, Clare, will never change. And for this you must have fortitude and deep understanding to be able to weather disappointments. But I will always be inside of you, bringing deep inner peace and joy, no matter how sad the outer circumstances."

"Will there be death in the Millennium?"

"Yes, there will be birth and death, though circumstances will allow for a longer life span and perfect health due to the atmosphere and absence of sin and demons. It is yet a pity that evil will manifest without provocation by the enemy. This is the weakness of Adam and Eve. It will be a shock to many that evil can still raise its ugly head without demonic assistance.

"You will have joy in everything you put your hand to. You will see conversions, healings, restorations and complete transformation of hearts. This will bring you unspeakable joy as it does for all the angels and saints in Heaven.

"You see My Daughter, so many on Earth in this hour long with all their hearts to minister but the forces allied against them are tremendous, both of a personal nature and an impersonal nature. Few there are that break through this wall, for great perseverance is required and great reliance on Me.

"And there are those who have been chosen and equipped for this, there are others who have not. And to them I give the grace of prayer. Their desires are manifested in the arenas of evangelism, and while they are not a direct part of the conversions as man sees it, they are the living prayer force behind these evangelists. And were you to see these evangelists without the great mass of prayer warriors offering prayers and supplications on their behalf, you would see them as just simple, pitifully weak men.

"The evangelists themselves must have very pure hearts, humility and an anointing from above. Their integrity must be impeccable. That is why we work so hard on issues of this sort. They cannot carry out the work and sustain the heat of the battle or hold up under pressures without a profound commitment to integrity and doing things My way.

"Yet, pull the curtain back and the man becomes very, very little in My plan. The intercessors behind the man are tremendous, making him look like a giant, when in reality it is the little ones behind him that are responsible for his perceived stature. In this way, the desires of those who wanted to minister are satisfied. And yet there is a time and a season for all. They will get their turn to touch souls with My Love. Everyone gets a turn to do what is on their heart to do, because their hearts are conformed to Mine."

"And what about worship, Lord?"

“You are now speaking of something out of the realm of understanding. When you are worshipping, you have ceased all human activity and are in the realm of God Your Creator. You cease to be apart and are molded into One with Your Creator. Your hearts expand right out of yourself in worship and when you come back to yourself, so to speak, you are totally renewed, energized and inspired. Whatever you went into worship with, when you come out, it is totally gone. There is really nothing more I can say about worship because it is so sublime.

"You will experience it. That's all I can promise. And, you will never, ever, be the same again. You are going to go from glory, to glory, just as it is written."

“Lord, is there anything else you want to talk to me about tonight?”

"I am asking you to keep watch with Me. Limit your interactions to necessary communications and return to the place of deep intercommunion with Me. Much is imparted to you through it.”

SECTION EIGHT

Prayer, Holy Spirit Baptism, Communion and Deliverance

THE BINDING PRAYER & Instructions

Revised on: 11-12-15

Instructions: *When you pray the Binding Prayer, speak with intention directly to the spiritual forces of the air, speak deliberately and firmly.* Kick the filthy dogs out of your kitchen!

We have defined US, WORK & EQUIPMENT for our ministry. You may not need this part of the prayer.

Always strive to forgive your human enemies from the heart. After all, they are pitiful to oppose God, and sooner or later it will catch up to them.

Then you are addressing Satan worshipers, demons and demons who pretend to be aliens, but are in fact, fallen angels & their dark matter weapons. You are not doing this on your own, but by the power of the NAME.

Protection is very important and these are the things we have found that come against us. As far as the forces of opposition, you can delete things that do not affect you and add things that you struggle against.

Prayer Against Curses

3xThe prayer against curses, etc. came from Francis MacNutt, who has a world-class deliverance ministry and found this prayer important for anyone who wants to be free, repeating it three times – x3

Glory: We want to be walking in the Glory and protected by it as well. Speaking favor was given to us by an Apostle for this ministry. The Blood is our protection, along with the Name: "Every knee shall bow." The demons are required to retreat when the Name is used or suffer the consequences of serious "electrical shock" (my best thought on what they use) from the angels who protect us and enforce the use of the Name.

Thanksgiving is so important. Without these weapons, we'd all be road kill – how grateful we should be! Life drains us of these attributes: love for others, health, strength, etc. so, here we are asking to be restored from what has been done to us by others and what we have done to ourselves as well.

Restitution is so important, since we have lost much to the enemy. Seeing the Father smiling upon us washes away the never-ending attempts of the enemy to make us feel badly about ourselves.

Jesus, I trust in You is the greatest statement of faith against the lies of the enemy when you are attacked. I use it constantly. They hate it. It reinforces in our being that God is Greater than any of these petty forces.

And finally, I wanted to put a few pointers for repentance here, so that when you feel the need to come before the Lord repenting, you'll have some ideas to work with.

Repentance

Repentance is something we should do the very moment we are convicted that we sinned. But it can be good to go over this prayer once in a while to make sure you are covering all the bases on your sins. So, this prayer and list of sins is just a guide. You know where you fall, so you can adjust this to your own personal needs.

Before we go into prayer it is good to ask Holy Spirit to reveal any misdeeds or neglects, and seriously repent asking for strength so we won't repeat them. Then you can go through the list, highlight what you are repenting from and call out the things you know you are guilty of, and ask for the grace so you will not repeat them.

Confession & Repentance

I renounce and repent of pride, rebellion, unforgiveness; bitterness, judgment, jealousy; greed, disobedience, unbelief, laziness, negligence, selfishness, self-pity, self-indulgence & gluttony; anger, depression, despair; lying, (adultery, fornication, impurity) and listening to lying accusations against Your character and the promises you've made to me.

Oh Lord, You are kind, merciful, faithful and true. Forgive me for having ever offended You and my neighbor. Grant me the grace and strength to sin no more, especially in the hidden places of my heart. Jesus, please send me a spirit of repentance for those things I have not recognized or repented of yet.

I present my contrite spirit to You, Jesus, and call upon your faithfulness and Mercy to forgive my sins. Restore and protect that which you wish to do with and through me for others.

Invocation To The Lord

Lord, You hear the desire of the poor: Your ear has heard the preparation of our hearts. We cling to your promise, "Blessed are the pure in heart, for they shall see God and He shall dwell in their hearts." I confess there is nothing I can do to 'earn' your fellowship, to hear Your precious voice, to see Your precious face, no amount of fasting or good works can earn it; I rely solely on Your Mercy. For as You can see, I am faint of heart and longing for You. As the deer pants for streams of living water, so my soul pants for You, O my God. I appeal to Your Mercy Lord. Please visit me.

The Binding Prayer

Use this prayer, whenever it is needed, whenever there is trouble or oppression in the air, every morning or just before going into your prayer time.

Speak This Prayer Directly to the Demons,
Out Loud With Intention
(Kick the filthy dogs out of your kitchen!)

“US” = volunteers, staff member, viewer, friend, family. "WORK" = web sites, channels, pod casts, books, recordings, pdf's, and all materials produced for the Lord. “EQUIPMENT” = everything used to produce work for the Lord: house, computers, cars, electricity, etc.

Forgive & Bless Our Enemies From the Heart

Father, I forgive and bless from my heart those people who have chosen to be our enemies, and pray that Your love would heal and convert them. "Father, forgive them for they know not what they do."

Satan Worshipers

In the Name of Jesus, I block all who astral project from trespassing into our space wherever we are, along with all projected thoughts and weapons sent against us. I also bind everything and everyone attached to them, including their leaders and underlings, in Jesus' Holy Name.

Demons & Aliens

In Jesus' Name, I bind and disable all: demons, demon-aliens, with your weapons and anyone or thing attached to or being used by you, who have or will come against us along with your reinforcements, replacements and retaliations.

Dark Matter Weapons

In the Name of Jesus, I bind and disable all inter-dimensional dark matter weapons used or to be used against us or those we are to touch. By the power of the Name of Jesus, I disable and send you operators, vehicles, reinforcements, replacements and dark matter weapons to the abyss, with all retaliation bound, never to return until the Lord releases you.

The Lord's Protection

The Blood of Jesus cover & protect us body, soul and spirit, our work & equipment, housing and resources from those sent to hinder or destroy us.

"Lord deliver us from evil, sever the cords of the wicked, and fortify a globe of angelic protection surrounding us our property, and equipment wherever we go."

Spirits of Deception

In Jesus' Name, I bind all Jezebel spirits, Lying, Religious, Beguiling, Hindering, Deceiving and Seducing Spirits with your backup pools, those attached to or used by you and every one of your leaders who have sent you against us. As well as all those who provoke every manner of sin against us, namely;

Forces of Opposition
(name your own personal ones)

Fear of Man, PTSD, co-dependent behavior, overwhelm, bullying, panic, confusion, fight or flight chemical and emotional response, and all dynamics of Oppression & Apathy; brain imbalance, pain response: anxiety, fear, anger, depression, despair, and suicide; unhealthy cravings, gluttony, weight gain, doubt and unbelief, false guilt, self-hatred, bitterness.

Lying symptoms, spiritual & physical parasites, infirmity, sickness & death, vapid spirits of heaviness, fatigue, luke-warmness, weakness and sleep; avarice, greed, pride, rebellion, opposition, self-pity; distraction; restlessness, curiosity, compulsive-addictive behavior; sexual arousal, spousal & child abuse, incest, pornography and all sexual addictions, rejection and abandonment.

Spiritual deafness-dumbness-blindness and fog; Apathy, laziness, jealousy, judgment, condemnation and gossip against self & others; lying and deceiving voices, twisted communication; contentiousness, division, alienation. I declare all of you coming against us, your leaders and replacements, bound and permanently disabled in Jesus' Holy Name, never to return.

Curses Hexes Spells Strongholds

x3"I break and forever disable, every curse, hex, evil wish, spell, seal, link, generational curse, soul tie, restraint, assignment, devilish wile, and stronghold in Jesus' name, for it is written, "No weapon formed against us will prosper."**x3**

The Glory

Lord, I humbly ask you to release the Glory and protection that You sent with Your People Israel, fire in the midst of them wherever they went. And in Jesus' Holy Name, to restore seven-fold all the enemy has stolen from us. Please immerse us in Gratitude, Worship and Divine Love, gazing upon Your smile.

Favor

I speak Divine and Supernatural favor, Double favor, Additional favor, Abundant favor, Extended favor, over us and our works.

The Name & The Blood

Thank you, Jesus, for the use of Your Name and the power it has over every evil. Please cover and sanctify us, with Your Blood, to be conformed to You, Lord, in Humility, Charity, Courage and Purity.

Healing From Our Sins and Attacks

I pray, Holy Spirit, that You would pass over our whole beings: body, soul, and spirit with Your Glory and increase and restore: love for others, health, strength, vigor, faith, purity, wholeness, peace and joy to the places the enemy, the world and our own flesh have defiled.

Jesus, I trust in You. Jesus, I trust in You. Jesus, I trust in You. Amen

HOW TO BE BAPTIZED IN THE HOLY SPIRIT

Originally published in Charisma Magazine 3/23/2010
J. LEE GRADY

When we meet Christ and put our trust in Him, we are "born again" (John 3:3) and we receive the Holy Spirit in our hearts. This is the most important decision we will ever make. This happened to the disciples of Jesus in John 20:22, which says: "[Jesus] breathed on them and said to them, 'Receive the Holy Spirit.'"

But before Jesus ascended to heaven He told His disciples to wait in Jerusalem until the "promise of the Father" had come (Luke 24:49). He told them that if they would wait there they would be "clothed with power from on high." In Acts 1:8 Jesus told His followers that they would receive "power" to be His witnesses.

So the disciples waited in Jerusalem for many days, praying near the temple. On the day of Pentecost, which was 50 days after Jesus had died on the cross, something amazing happened. The Holy Spirit was poured out on the early church . This is described in Acts 2:1-4. The Bible says that when the Spirit came, the disciples were filled (another word is "baptized") with the Spirit.

This shows us that there are two separate experiences we can have with God. One is salvation, in which we receive God's amazing forgiveness a new nature. The Holy Spirit comes to live inside us, and He becomes our Teacher, our Comforter and our Helper.

The second experience is the baptism of the Holy Spirit, in which the Holy Spirit who is already in us overflows. "Baptized in the Spirit" means "completely immersed in the Spirit." Jesus never wanted us to rely on our own ability to do the work of ministry. He wants to do it through us. So He fills us with the Holy Spirit in order to empower us with His ability.

When we have this experience, the Holy Spirit's power fills us so full that He spills out. Also when we are baptized in the Spirit, unusual "gifts of the Holy Spirit"-which are listed in I Corinthians 12:8-10)-begin to be manifested in our lives. We begin to experience His supernatural power. These gifts include prophecy, discernment, miracles, healing and speaking in unknown tongues.

When people were baptized in the Holy Spirit in the New Testament church, the Bible says they all spoke in tongues (see Acts 2:1-4, Acts 4:31, Acts 10:44-48 and Acts 19:1-7). A lot of people get hung up on speaking in tongues because it seems like a weird thing. It's actually not strange at all. It is a very special form of prayer that any Christian can experience.

When we pray in our heavenly prayer language, we are praising God and also strengthening ourselves spiritually. Speaking in tongues helps us become mighty in the Spirit. The apostle Paul, truly a giant in the New Testament church, told the Corinthian believers: "I thank God that I speak in tongues more than you all."

Being baptized in the Holy Spirit is not something you have to qualify for. Any Christian can ask, and Jesus is ready to do it. You can pray by yourself or you can ask someone else to pray for you.

Here are the simple steps you can take to be filled with the Holy Spirit:

1. Prepare your heart. The Holy Spirit is holy. He is compared to a fire (see Matt. 3:11), which means He purifies sin and burns up that which is not Christ-like in our lives. Make sure you have confessed all known sin and made your heart ready for His infilling.

2. Ask Jesus to baptize you in the Spirit. You do not need to jump through hoops to get God's attention. He is eager to answer your request. Jesus is the one who baptizes us in the Spirit, so ask Him—and expect Him to answer.

3. Receive the infilling. Begin to thank Him for this miracle. The Holy Spirit's power is filling your life. If you feel your mind is clouded with doubts, just praise the Lord. Focus your mind on Him and not on yourself.

4. Release your prayer language. The moment you are filled with the Spirit, you will receive the ability to speak in your heavenly prayer language. You may feel the words bubbling up inside of you. You may begin to hear the words in your mind. Open your mouth and began to speak, trusting the Lord to give you this new, supernatural language.

Some people ask me, "Do I have to speak in tongues?" Certainly God will not force you to do it, and it has nothing to do with salvation. But I believe He offers this gift to anyone who wants it. It could be considered the least of the gifts—but it serves as a doorway to the supernatural realm and helps usher you into the deeper things of God.

5. Step out in boldness. After you have been baptized in the Holy Spirit, one of the first things you will notice is a new boldness. The Holy Spirit does not like to hide. He wants you to speak about Jesus to those around you—and He will give you surprising courage.

Communion

July 30, 2015

The Lord's Blessing is Truly with us, Youtube Family.

The Lord had a teaching about communion today. Before I start to share with you about what He had to say, I would ask that we don't get into any strife or fighting or disagreement about who's got the best communion and what's valid and what's not, and 'pagan worship' and what is not...all of that is just abhorrent to the Lord. He just has a simple message to His Bride today, and it's about you receiving communion. It's very, very important to Him, especially as our environment grows darker and darker, you need to be strengthened

more and more.

And I'd like to say that, in MY life, receiving communion every day has been a tremendous strength for me, and a pivotal point in my conversion to the Lord. Even Smith Wigglesworth – a great revivalist – received communion every day. What a great testimony!

So, this is the way He wants to manifest to us and to strengthen His Bride for the journey, and to be One with Her – physically – through communion.

The Lord said, "I want to talk to you about Communion."

Oh boy, that's a touchy subject...kind of a 'no go zone', isn't it? Since so many are at odds about what

communion truly is.

"Haven't I made Myself perfectly clear on this? At the very least seven times in the Scriptures?

"If you believe in your heart, and confess with your lips in all sincerity, I will be present to you in a miraculous way in communion. This IS My provided way, for the times you live in."

And when He said that, I sensed what He was saying was, "This is not my ideal way, but this is the way I am providing for you, because the times are so evil."

"I have already provided the Scriptures to convince any skeptic that I am truly present in the Bread and Wine. It may look like bread and wine, but nonetheless, I have chosen to be there with you, that you might be nourished for the journey."

Whoever eats my flesh and drinks my blood remains in me, and I in them. John 6:56

I'm going to be quoting from John chapter 56 quite a bit, because He did. But, I wanted to give you the address for the Scriptures so you could look at it yourself.

"There is absolutely no sense in arguing about the way different faiths approach the communion table. This channel is not for that purpose. But, all Christian faiths are agreed that I have declared, 'This is My Body and My Blood.' Their particular way of approaching the communion table may be different, though.

"But you, My Bride, must be nourished on My Body and My Blood as well. This is our point of physical union: the bread becomes a part of you physically, and because of that, you and I become One. You are fruitful and bear spiritual children, as well as being strengthened for the journey.

"If you are from a liturgical church and receive communion from a priest, make sure to reinforce the words –' truly, Jesus - this is Your Body, and truly – this is Your Blood'. In this way, any lack of intention due to the destruction of the church and the faith from the inside out will be accounted for and made up for in your confession. Yes, you will repair for any lack of faith by your deep reverence and the faith proclamation of your heart. I will honor the sincere prayer of faith."

I think what the Lord is alluding to here is that, in this day and age there's so many different kinds of ministers and priests, who then they say, "This is Your Body and Your Blood" – they don't really mean it, they don't really believe it. And what the Lord is saying is that, YOUR confession of faith, that it truly IS His Body and Blood...that it will make up the difference for their lack of faith.

"May I say, I ALWAYS honor the sincere prayer of faith, although I might not always answer it the way you wish. But, in matters of communion, I will.

"Not all of you will agree with Me. You have the right to disagree, but I would ask you to consider that these times in which you live, what seems to be the truth on the outside is sometimes lacking in internal form and this is to be considered in any church you receive communion.

"It is a Mystery of redemption and salvation, sanctifying you for all eternity."

And then He quoted: John 6:53 Very truly I tell you, unless you eat the flesh of the Son of Man and drink his blood, you have no life in you.

"I want each of you to design your own communion service using, the Last Supper as your guide. To the degree that you believe, to that degree I will be present to you."

And, may I say also as an aside, I think that if you really believe that it is the Body and Blood of Jesus, that you ought to dispose of whatever is left over VERY respectfully. Rinse it off and put it in a plant, dissolve it in water and then pour it into a plant or somewhere where it won't be tread upon. Certainly, don't feed it (leftover bread) to the birds! Dispose of it very, very respectfully, not putting it down the drain, but, pouring it on a plant or someplace special.

"As things become darker and darker, I want to strengthen you completely in every possible way. The reception of My Body and Blood is one of many ways, but profoundly important to Me."

John 6:47 Very truly I tell you, the one who believes has eternal life. 48 I am the bread of life. 49 Your ancestors ate the manna in the wilderness, yet they died. 50 But here is the bread that comes down from heaven, which anyone may eat and not die. 51 I am the living bread that came down from heaven. Whoever eats this bread will live forever. This bread is my flesh, which I will give for the life of the world.

"For those of you who come from a tradition, continue to receive communion as you do. But, if that should ever be brought to an end through persecution, have your own private service in reverence and faith and I will be present to you in a special way.

"I long to be received into the heart of My Bride. I long to share this communion with you. I long that we should be One in every possible way. Do not deny Me access to your bodies through communion. Do not abstain from receiving Me because you have fallen. It is the sick that need communion the most. First, confess to Me what you have done, sincerely from the heart repenting, and then you may receive.

"I want you to follow the conviction of your hearts. If you receive from a priest, continue to receive, remembering to confess in faith My presence. If you receive at a non-liturgical church, continue to do so as long as your conscience bears witness – but, be sure to confess in faith My presence.

"There is so much the many denominations teach that is error, and because of men's egos, the Truth - for now - shall only be known in Heaven. Do not let a Religious spirit dominate your thinking on this. Do not bicker over traditions. May I say, I hate your bickering. It is filthy vomit in My eyes. Do you know it is better to be silent and maintain the bond of brotherhood and love than to dissemble and contend with one another? What was ever accomplished by that, but enmity.

"For your information, I will reveal truth to you in your conscience but you are not to force it upon anyone else and say 'I am of Paul, his way is better. I am of Peter, no! His way is better!' Do you see how foolish you are in the sight of the angels??? Rather pray for one another that the truth will prevail and the rest I shall do in My Own Timing.

"In the meantime, love one another as I have loved you."

Song: John Michael Talbot “The Bread of Life”

HOW TO PREPARE FOR DELIVERANCE OF DEMONIC SPIRITS

Yes, Jesus can appear to you and deliver you in the spirit. He did that for me.

Do you have the Baptism of the Holy Spirit? Very important to receive the gift of tongues and be praying or singing in tongues because that is God praying through you. VERY IMPORTANT!!! You should worship and pray in this way for at least 30 minutes to two or three hours before deliverance.

Make a complete list of the people who have hurt you. If there is anyone you haven't forgiven, you need to at least make an act of the will to forgive them, and ask Jesus to help you forgive them and love them and pray for them, through you. Make a list of those you have hurt, ask God to forgive you and to bless them.

Also, if you are in any kind of sin: living with a man, or any kind of sex outside of marriage, that has to be stopped or you need to get married. If you are in any way being dishonest, disrespectful to parents, basically violating the ten commandments, and the beatitudes in Matt 5. Check to see if you are following all these things, and there is NO SIN in your life, no dirty magazines, violent or sexual movies, or movies about the supernatural outside of God like Harry Potter.

Make sure there are no cursed objects in your home, especially things made by natives or people who have cursed images, and no false Gods like Buddha, Tikis. Celtic new age items, no dragons or dragon games, nothing from the occult. No Tarot cards, astrology books, jewelry or symbols, charts... anything occult has to be removed from your house. No occultic jewelry. If you are clean, then you can be delivered. But if you are still attached to any form of witchcraft, Santa Ria, etc. you cannot be delivered. The demons may leave but then will return with more.

So, you have to be prepared for deliverance first. When you decide to get rid of all these things (that is, if you have them) you need to renounce all your involvements with them. If you have a long list of occultic practices you should put them on paper and repent and renounce each one as I have given you example below:

"In the Name of Jesus, I repent of using the Tarot Cards and renounce the Tarot. Leave and never return, in Jesus Name. Jesus, have mercy on me and deliver me from evil."

"In the Name of Jesus, I repent of using the Ouija board and renounce the Ouija Board. Leave and never return, in Jesus Name. Jesus, have mercy on me and deliver me from evil."

"In the Name of Jesus, I repent of praying to Buddha and renounce Buddha and meditation. Leave and never return, in Jesus Name. Jesus, have mercy on me and deliver me from evil."

"In the Name of Jesus, and by the power of His Blood, I repent and renounce my involvement in witchcraft ceremonies, going to mediums and Tarot card readers, and all practitioners of all forms of witchcraft. Lord deliver me from evil."

Also with sexual relationships, make a list of who you have had relations with on paper and repent before the Lord of every single one.

Then "In the Name of Jesus, I renounce ______ ______.
And I repent for ever having committed this sin, in Jesus Name. I break the soul tie to _____ ________ in Jesus Name. Lord deliver me from evil."

"In Jesus name, I break every generational curse put on me from my ancestors. I am covered by the blood of Jesus that wipes away all curses. Lord, deliver me from evil."

When you are done renouncing, burn that list and ask God to remove all the evil from your life, even if you forgot something. Ask Him to make you strong in discernment and self-control so you will never touch anything like that again.

Here are some objects that may be inviting the demons in: Newspapers, or magazines in the house because witches curse their ads in these things to draw people in, and open the door for demons to enter the house.

No demonic, occultic, witchcraft, scary or brutal movies, videos or video games OR BOOKS in the house. No Egyptian artifacts or symbols - they are extremely evil. Buddhas, Native American Medicine Men, Swammis, Spiritual leaders from other religions, Tiki images, ANYTHING SPIRITUAL IN NATURE that is not Christian.

You may have Christian crosses or other objects used for devotions. A picture of Jesus is fine, you aren't worshiping the image, you are worshiping the person in the image. That's very helpful to get your focus back on Jesus.

The standard the Lord gave me about movies was not to watch any movies that depict sin, like mafia, black market dealings, war movies, movies with adultery or sex. What's left? Older Disney family movies, nature movies, or movies that are about conversions, and biographies. That's about it.

Love, Clare

ccci

Made in the USA
Lexington, KY
29 May 2016